AF574011

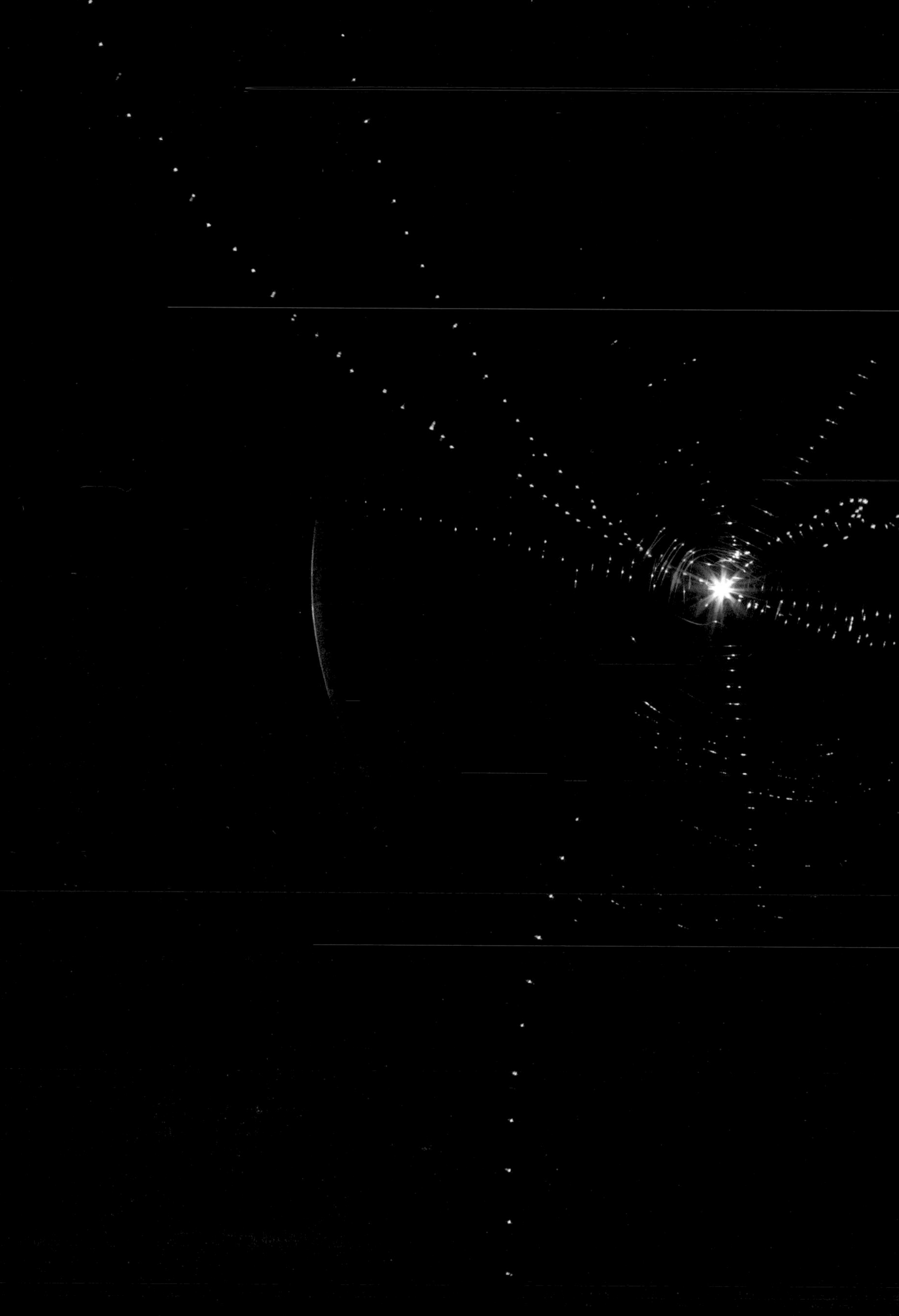

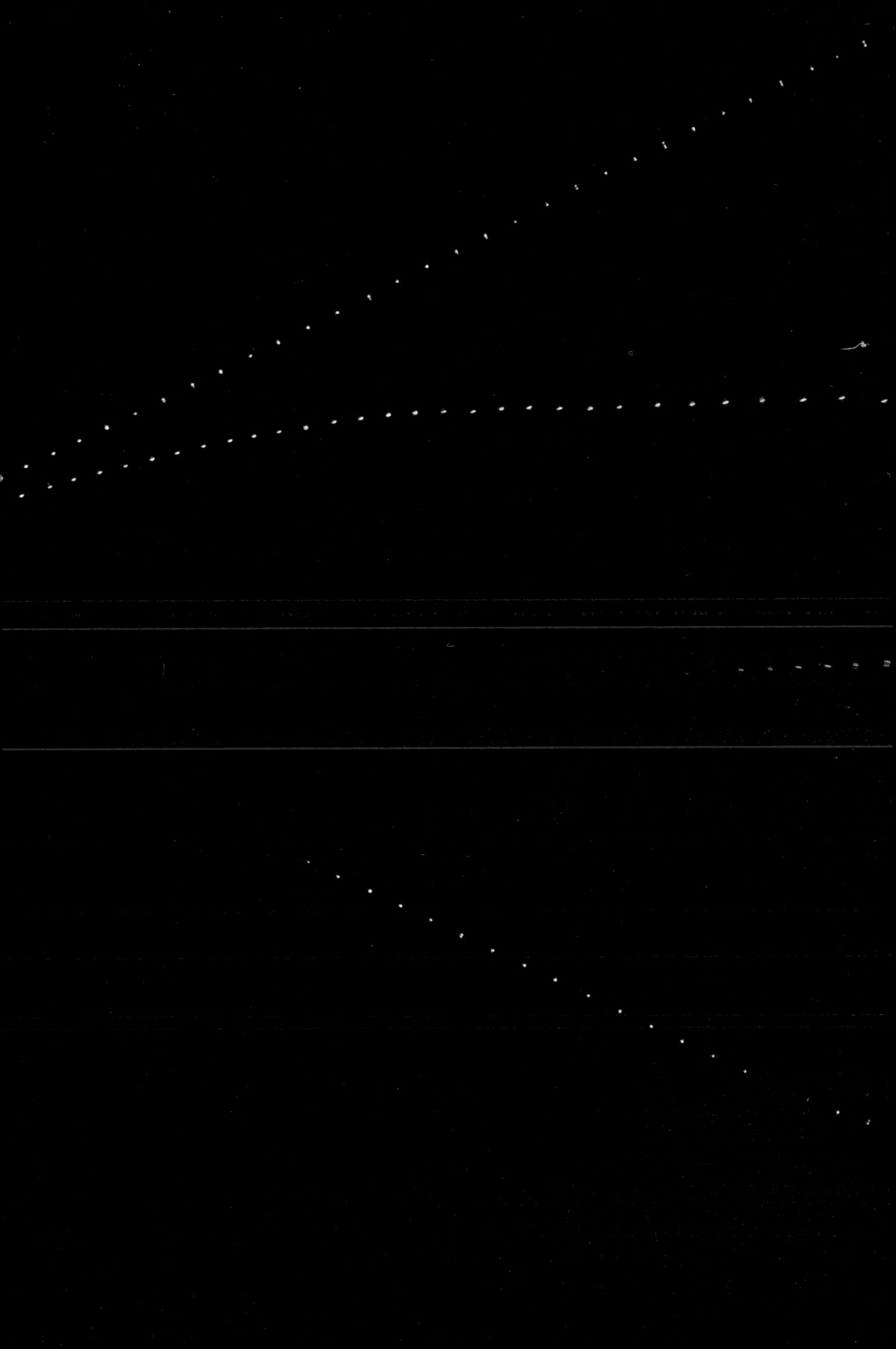

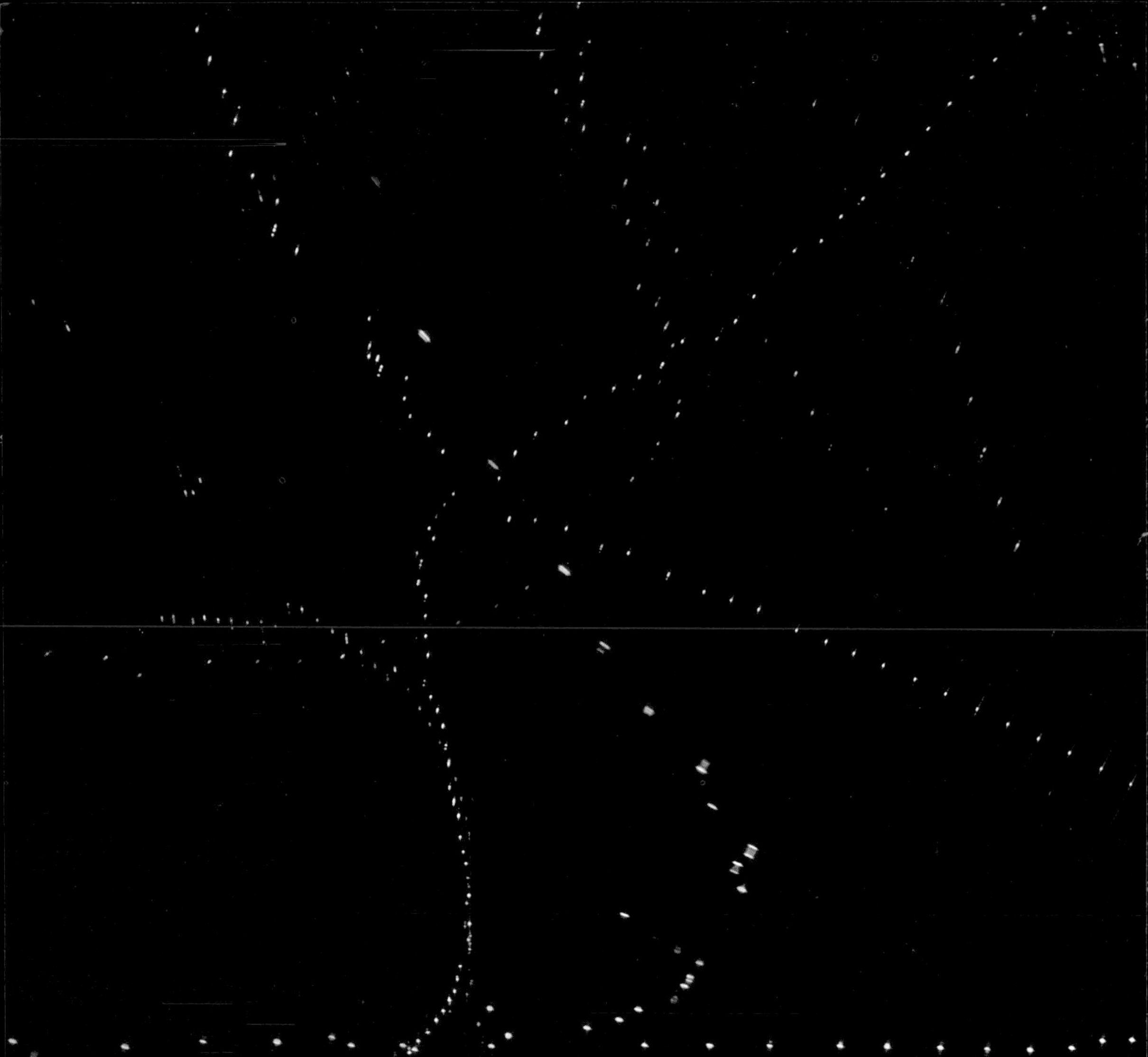

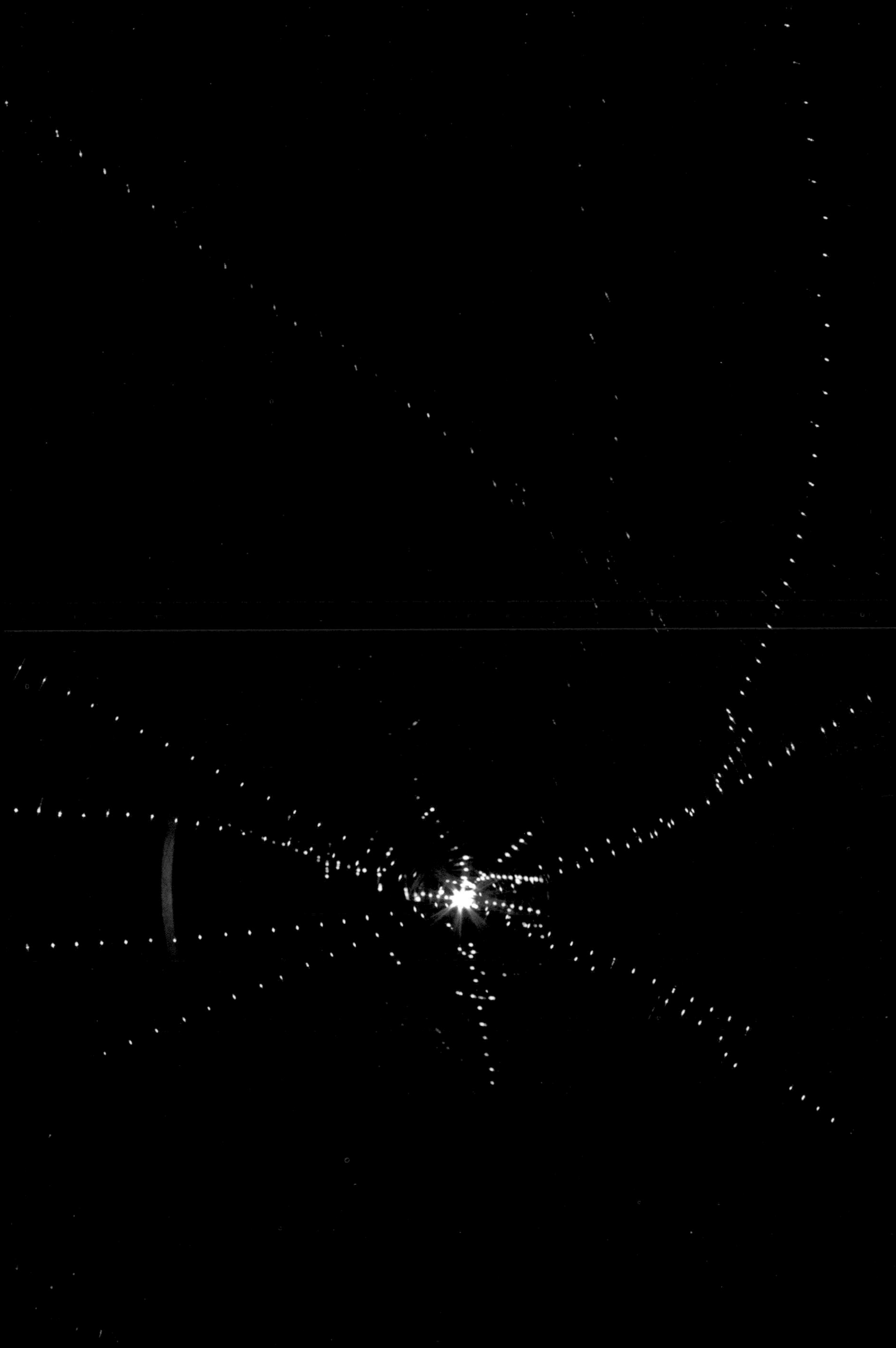

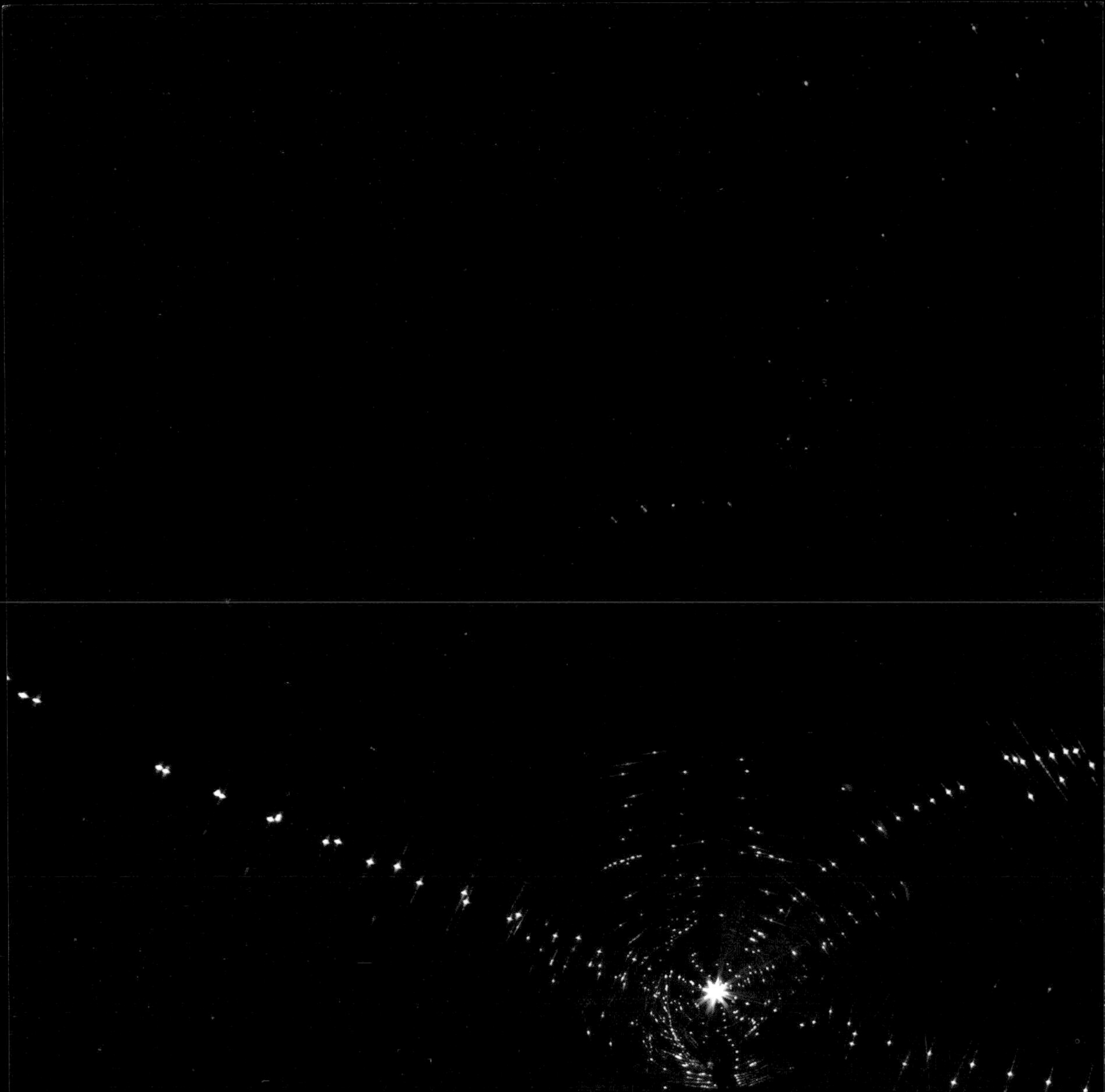

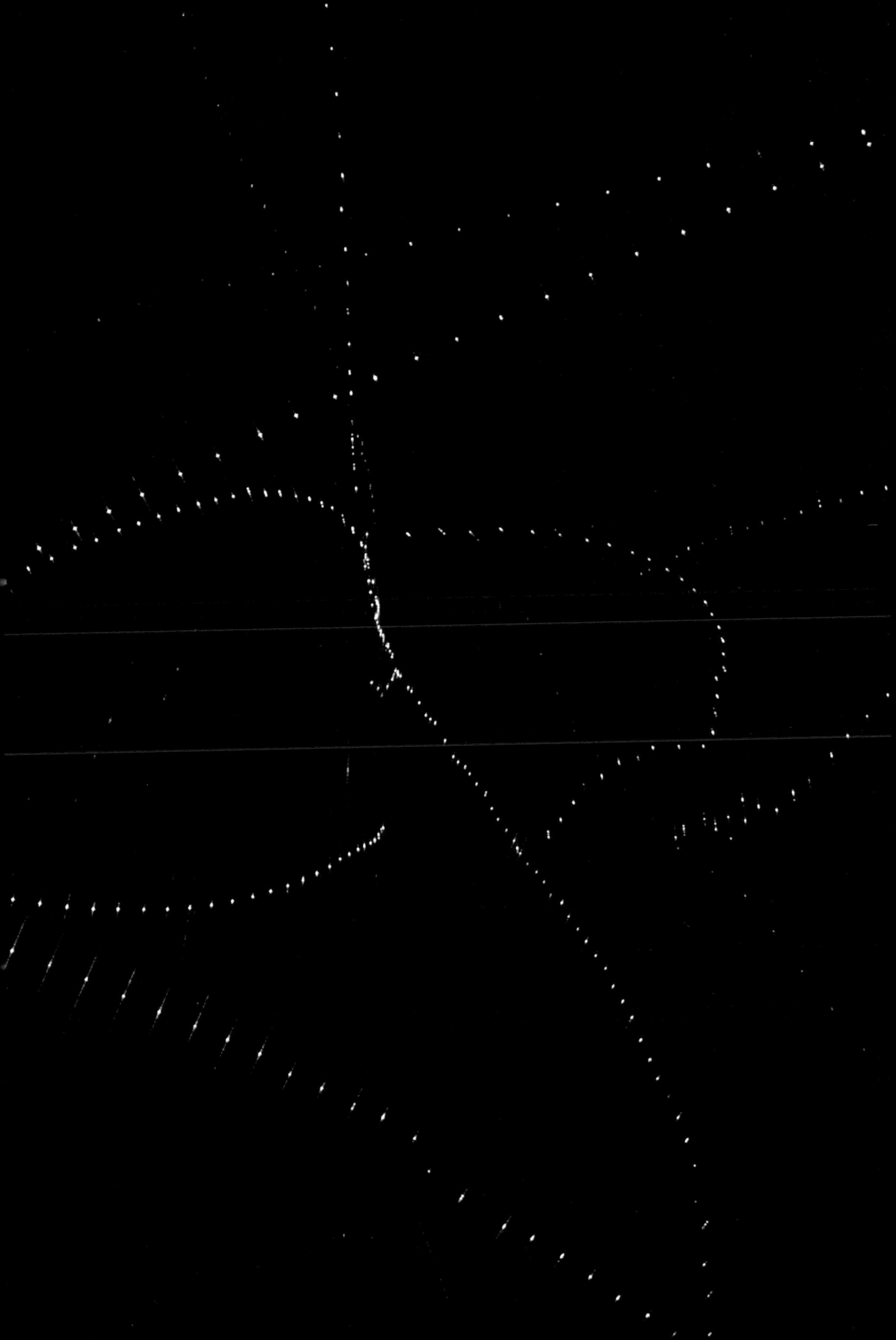

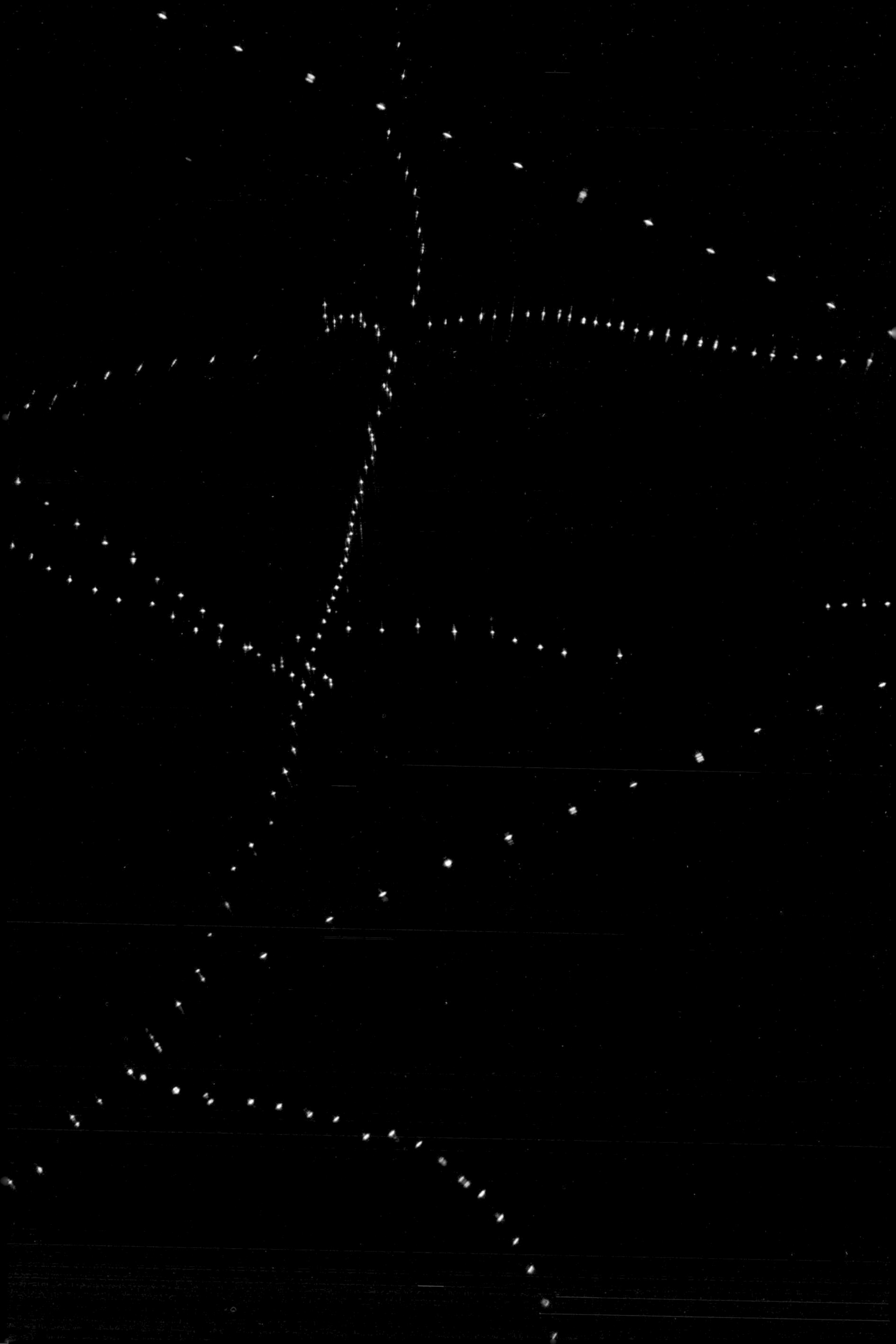

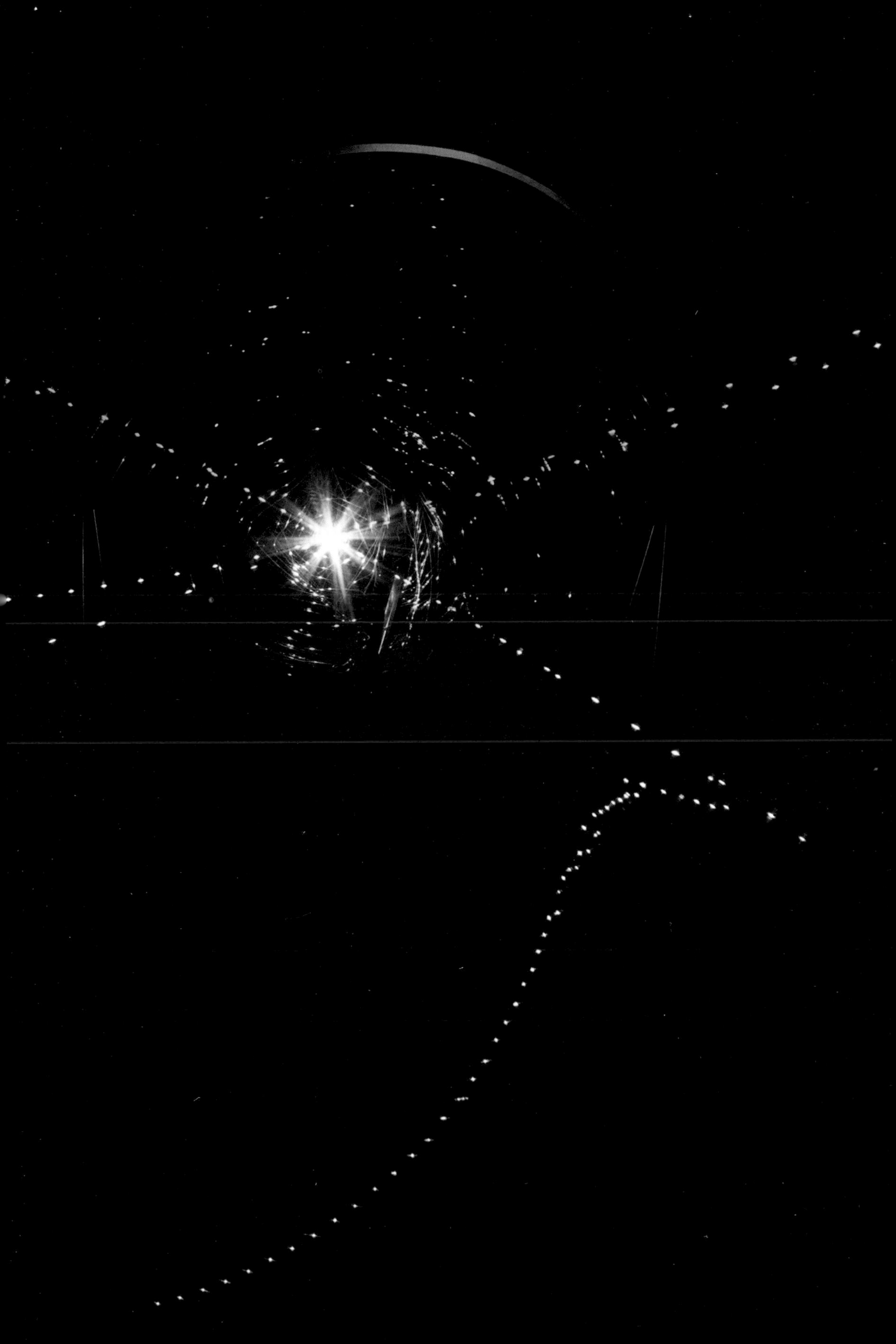

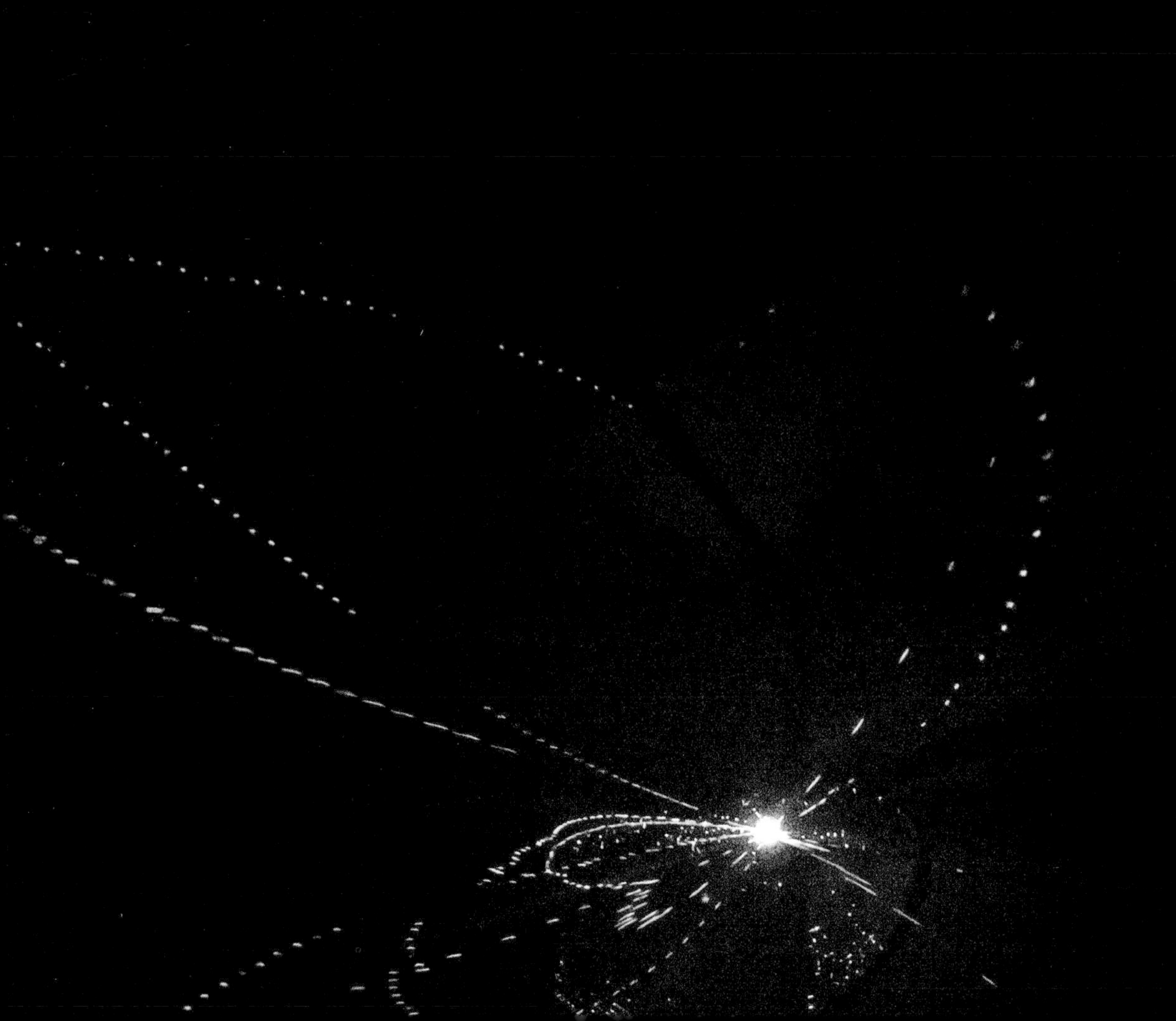

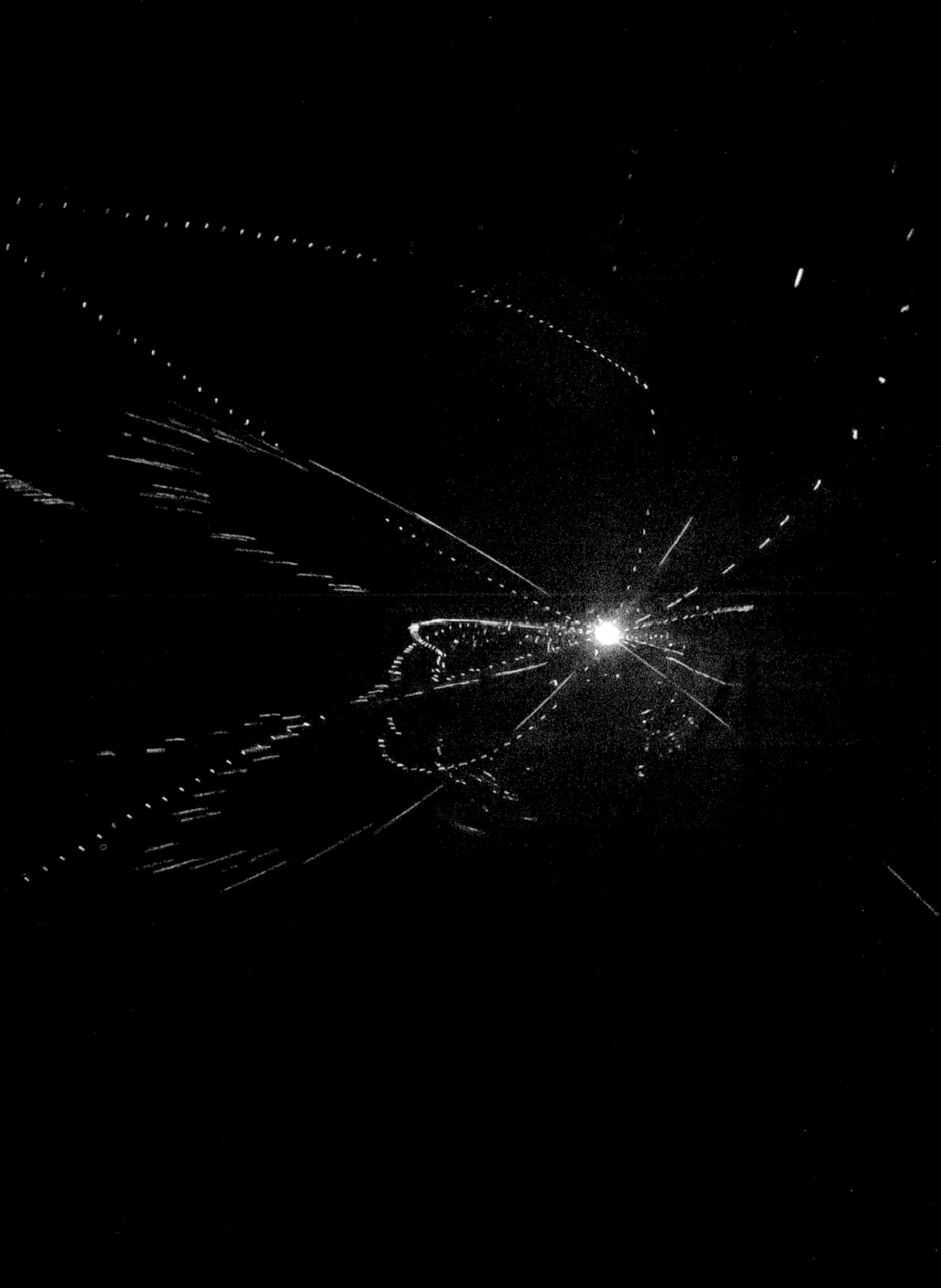

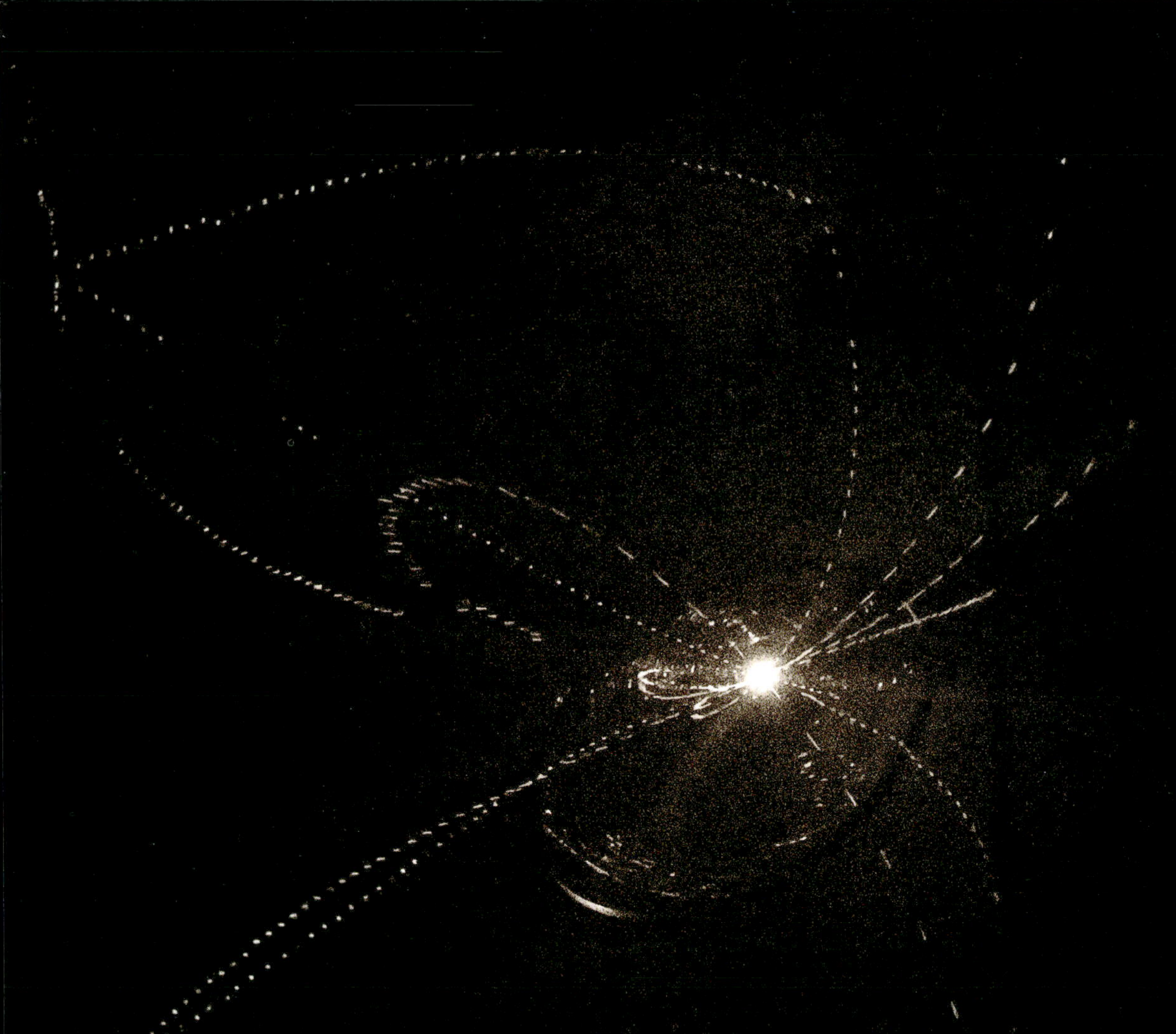

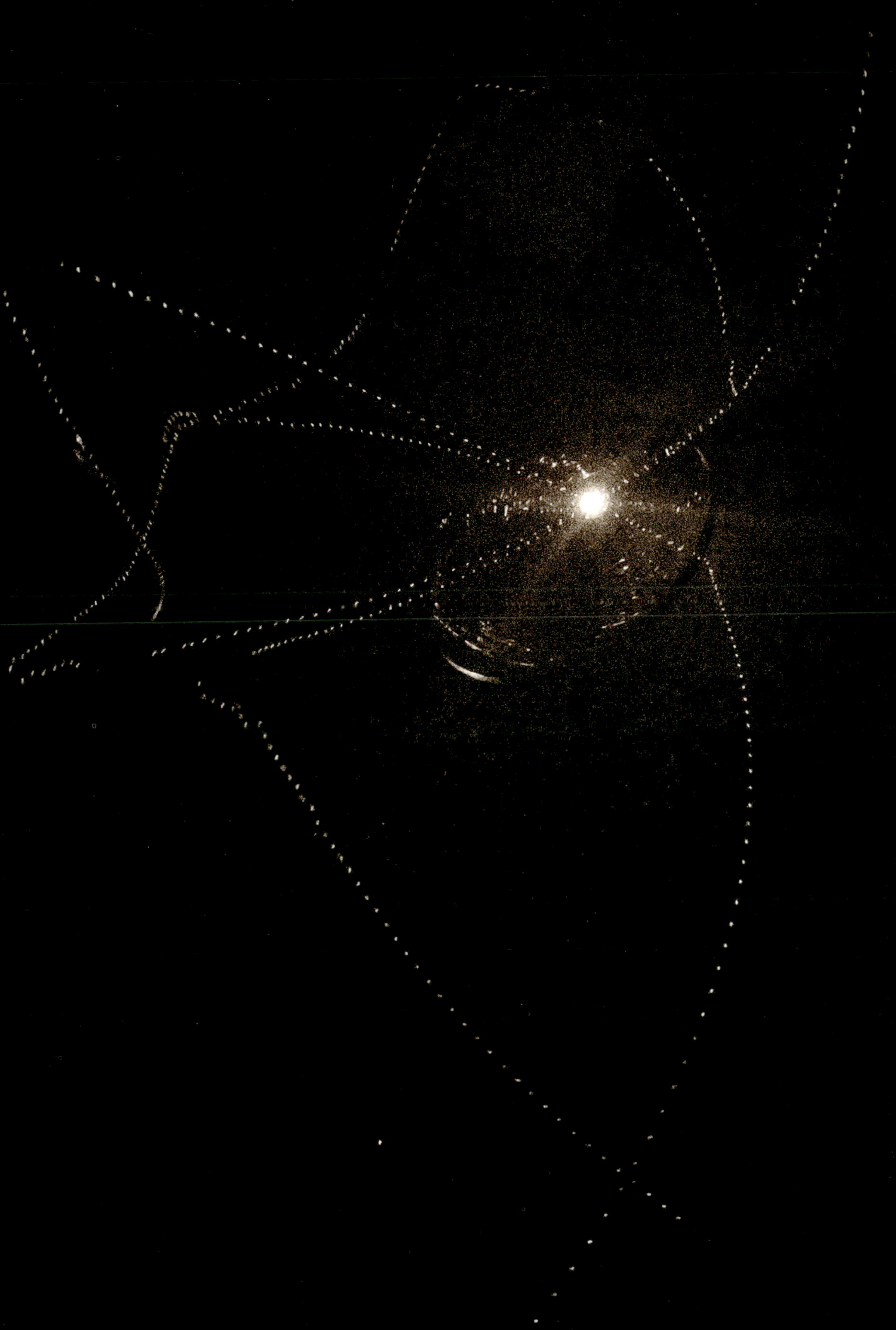

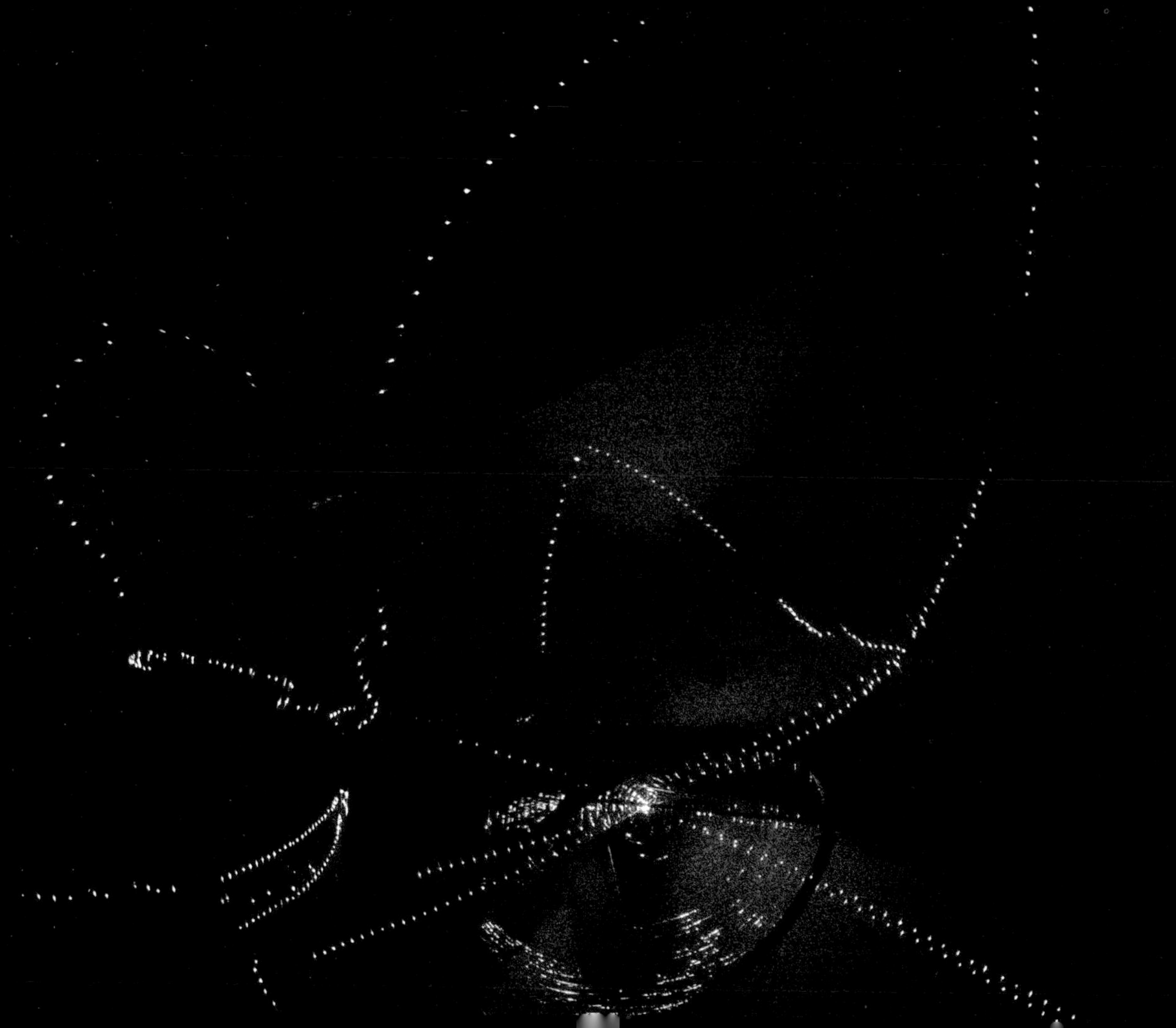

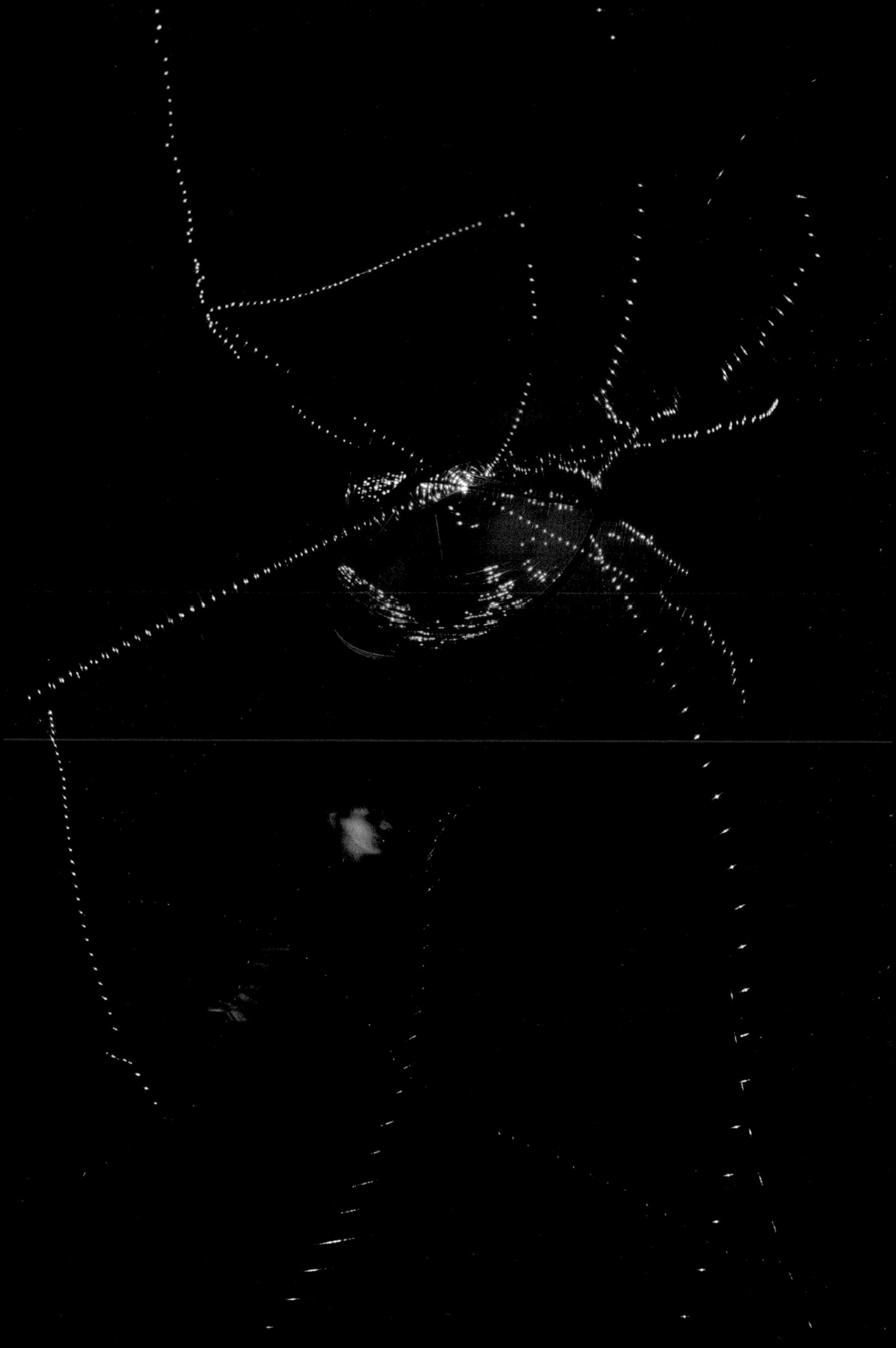

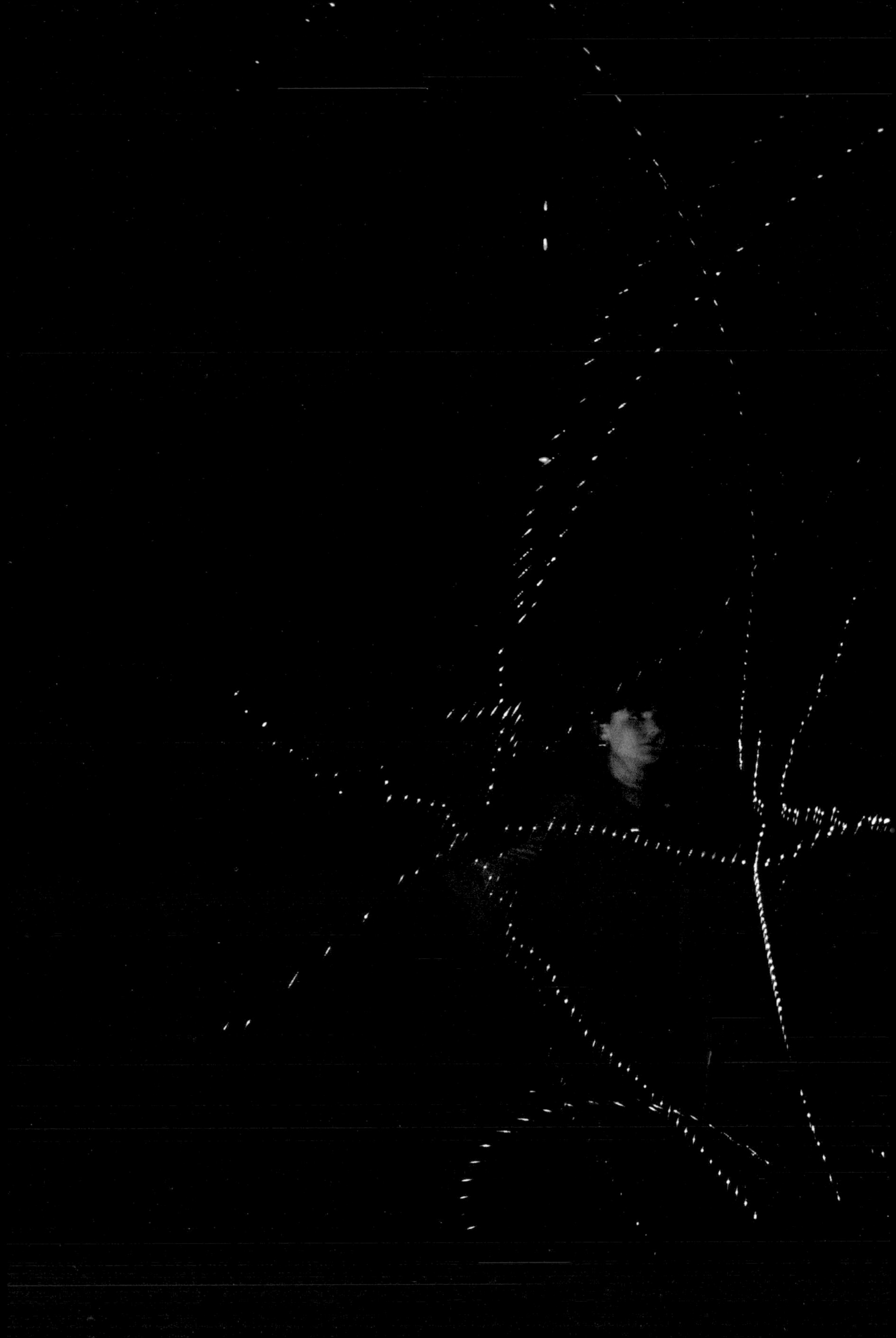

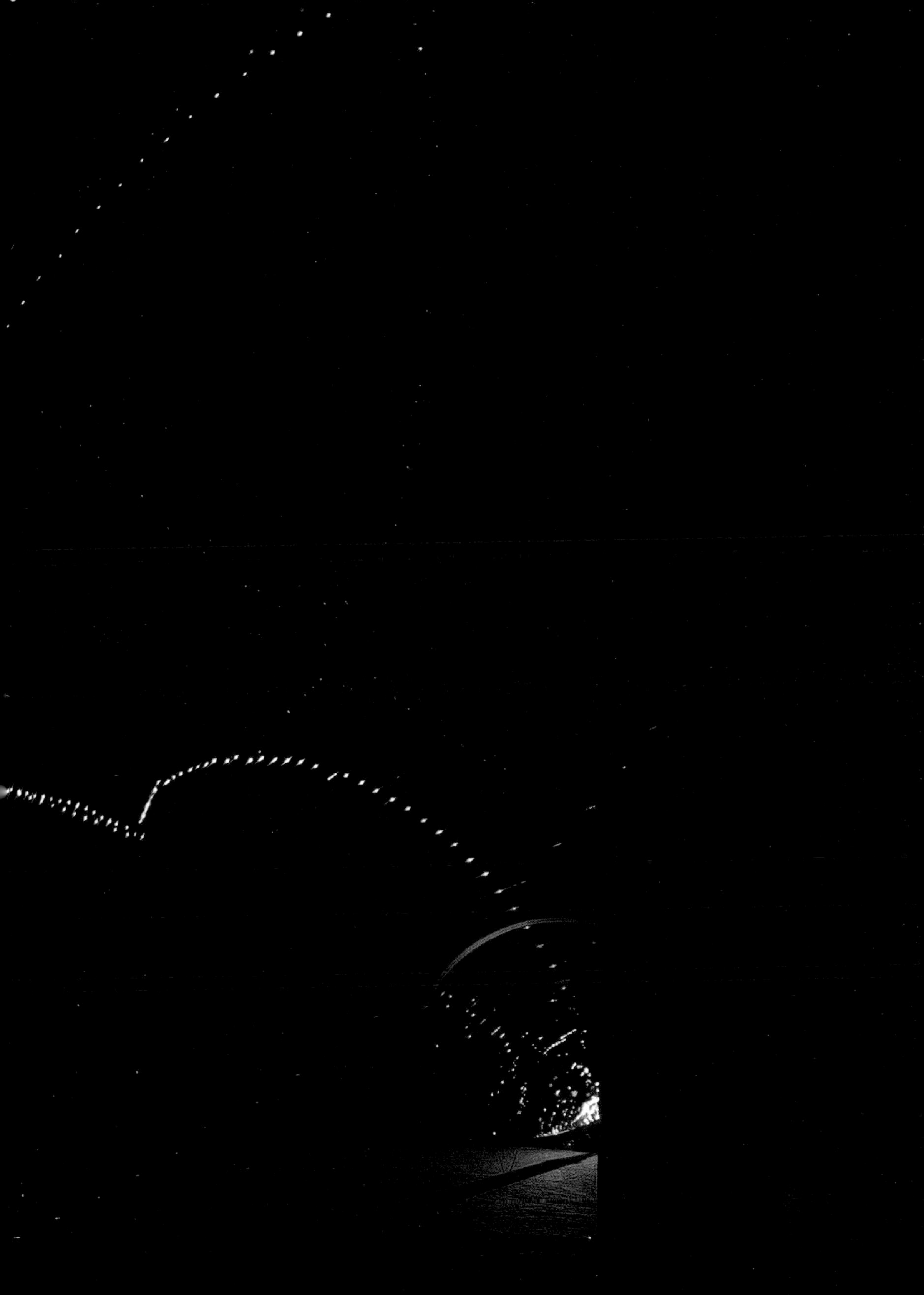

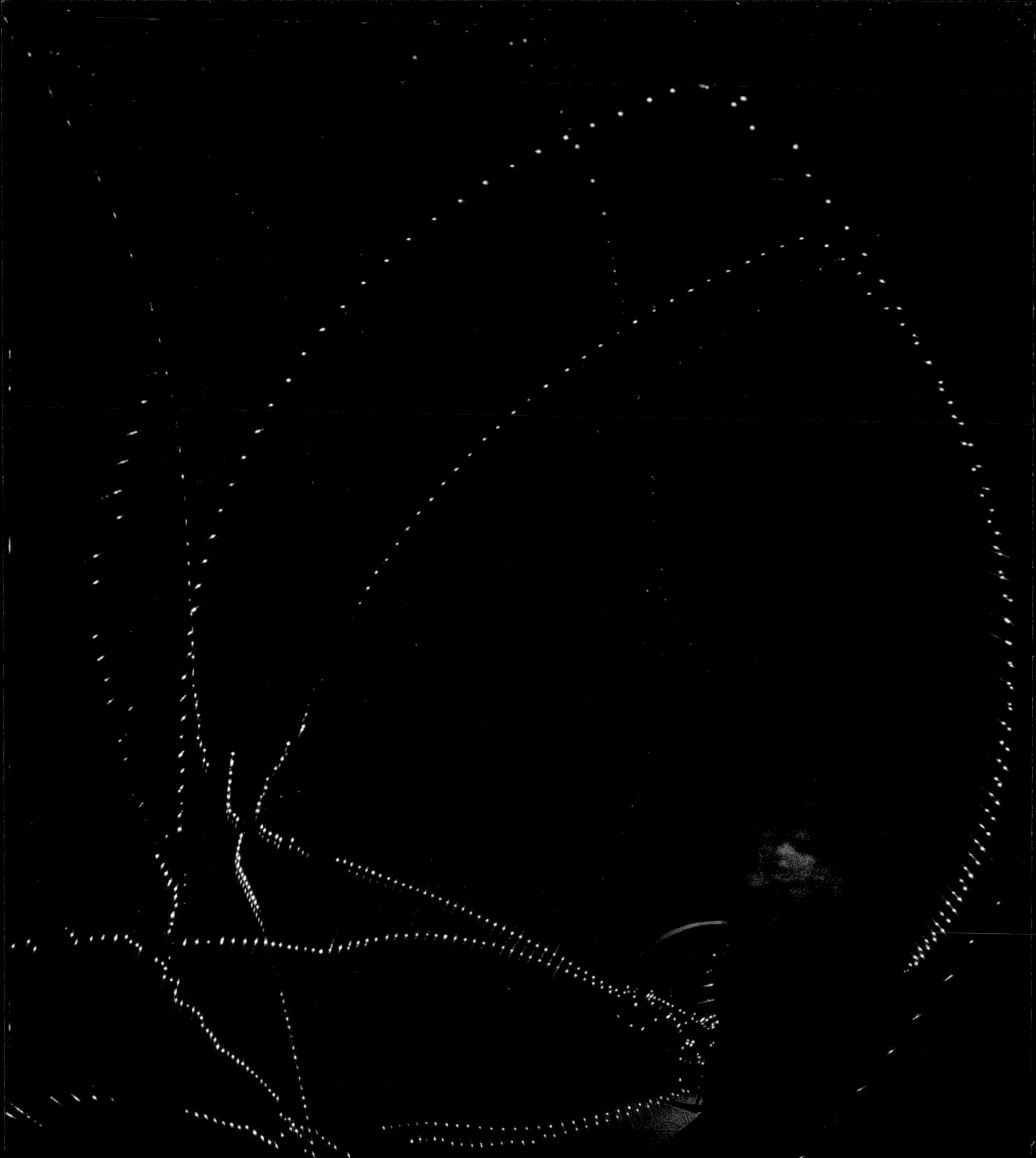

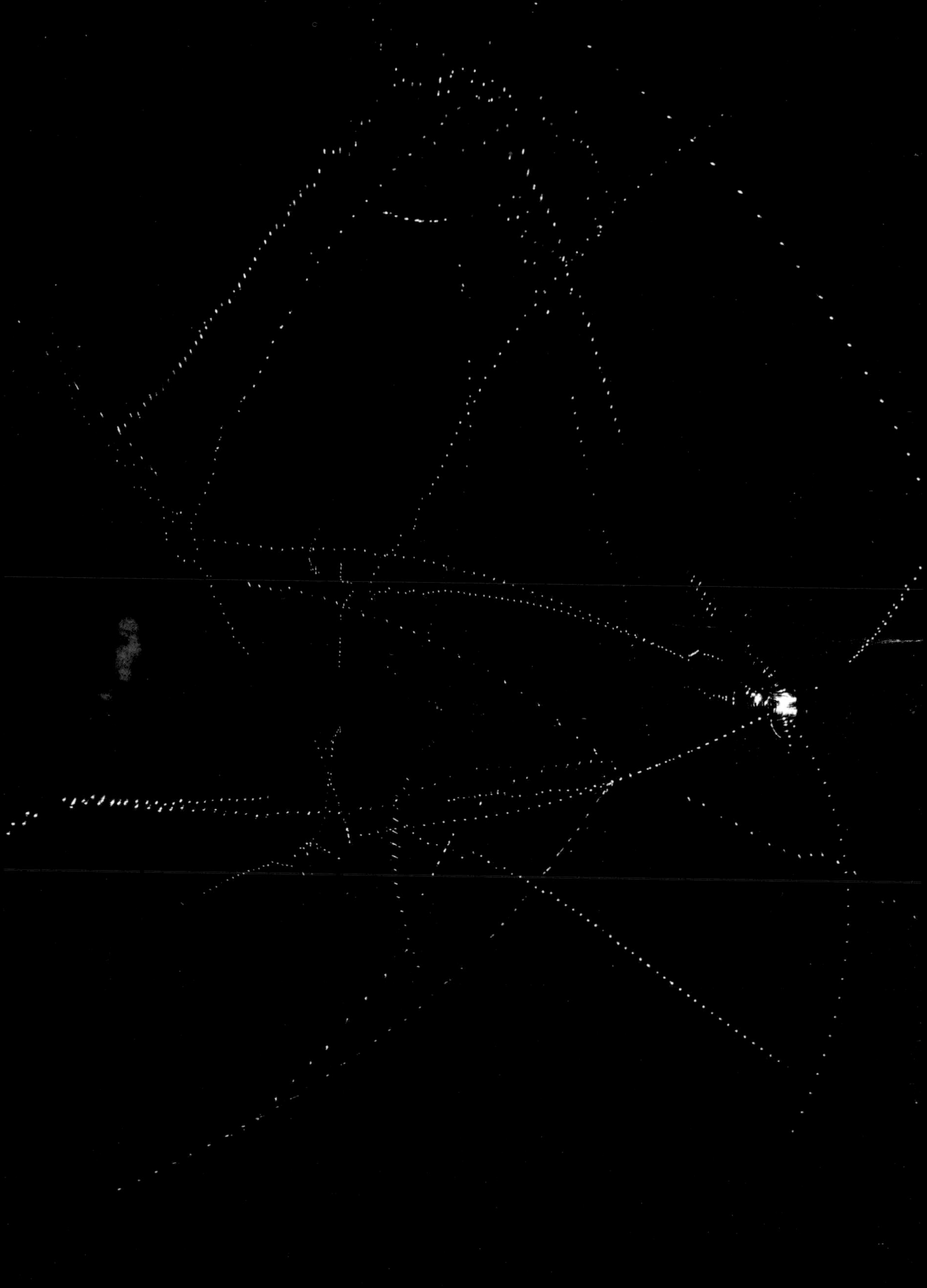

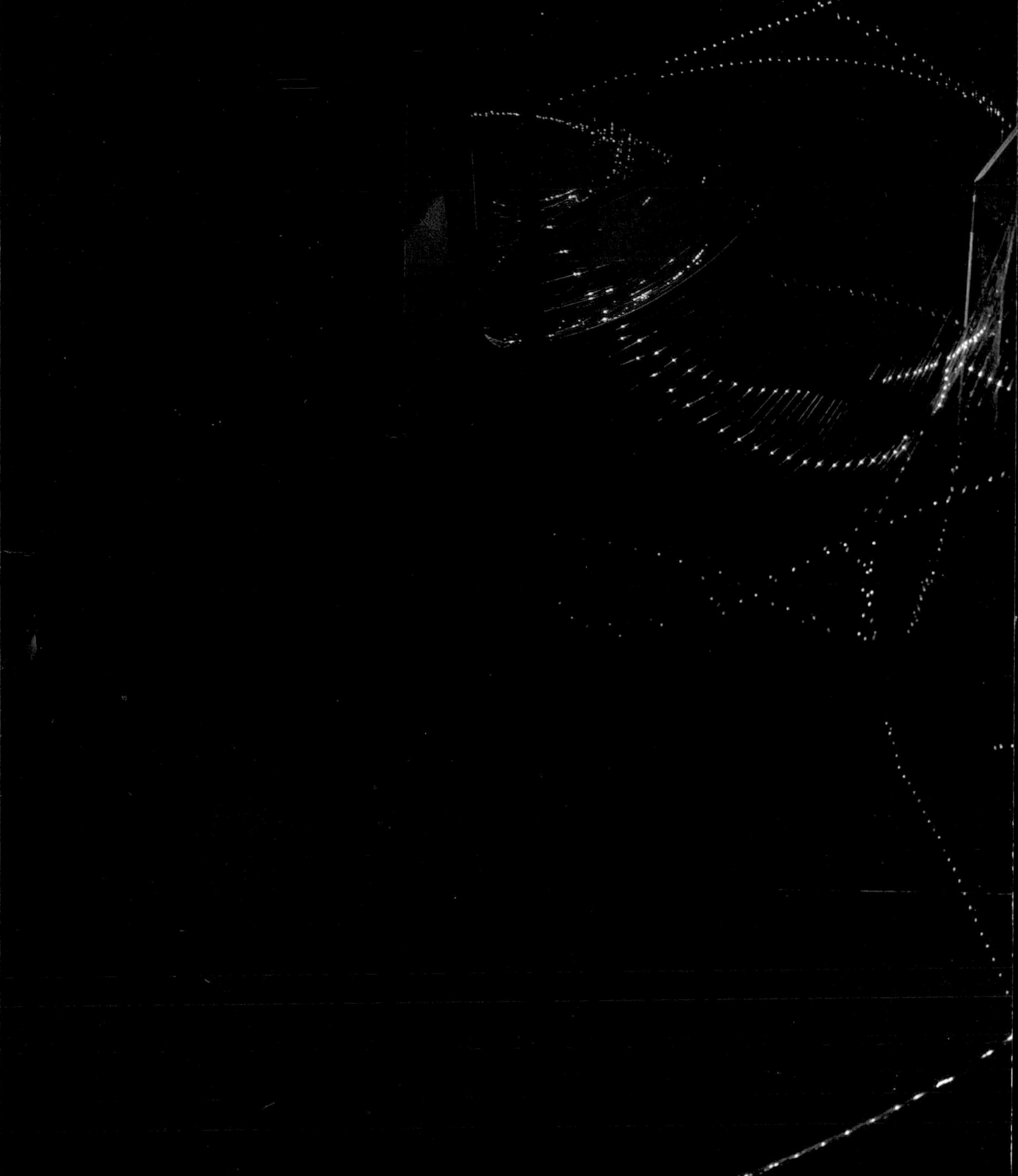

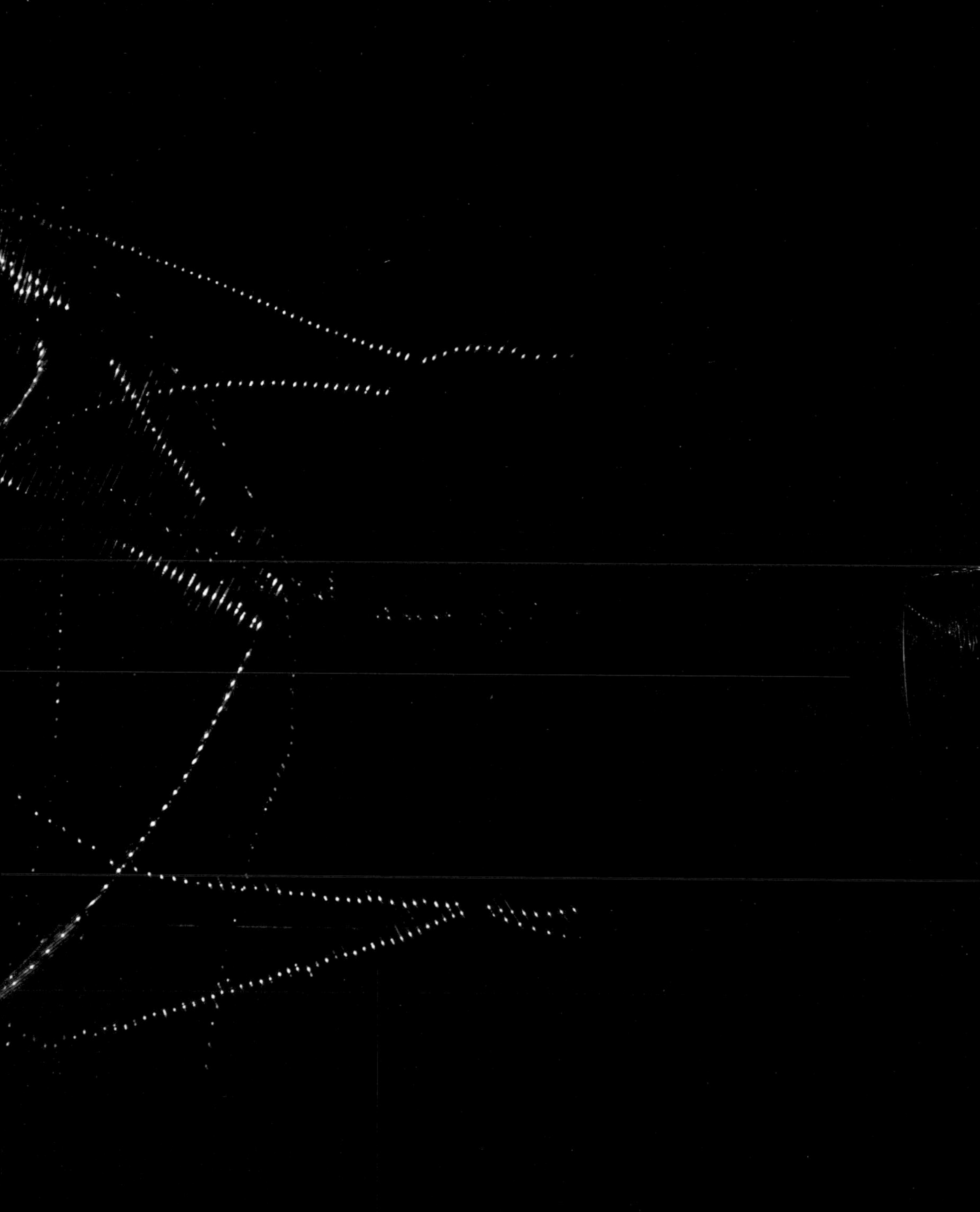

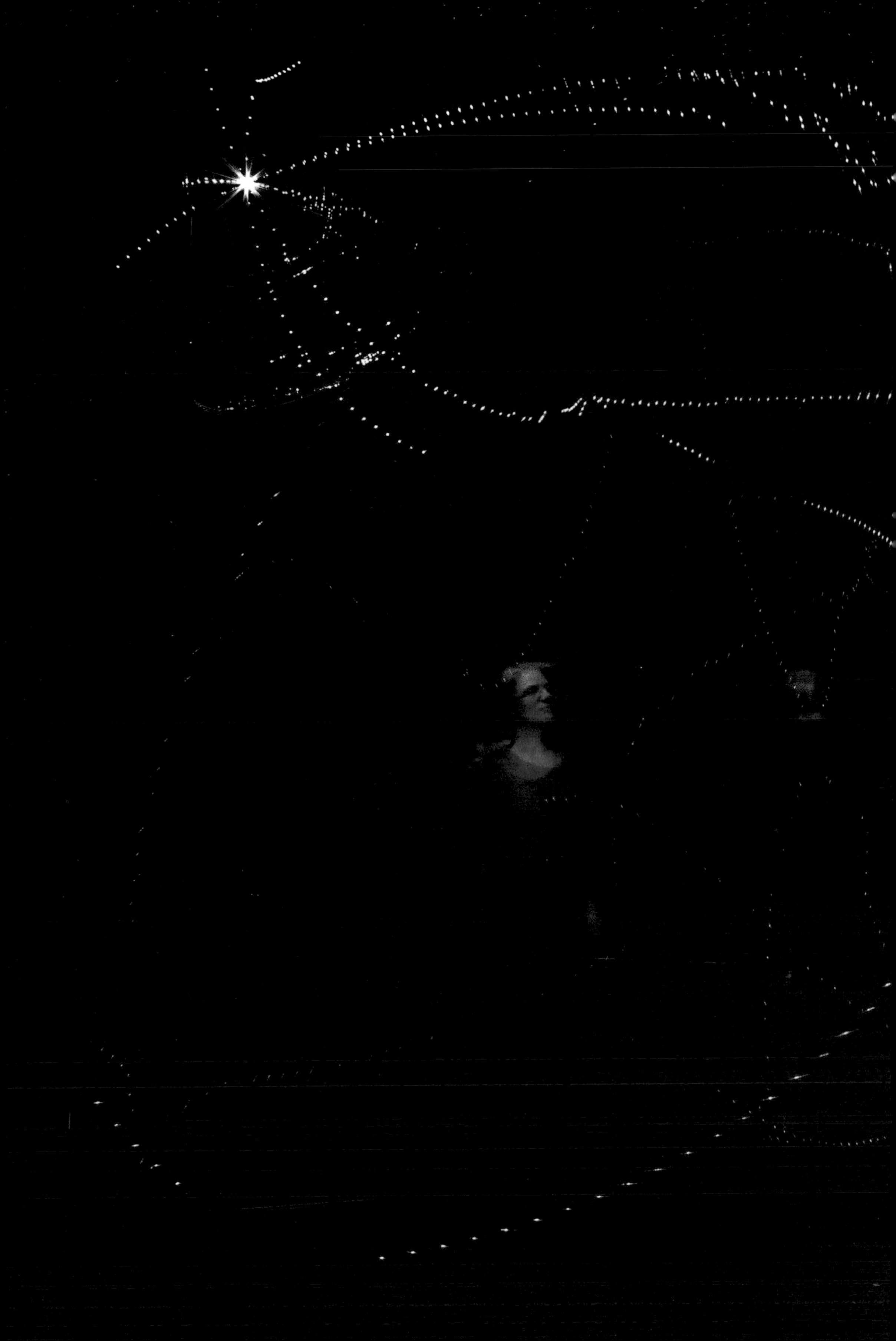

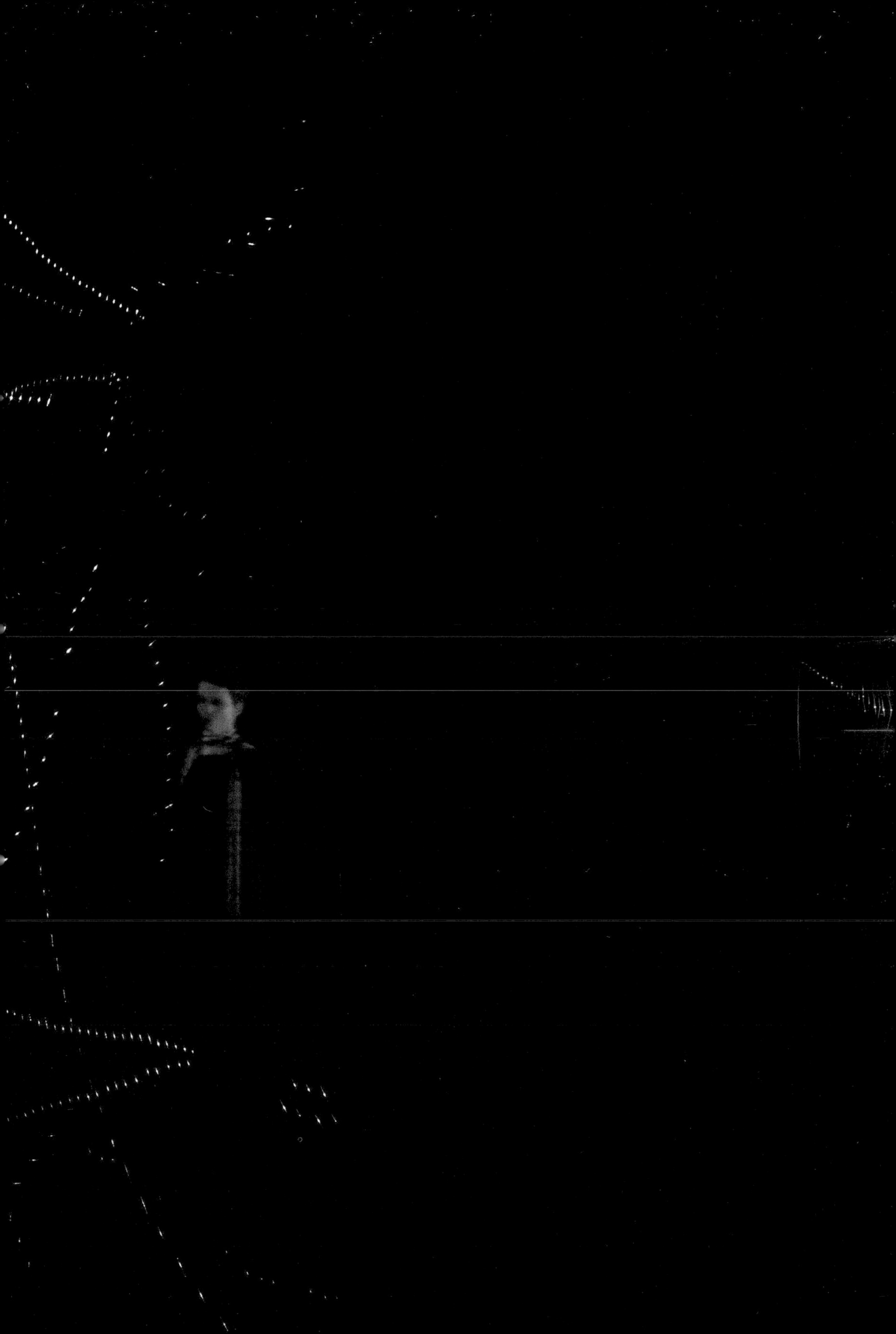

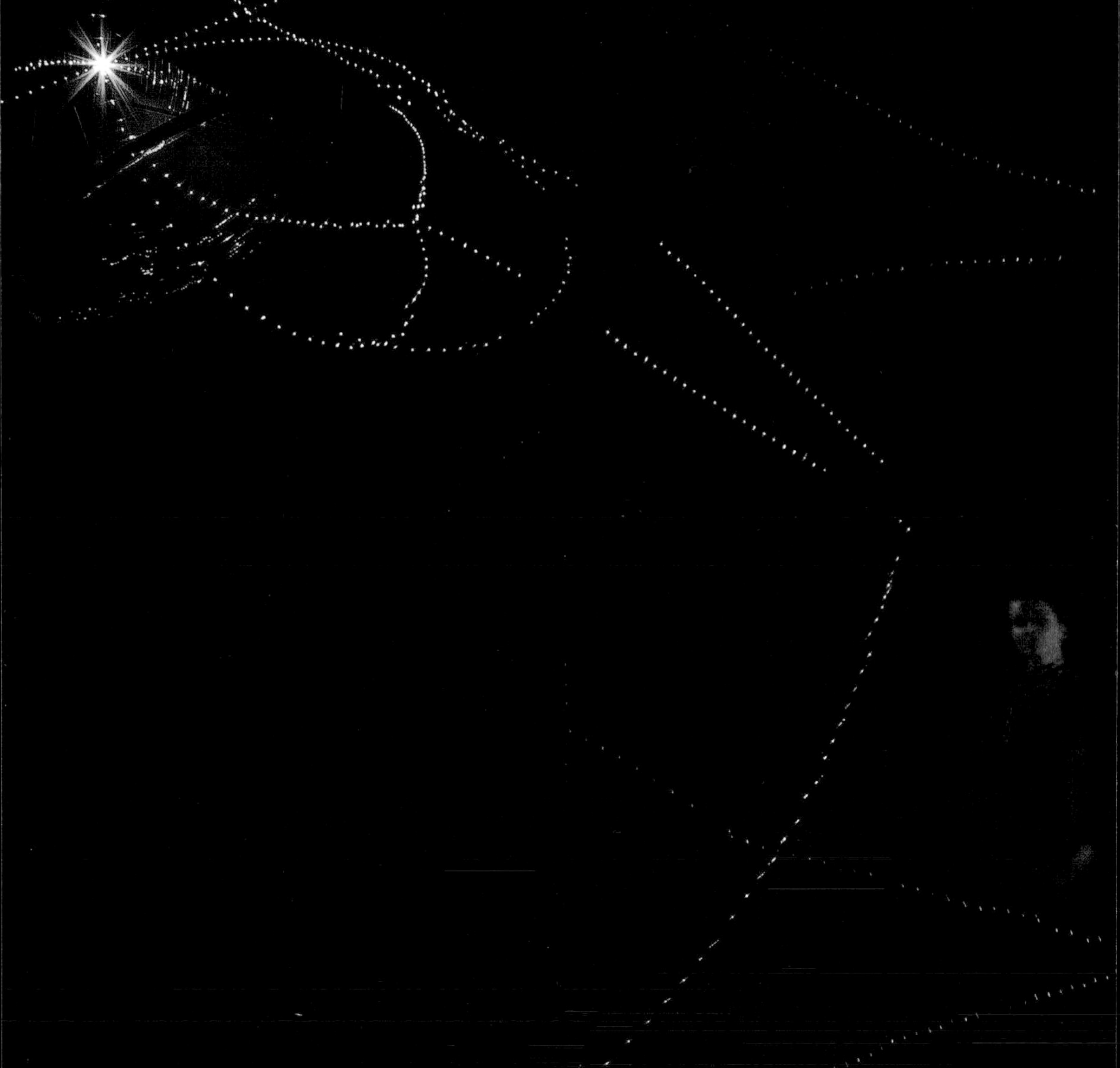

S. **pp.** 1–24:
Ivana Franke: Retreat into Darkness. Towards a Phenomenology of the Unknown,
Ausstellungsansichten **Exhibition views,** Schering Stiftung, Berlin, 2017
Installation im abgedunkelten Raum mit vier Objekten aus Aluminium mit Monofilament bespannt, drei Lichtquellen, vier Kontrolleinheiten. **Installation in a dark space with four aluminum constructions with monofilament nets, three light bulbs, four control units.**
Ø 100 × 86 cm, Ø 120 × 113 cm, Ø 150 × 129 cm, Ø 300 × 270 cm.

Ivana Franke

Retreat into Darkness

Towards a Phenomenology of the Unknown

Hg. von **Ed. by**
Heike Catherina Mertens und Katja Naie

Inhaltsverzeichnis

Content

Vorwort

Preface

Heike Catherina Mertens & Katja Naie

»Die Eigenschaft des reinen Geistes ist das Schauen und nicht das Wissen«, schrieb der Dichter und Arzt Justinus Kerner 1829 in *Die Seherin von Prevorst*. Darin beschreibt er die Krankengeschichte seiner Patientin Friederike Wanner, die Stimmen und Lichterscheinungen wahrgenommen und spätere Ereignisse vorhergesagt haben soll. Einige Jahrzehnte später spricht der Physiologe und Physiker Hermann von Helmholtz vom Gehirn als »Vorhersagemaschine« und heute kennen die Neurowissenschaften »prädikative Wahrnehmungsprozesse« und »kontrollierte Halluzinationen«, wie Anil Seth in seinem Beitrag zu diesem Buch aufschlussreich darlegt.

Ivana Franke geht diesen wissenschaftlichen Erkenntnissen mit ihren begehbaren Rauminstallationen und Skulpturen nach und thematisiert das »reine Schauen« als konstitutives Element ihrer künstlerischen Arbeit. In ihrem Projekt *Retreat into Darkness. Towards a Phenomenology of the Unknown*, das eine Einzelausstellung, verschiedene Experimente in Kooperation mit dem Kognitionspsychologen Bilge Sayim, ein interdisziplinäres Symposium und diese nun vorliegende Publikation umfasst, geht es um keinen geringeren Versuch, als die Wahrnehmung von erfahrungsbasiertem Wissen zu entkoppeln und den Schauenden in eine Art pränatalen Zustand zu versetzen. Ivana Franke möchte uns sehend machen, wie wir noch nie zuvor gesehen haben. Dass ihr dies gelingt, beschreibt Jimena Canales in diesem Buch anschaulich.

Die menschliche Wahrnehmung ist seit Jahrhunderten Gegenstand künstlerischer wie psychologischer und philosophischer Auseinandersetzungen. Ivana Franke antwortet darauf mit einer radikalen Entscheidung: Sie setzt die Besucher ihrer Rauminstallation in der Schering Stiftung der absoluten Dunkelheit aus. Sie können weder die räumliche Architektur noch Gegenstände im Raum wahrnehmen noch wissen sie, was sie erwartet. Dies ist eine zutiefst körperliche Erfahrung, auf die der Mensch nicht selten mit Angst reagiert. Das Auge benötigt zwischen fünf und zehn Minuten, bevor es die im Raum umherschwirrenden Lichtpunkte wahrnimmt. Und selbst wenn der Besucher nach einer Weile die Lichtquellen ausmachen kann, bleibt das Rätsel um die im Raum kreisenden Lichtfäden bestehen.

Ivana Frankes Wahrnehmungsraum kann als poetisches und minimalistisches Konzentrat langjähriger, künstlerischer wie wissenschaftlicher Forschung bezeichnet werden. Zum einen basiert er auf dem genauen Studium der Rezeption hochkomplexer geometrischer Strukturen, zum anderen auf aktuellen neurowissenschaftlichen Forschungsergebnissen. Das Resultat ist auf ästhetischer Ebene ein mit minimalen Formen und Lichtquellen bestückter Raum, der ein Maximum an Wirkung auf den Betrachter ausübt.

"The characteristic of pure intellect is seeing and not knowing," wrote the poet and physician Justinus Kerner in his book *Die Seherin von Prevorst* (The Seeress of Prevorst) from 1829, in which he describes the case history of his patient Friederike Wanner. Wanner apparently heard voices, saw light phenomena, and correctly predicted future events. A few decades later, the physiologist and physicist Hermann von Helmholtz described the brain as a "prediction machine." Today neurosciences refer to "predictive perception processes" and "controlled hallucinations," as Anil Seth explains in his enlightening contribution to this catalog.

Ivana Franke explores these scientific insights in her room-filling, accessible installations and sculptures in which she addresses "pure vision" as a constitutive element of her artistic work. Her project *Retreat into Darkness. Towards a Phenomenology of the Unknown*, which comprises a solo exhibition, various experiments conducted in cooperation with the cognitive psychologist Bilge Sayim, an interdisciplinary symposium, and now this publication, represents Ivana Franke's attempt to do nothing less than to separate perception from experience-based knowledge and return beholders to a kind of prenatal state. Ivana Franke wants to make us see in a way we have never seen before. In her essay in this catalog, Jimena Canales vividly describes how she succeeds in doing just that.

Human perception has been the subject of artistic, psychological, and philosophical investigation for centuries. Ivana Franke's answer to this debate is radical: She subjected the audience to total darkness in a room-filling installation in the Schering Stiftung. Visitors could not perceive the room's architecture or any objects within it, and they did not know what to expect. This was an intensely physical experience, and people often reacted with fear. They needed five to ten minutes for their eyes to adjust before they could begin to perceive the points of light hovering about the room. Even when the audience was able to make out the light sources after some time, the strings of light encircling the room remained a mystery.

Ivana Franke's sensory space can be seen as a poetic and minimalist culmination of many years of artistic and scientific research and was based not only on her in-depth study of the human reception of highly complex geometric structures, but also on current neuroscientific research. On an aesthetic level, the result was a room filled with minimal forms and light sources that had a maximal impact on the beholders.

We've all had that experience when we're looking for something but can't find it because we have the wrong mental image in our minds. If we're looking for a supposed red book in a bookshelf that is actually blue, we will be searching that bookshelf up

Im Alltag kennen wir alle das Phänomen, einen Gegenstand zu suchen und nicht zu finden, weil wir dessen Aussehen falsch vor unserem geistigen Auge imaginieren. Wer ein vermeintlich rotes Buch sucht, das in Wirklichkeit blau ist, kann lange vor dem Bücherregal auf- und abgehen. Diese Blindheit einem unerwartet auftretenden Objekt gegenüber bezeichneten Arien Mack und Irvin Rock 1992 erstmals als Unaufmerksamkeitsblindheit (inattentional blindness). Unsere selektive Wahrnehmung demonstrierten Christopher Chabris und Daniel Simons anschaulich 1999 in ihrem berühmten Experiment »The Invisible Gorilla«. 2015 konnte Carina Kreitz an der Deutschen Sporthochschule Köln nachweisen, dass diese »Unaufmerksamkeitsblindheit« nicht von unserer geistigen Leistungsfähigkeit abhängt, sondern »normal« ist. Doch in *Retreat into Darkness. Towards a Phenomenology of the Unknown* geht es nicht nur um diese Unaufmerksamkeitsblindheit, die ohnehin vereitelt wird, weil der Betrachter zum einen seinen (Seh-) Erwartungen enthoben und zum anderen durch die absolute Dunkelheit gezwungen wird, sich auf *alles* in Erscheinung Tretende zu konzentrieren. Ivana Franke möchte vielmehr die Grenzen unserer Wahrnehmung, die durch unseren Körper und das darin gespeicherte, erfahrungsbasierte Wissen geprägt ist, aufbrechen und aushebeln. Ein Abgleich von Gesehenem mit bereits Erfahrenem ist in ihrem zum Verschwinden gebrachten, physikalischen Raum kaum möglich.

Schwarz und Weiß, Dunkelheit und Licht sind die prägenden Elemente in Ivana Frankes künstlerischem Werk. Denn auch das Licht, mit seiner Fähigkeit zu blenden oder nur Teilphänomene zu erhellen, fordert unsere Wahrnehmung heraus. Die Künstlerin hinterfragt damit auch die gängige Praxis in unserem Kulturraum, Dunkelheit mit dem Unbekannten gleichzusetzen (»Dunkle Materie«; »im Dunkeln tappen«). Ist die Dunkelheit tatsächlich der Ort des Nicht-Wissens oder enthüllt sie nicht vielmehr Phänomene, die wir bei Licht nicht wahrnehmen, weil wir eben nur selektiv sehen?

Dieses Buch setzt Ivana Frankes Erforschung unserer Wahrnehmung auf künstlerischer wie wissenschaftlicher Ebene fort. Wir danken Elena Agudio, Jimena Canales, Pierre Gallais, Sylvia Pont, Bilge Sayim und Anil Seth für ihr leidenschaftliches Engagement, ihre Wahrnehmungsperspektiven mit uns zu teilen und ihre Erkenntnisse und Forschungsergebnisse für diesen Band niederzuschreiben. Besonders aber gilt unser herzlicher Dank Ivana Franke, die uns auf ihre Reise zu den Phänomenen des Unbekannten mitgenommen hat. Es hat sich wieder einmal bestätigt, was schon Karl Julius Weber wusste: »Reisen sind das beste Mittel zur Selbstbildung«. Auch eine Reise in die Dunkelheit.

and down and back and forth for ages. This blindness to an object's unexpected appearance was first called "inattentional blindness" by Arien Mack and Irvin Rock in 1992. Christopher Chabris and Daniel Simons also conducted a famous experiment called "The Invisible Gorilla" in 1999 that vividly demonstrated our selective perception. Furthermore, in 2015, Carina Kreitz from the Deutsche Sporthochschule (German Sport University) in Cologne was able to show that inattentional blindness is "normal" and does not depend on our mental ability. However, *Retreat into Darkness. Towards a Phenomenology of the Unknown* is not about inattentional blindness. That is because it obstructs inattentional blindness—beholders are prevented from harboring any (visual) expectations, while the absolute darkness forces them to concentrate on *anything* that appears. Instead, it was Ivana Franke's intention for us to overcome and undermine the limits of our perception defined by the body and the experience-based knowledge it stores. A comparison between what we see and what we already know is thus hardly possible in this dissolving physical space.

Black and white as well as darkness and light are defining elements in Ivana Franke's artistic work. Light has the ability to blind us or to illuminate only parts of scenes; it therefore also challenges our perception. The artist thus questions the common practice in our culture of equating darkness with the unknown ("dark matter," "groping in the dark"). Is darkness really the site of non-knowledge, or does it rather unveil phenomena that we fail to perceive in the light? Do we have selective vision after all?

This publication is the continuation of Ivana Franke's exploration of perception on both an artistic and scientific level. We would like to take this opportunity to thank Elena Agudio, Jimena Canales, Pierre Gallais, Sylvia Pont, Bilge Sayim, and Anil Seth for their dedicated commitment and for sharing their views on perception with us and writing about their insights and research in this book. Moreover, our special thanks go to Ivana Franke, who took us with her on her journey towards the phenomena of the unknown. This confirms once again what Karl Julius Weber already knew: "Traveling is the best way to educate yourself." This includes a journey into darkness.

Retreat into Darkness. Towards a Phenomenology of the Unknown

Gedanken zu Desorientierung, epistemologischen Brüchen und Nicht-Wissen

Retreat into Darkness. Towards a Phenomenology of the Unknown

On Disorientation, Epistemological Rupture, and Non-Knowledge

Elena Agudio

»Was dir weh tut, segnet dich. Die Dunkelheit ist deine Kerze.«
— Dschalāl ad-Dīn ar-Rūmī

Retreat into Darkness. Towards a Phenomenology of the Unknown (Rückzug in die Dunkelheit. Annäherung an eine Phänomenologie des Unbekannten) – der Titel, den Ivana Franke ihrer Installation in der Schering Stiftung[1] gegeben hat, klingt wie ein Manifest. Nicht wie eine Neuauflage eines »kynischen« Manifests im Sinne des Philosophen Diogenes von Sinope, der in einem Fass lebte, sondern wie eine hintergründige Reflexion der Rolle und der positiven Effekte der Desorientierung und der Dunkelheit. In diesem Zeitalter der totalen Transparenz der Daten,[2] im Alles überstrahlenden Licht der neoliberalen Gesellschaft, was ist da Dunkelheit? Wofür steht sie? Welches Verhältnis hat die Dunkelheit zum Wissen? Wir sollten versuchen, für einen Moment die westliche Tradition der Aufklärung außer Acht zu lassen; denn es ist eine Tradition, in der Schatten und Dunkelheit mit Ignoranz identifiziert wurden und die uns konsequenterweise dazu gedrängt hat, Licht und Transparenz mit Wissen und Rationalität gleichzusetzen. Dunkelheit ist aber nicht die Abwesenheit von Erkenntnis, sondern könnte hier als das Recht auf Undurchsichtigkeit, auf das Umherschweifen, auf das permanente Hinterfragen und Verflüssigen der erstarrten Normen gesehen werden. Dunkelheit kann eine Metapher sein für die »Magie der Schatten, die Magie des Ungesehenen, das notwendigerweise einer Initiation bedarf, um verständlich zu werden«.[3]

Genau so sollten wir uns Ivana Frankes Installation annähern: als eine Initiation in eine Phänomenologie des Unbekannten, so wie auch die Untertitel ihrer Installation und des begleitenden Symposiums lauten, die grundlegende Teile von Frankes künstlerischer Untersuchung waren.

In diesem Beitrag konzentriere ich mich auf drei zentrale Vorstellungen und Konzepte, die ich als wesentlich für die Annäherung an ihre Arbeit betrachte: Desorientierung, epistemologische Brüche und das Nicht-Wissen der Glühwürmchen.

1 Dieser Essay ist eine Transkription der Rede, die ich anlässlich der Ausstellungseröffnung am 26. April 2017 gehalten habe.

2 Eine bestimmte »Tyrannei der Transparenz«, die typisch für die Informationsgesellschaft ist.

3 Simon Njami, »The Mother Of All Dances«, in: *Doppiozero International*, 17. September 2015.

"What hurts you, blesses you. Darkness is your candle."
— Jalāl ad-Dīn Muhammad Rūmī

Retreat into Darkness. Towards a Phenomenology of the Unknown, the title chosen by Ivana Franke for her installation at Schering Stiftung,[1] sounds like a manifesto. Not a revival of a cynical manifesto, like the one written by Diogenes of Sinope, the philosopher who lived in a barrel, but a subtle reflection on the role and the positive effects of disorientation and darkness. In this age of the total transparency of data,[2] in the tremendous light of neoliberal society, what is darkness? What does it represent? How does darkness relate to knowledge? We should try for a moment to subvert the Western tradition of Enlightenment, that tradition that understands shadows and darkness as ignorance and has been consequently pushing us to see light and transparency as knowledge and rationality. Darkness is not the absence of knowledge; rather, it could be read here as the right to opacity, to errantry, to constant questioning and to making fixed norms fluid. Darkness can represent a metaphor for the "magic of the shadow, the magic of the unseen that necessarily requires an initiation to become intelligible."[3]

This is the way we should approach Ivana Franke's installation: as an initiation into a phenomenology of the unknown, as she has subtitled her installation and the consequent symposium that should be considered as an essential part of Franke's artistic inquiry.

In this essay, I would like to focus on three major ideas and concepts that I consider crucial to approaching her work: disorientation, epistemological rupture, and the non-knowledge of fireflies.

1 This essay is a transcription of a lecture held on the occasion of the exhibition opening on April 26, 2017.

2 A certain "tyranny of transparency" peculiar to the information society.

3 Simon Njami, "The Mother Of All Dances," *Doppiozero International*, September 17, 2015.

Desorientierung

Meiner Meinung nach handelt es sich bei Ivana Frankes *Retreat into Darkness* um eine Einladung zur Desorientierung.

Im Kontext des diskursiven Begleitprogramms zum Ausstellungs- und Performanceprojekt *The Incantation of the Disquieting Muse. Von Göttlichem, Supra-Realitäten oder der Austreiberei von Hexerei* am SAVVY Contemporary, Berlin, im Sommer 2016, sprach die algerische Philosophin Seloua Luste Boulbina in einem Vortrag über die Notwendigkeit der Desorientierung als ein Mittel, um das Wissen zu dekolonisieren. Dabei präsentierte sie Desorientierung »nicht als ein Scheitern oder eine Abwesenheit, sondern als eine Handlung und Haltung«. Sie sagte: »Tatsächlich glaube ich, dass wir lernen müssen, desorientiert und auf diese Weise dezentriert zu werden – in uns selbst und auch von uns selbst – um menschliche Regionen, die von den Europäern lange als »rückständig« angesehen wurden, richtig oder auf eine korrekte Weise zu erreichen.«[4]

In unserer heutigen Zeit der Unsicherheit brauchen wir Gelegenheiten, den Rahmen der vorgegebenen Karte zu verlassen und uns zu verirren, damit wir beginnen können, neue Vorstellungen von der Welt und unserer Position im Kosmos zu entwerfen. Meiner Meinung nach kann man sich der Dekolonisierung nicht nur aus einer postkolonialen Perspektive annähern, sondern diese auch – in einem weiter gefassten Sinn – als eine Möglichkeit ansehen, die vorgefassten epistemologischen Parameter abzuschütteln, in die wir eingebettet sind, und die Gelegenheit nutzen, diese zu verlernen und uns neue mögliche Zukünfte vorzustellen.

Mit ihrer neuen Installation lädt Franke uns ein, eine visuelle und körperliche Erfahrung zu machen, durch die es gelingt, unsere vorurteilsbehafteten Vorstellungen über die Realität zu überwinden und diese in andere Dimensionen zu überführen, die dezidiert fiktiv, imaginär und kosmisch sind. In einer bestimmten Hinsicht sind diese Dimensionen, so wie die Künstlerin sie definiert, fremdartig.

Aber zurück zum Konzept der Desorientierung. Desorientierung bedeutet zu vermeiden, auf ausgetretenen Pfaden zu wandeln, um stattdessen neue und wenig bereiste Wege zu erforschen. Heidegger bezeichnete diese als »Holzwege«, Pfade im Wald, auf denen normalerweise selten jemand entlang geht – weit entfernt von den Hauptwegen, die Menschen in ihrem täglichen Leben benutzen – und die in viele verschiedene Richtungen abzweigen, oft unterbrochen und umgeleitet. Wege, die kein ultimatives und klares Ziel anstreben, aber die von einem fundamentalen Zustand des Umherschweifens und des Forschergeistes geprägt sind. In einer teleologischen Gesellschaft, wie unserer westlichen Zivilisation,

4 Seloua Luste Boulbina, in: *The Incantation of the Disquieting Muse*, hg. von Bonaventure Soh Bejeng Ndikung und Federica Bueti, Berlin: GreenBox, 2017.

Disorientation

For me, Ivana Franke's *Retreat into Darkness* works as an invitation to disorientation.

In a recent lecture held at SAVVY Contemporary, Berlin, in the summer of 2016 in the context of the discursive program of the exhibition *The Incantation of the Disquieting Muse. On Divinity, Supra-Realities or the Exorcisement of Witchery,* the Algerian philosopher Seloua Luste Boulbina talked about the necessity of disorientation as a means of decolonizing knowledge. Boulbina presented disorientation "not as failure or absence but as action and posture." She said: "Indeed, I believe that we must learn to become disoriented and thereby, to become decentered—within oneself and from oneself—to properly or correctly reach regions of humanity long considered 'backward' by Europeans."[4]

In our current times of uncertainty, we need opportunities to practice these acts of unmapping and getting lost, to reimagine the world and our position in the cosmos. I am of the opinion that decolonization can be approached not only from a postcolonial perspective, but also—more generally—as a possibility of getting rid of the preconceived epistemological parameters we are embedded in, as a chance to unlearn them, to imagine new possible futures.

With her new installation, Franke takes us into a visual and bodily experience that is able to break with our prejudiced idea of reality by lending it other dimensions that are decidedly fictive, imaginary, and cosmic—dimensions which, in some ways (as the artist likes to define them) are alien.

But let me first get back to the concept of disorientation. Disorientation means to avoid traveling the beaten tracks in order to explore new and untraveled paths. These paths are what Heidegger called *Holzwege*, tracks in the woods that are usually rarely walked, far from the main trajectories followed by people in their daily lives. They go in many different directions and are often interrupted and diverted. These are ways that are not committed to an ultimate and definitive goal, but perpetuate an irreducible state of errantry and a spirit of investigation. In such a teleological society as Western civilization, which is still intimately driven by the Enlightenment's project of progress and by goal-oriented thinking, ambivalent concepts such as errantry and disorientation are seen in all their negative peculiarity and are mainly read as dangerous deviations from the social norm of productivity and success. Since the first formulations of cybernetics in the 1950s, today more than ever our permanently controlling systems of social engineering have been using

4 From Seloua Luste Boulbina's public intervention in the discursive program of *The Incantation of the Disquieting Muse*, ed. Bonaventure Soh Bejeng Ndikung and Federica Bueti (Berlin: Greenbox, 2017).

die immer noch sehr stark vom Fortschrittsgedanken der Aufklärung und vom zielorientierten Denken angetrieben wird, werden ambivalente Konzepte, so wie das Umherschweifen und die Desorientierung, eher als negative Ausprägungen betrachtet und hauptsächlich als gefährliche Abweichungen von der sozialen Norm der Produktivität und des Erfolgs angesehen. Seit den Anfängen der Kybernetik in den 1950er-Jahren arbeiten die beständigen, sozialtechnischen Kontrollsysteme heute mehr denn je mit Methoden der Regulierung, die auf Fehlerkontrolle und Feedbackmechanismen aufbauen, um Störeffekte zu reduzieren und alle denkbar möglichen Ziele zu erreichen. Die Kontrolle von Fehlern durch Feedback macht es möglich, jeden Prozess der Abweichung zu kompensieren, der das System an die Schwelle der Instabilität bringen könnte.

Hier, in diesem Kontext, sind wir allerdings gerade an dieser Instabilität interessiert, am kritischen Potential der Desorientierung und an ambivalenten Konzepten der Umwälzung wie der klassischen Idee der »Katastrophe« oder dem Glissant'schen Konzept des »Umwegs«, genauso wie der Idee der Undurchsichtigkeit und der Gegenpoetik.

Zum einen bedeutet »Katastrophe« in einem etymologischen und ursprünglichen Sinn eine plötzliche Wendung und hängt mit dem Wandel des Schicksals und der finalen Auflösung in der griechischen Tragödie zusammen, die Aristoteles (wie er in seiner *Poetik* erläutert) als einen grundlegenden Moment eines kollektiven Prozesses der Katharsis und der Reinigung von Geist und Emotionen ansah: die Metamorphose einer problematischen Situation zu einer positiven. Zum anderen schlägt Glissant den »Umweg« als eine Strategie vor, um einer Situation auszuweichen ohne sie zu vermeiden, indem man um diese herum geht und sie so überwindet.

All diese Momente der Desorientierung und Instabilität gehören zu den Besonderheiten von Ivana Frankes künstlerischer Forschung über die Grenzen der Wahrnehmung, besonders was ihre Arbeit in der Schering Stiftung angeht. Und diese Momente sind auch grundlegend für meine aktuelle kuratorische Praxis, weil sie eine politische Reflexion über die Möglichkeiten darstellen, »im Zeitalter der algorithmischen Kontrolle und Gouvernementalität »unkalkulierbar« zu werden. Jenseits der Kontrollschleifen und des Totalitarismus der Daten.«[5] Hier bieten sich Möglichkeiten des Widerstands und der heuristischen Reflexionen.

5 Antonia Majaca / Luciana Parisi, »The Incomputable and Instrumental Possibility«, in: *e-flux Journal* #77, November 2016.

error-controlled regulation and feedback mechanisms to reduce the effects of perturbations for the achievement of any goal. The control of errors through feedback thus allows the compensation for any process of deviation that could push the system to the threshold of instability.

It is exactly this instability that we are interested in—the critical potentials of disorientation and ambivalent concepts of overturning, such as the classical idea of "catastrophe," or Glissant's concept of "detour," together with opacity and counterpoetics.

On the one hand, in its etymological and original sense, "catastrophe" means a sudden turn, and it corresponds to the change of fortune and final resolution in Greek dramas that Aristotle (as explained in his *Poetics*) considered the fundamental moment of a collective process of catharsis and purification of mind and emotion, the metamorphosis of a problematic situation into a positive one. On the other hand, "detour" is a strategy proposed by Glissant as a way of evading but not avoiding a situation by getting around it and negotiating it.

All these moments of disorientation and instability are peculiar to Ivana Franke's artistic research into the limits of our perception, especially in her work presented at Schering Stiftung. These moments are also fundamental for my current curatorial practice and represent a political reflection on the possibilities of "becoming incomputable in the age of algorithmic control and governamentality. Beyond the control loops and totalitarianism of data."[5]

Epistemological Rupture

I would like to understand the darkness that Ivana Franke asks us to face in her installation as a small act of sabotage, as a possibility, and as a heuristic violation of pre-packaged (spatial) rules, as the ultimate invitation to drive "Off the Beaten Track"[6] and follow the path of curiosity and of "epistemological rupture." Ivana Franke addresses us with the question: "Do we only see what we know? What can dislocate us from our comfortable, predefined point of view and challenge our gaze on the world?" She is interested in enhancing our capacity to imagine, in challenging existing common modes of knowledge, and in creating room for different possible futures.

Artistic vision often works in a catastrophic way, acting as a virus, insinuating into the social body and changing the "horizon of meaning" of a certain social context. However, processes of knowledge that are derived from fractures and breaks are not only peculiar to artistic research: They are a common ground

5 Antonia Majaca / Luciana Parisi, "The Incomputable and Instrumental Possibility," *e-flux Journal* 77 (November 2016).

6 Heidegger's collection of texts was originally published in German under the title *Holzwege*, in its English version under *Off The Beaten Track*.

Epistemologische Brüche

Ich begreife die Dunkelheit, der uns Ivana Franke in ihrer Installation aussetzt, als einen kleinen Akt der Sabotage, als eine Chance und eine heuristische Übertretung der vorgefertigten (räumlichen) Regeln. Es sei dies eine ultimative Einladung, die »ausgetretenen Pfade« (*Holzwege*)[6] zu verlassen und dem Weg der Neugier und der »epistemologischen Brüche« zu folgen. Ivana Franke richtet die Frage an uns: »Sehen wir nur das, was wir wissen? Wie können wir uns von unseren bequemen und vorgefertigten Sehgewohnheiten lösen und unseren Blick auf die Welt hinterfragen?« Sie interessiert sich dafür, unser Vorstellungsvermögen zu erweitern, die üblichen Erkenntnisweisen herauszufordern und einen Raum für verschiedene, mögliche Zukünfte zu schaffen.

Künstlerische Visionen arbeiten oft in einer katastrophischen Weise, sie verhalten sich wie ein Virus, dringen in den sozialen Körper ein und verändern so den »Bedeutungshorizont« eines bestimmten sozialen Kontextes. Aber Erkenntnisprozesse, die aus Frakturen und Brüchen abgeleitet sind, sind nicht nur typisch für die künstlerische Forschung: Sie sind die gemeinsame Basis aller kreativen Praktiken und auch in den Wissenschaften sehr bedeutend, wenn man bedenkt, dass der Erzählung nach einige der wichtigsten wissenschaftlichen Entdeckungen nur durch »Zufall« passiert sind. Die Regelübertretung, das Verkehren der Ziele, die Abweichung und das Ausscheren aus den ausgetretenen Pfaden sind fundamentale Momente der Befreiung und des heuristischen Denkens, die ebenfalls notwendig sind für das Auftreten und die Evolution wissenschaftlicher Erkenntnis. Wie der Historiker Gaston Bachelard argumentierte, beruht die wissenschaftliche Forschung auf der fundamentalen Veränderung der Grundkonzepte und experimentellen Praktiken eines Fachs. Er bezog sich auf die Notwendigkeit von permanenten »epistemologischen Brüchen« in der Wissenschaftsgeschichte und auf den diskontinuierlichen Charakter des wissenschaftlichen Fortschritts. In einer Reihe von Werken, die Bachelard in den 1930er-Jahren schrieb – das wichtigste davon war *La Formation de l'esprit scientifique* (dt.: Die Bildung des wissenschaftlichen Geistes) –, beschreibt er den Bruch, durch den sich wissenschaftliches Denken als das Resultat einer Reihe von Begegnungen mit »epistemologischen Hindernissen« etabliert. Wissenschaftliches Denken beinhaltet immer den Bruch mit der Barriere der unmittelbaren Erfahrung. Er beschreibt die daraus folgende Qualität der Wissenschaft mit den folgenden Worten: »Vor allem muß man sich darüber im Klaren sein, daß die neue Erfahrung *nein* zur alten Erfahrung sagt, denn ohne dies handelt es sich ganz eindeutig nicht um eine neue Erfahrung.«[7] Die Arbeit einer spezifischen, theoretischen Transformation etabliert eine Wissenschaft, indem sie sich von der Ideologie ihrer

6 Heideggers Textsammlung wurde auf Englisch als *Off the Beaten Track* veröffentlicht, was auf Deutsch »Jenseits des ausgetretenen Pfads« bedeutet. Der deutsche Titel ist *Holzwege*.

7 Gaston Bachelard, *Die Philosophie des Nein*, Wiesbaden: Heymann, 1978, S. 24.

in all creative practices, and they are especially crucial in science as well, if we consider that some of the most important scientific discoveries are said to have happened simply by "accident." The transgression of rules, the perversions of goals, the deviations and swerves from the beaten tracks are fundamental moments of liberation and heuristic thinking that are necessary for the emergence and evolution of scientific knowledge. As the science historian Gaston Bachelard asserted, scientific research consists of the fundamental changes of basic concepts and the experimental practices of its discipline. He was speaking about the necessity of continuous "epistemological ruptures" in the history of science and the discontinuous nature of scientific progress. In a series of books written in the 1930s, chief among them *La Formation de l'esprit scientifique*, Bachelard described the rupture that establishes scientific thought as the result of a series of encounters with "epistemological obstacles." Scientific thought always involves a break with the obstacle of immediate experience. He described the ruptured quality of science with the following words: "Above all, we must be cognizant of the fact that the new experience says no to the old experience; without that, by any measure, it is not a question of a new experience."[7] The labor of a specific theoretical transformation establishes a science by detaching it from the ideology of its past and by revealing this past as ideological, for today's truth in science is often tomorrow's error.

Non-Knowledge

The ultimate quality of an image, as suggested by Georges Didi-Huberman, lies in its openness, in its mutability, and eventually in its fragility: It has the intrinsic quality of being able to condense cultural memory, to project the past onto the present, and to transform ancient visual symbols into new forms.

Like fireflies, images are "the most fragile and the most fleeting things in existence."[8]

In the glow of their fugacity, the intangible appearances that Ivana Franke invites us to observe and to fix in our minds present themselves as intermittent glimpses behind Maya's veil of individual memory, like mysterious and always unrepeatable epiphanies. They do not manifest themselves through a physical medium; they happen directly in the stream of consciousness of the viewer, then they fade away and become non-representable again. They are not transcendental entities capable of existing on their own: They do not have a bodily substance, but are rather the result of a complex process of interaction between specific

7 Gaston Bachelard, *Philosophy of No: A Philosophy of the New Scientific Mind.* Trans. G. C. Waterston (New York: Orion Press, 1968).

8 Georges Didi-Huberman, *La survivance des lucioles* (Paris: Minuit, 2009).

Vergangenheit löst und aufdeckt, dass diese Vergangenheit ideologisch ist, denn in der Wissenschaft ist die Wahrheit von heute oft der Fehler von morgen.

Nicht-Wissen

Die ultimative Qualität eines Bildes, so Didi-Huberman, liegt in seiner Offenheit, in seiner Wandelbarkeit und letztlich in seiner Zerbrechlichkeit: Ihm wohnt die Qualität inne, das kulturelle Gedächtnis zu kondensieren, die Vergangenheit auf die Gegenwart zu projizieren und uralte visuelle Symbole in neue Formen zu verwandeln.

So wie ein Glühwürmchen ist ein Bild »das flüchtigste und zerbrechlichste Ding, das es gibt.«[8]

In ihrem flüchtigen Leuchten präsentieren sich die ungreifbaren Erscheinungen, die Ivana Franke uns beobachten und in unserem Geist fixieren lässt, als gebrochene, ephemere Blicke durch den Maya'schen Schleier der individuellen Erinnerung, wie geheimnisvolle und immer unwiederholbare Erleuchtungen. Sie manifestieren sich nicht durch ein physisches Medium, sondern direkt im Bewusstseinsstrom der Betrachter. Dann lösen sie sich auf und werden wieder unrepräsentierbar. Es handelt sich nicht um transzendentale Entitäten, die auf sich alleine gestellt existieren können: Sie haben keine körperliche Substanz, sondern sind das Ergebnis eines komplexen Prozesses der Interaktion zwischen von der Künstlerin modulierten, spezifischen Stimuli und unserem Gehirn und zwischen der äußeren Welt und unserer Wahrnehmung. In ihrer Arbeit in der Schering Stiftung möchte Ivana Franke, dass wir uns als Betrachter, genau wie sie selbst, mit Didi-Hubermans Idee des Nicht-Wissens auseinandersetzen. Der französische Kunsthistoriker schrieb dazu:

> Aber das Verhältnis von Nicht-Wissen zu Wissen ist nicht das von totaler *Finsternis* zu hellem *Licht*. Nicht-Wissen ist imaginiert, gedacht und geschrieben. Deshalb wird es zu etwas anderem, als das »Nichts« einfacher Ignoranz oder Dunkelheit: Es wird zur Nacht, die sich bewegt; in der schwache *Schimmer* vorbeiziehen und uns in der Dunkelheit mit Erstaunen füllen und uns dazu bringen, sie wieder sehen zu wollen. Wie Glühwürmchen, die ihr Licht in der Sommernacht aufblitzen lassen, zum Beispiel.
>
> Wir müssen deshalb annehmen, dass das Verhältnis zwischen Nicht-Wissen und Wissen – wie zwischen Verschwinden und Erscheinen – etwas anderes ist, als ein einfacher Mangel: Es handelt sich eher um das Verhältnis von Blickwinkeln. Wir können also die These aufstellen, dass Nicht-Wissen sich zum Wissen verhält, wie das Glühwürmchen zum Licht – oder wie ein kleines Bild zum weiten

8 Georges Didi-Huberman, *La survivance des lucioles*, Paris: Les Edition de Minuit, 2009. (Im Original Französisch: »[...] la chose la plus fugace, la plus fragile qui soit«, S. 21.)

stimuli modulated by the artist and our brain, between the external world and our perception. In her work at Schering Stiftung, Ivana Franke confronted herself (and would like us to be confronted) with Didi-Huberman's idea of non-knowledge. As the French art historian wrote:

> But non-knowledge is not to knowledge what total *darkness* would be to full *light*. Non-knowledge is imagined, thought and written. It thus becomes something other than the 'nothing' of simple ignorance or obscurity: it becomes the night that moves, where faint *glimmers* pass and fill us with wonder in the dark, and make us want to see them again. Like fireflies, when they make a summer night flicker, for example.
>
> We must hypothesise, therefore, that the relationship of non-knowledge to knowledge—like disappearance to appearance—is something other than one simple privation: it is rather a relationship of point of view. We can thus hypothesise that non-knowledge is to knowledge what the firefly is to the light or what a small image is to the wide horizon. We see entirely different things, in effect, depending on whether we expand our vision to take in the *horizon* that stretches, immense and immobile, beyond us; or direct our attention towards the *image* that passes, tiny and mobile, close by us in the night. The image is indeed like a firefly, a little glimmer, the *lucciola* of transient, sporadic events.[9]

In these lines, Didi-Huberman talks not only about the instability of images, but also about firefly-knowledge as a dim but still resistant light. He analyzes cultural crisis using a metaphor borrowed from Pier Paolo Pasolini, who in 1975 wrote his famous article "Il vuoto del potere" also known as "L'articolo delle lucciole."[10] He says that talking about fireflies is like talking about the memories and cultural historical values that are becoming lost because of the blinding light of the neo-capitalistic system, or "the neo-fascism of consumerism," as he calls it.

But again, this is a problem of perspective and orientation. He suggests that it is not fireflies that are disappearing; rather, it is the disenchanted gaze that is becoming unable to see them, incapable of recognizing them in the river of light and transparency imposed by our society.

Beyond these two thinkers' perhaps misoneistic and even romantic passive nostalgia for better times that are long gone, let us take Ivana Franke's invitation to "Retreat into Darkness" as an occasion to break with our epistemological paradigms, to actively reflect and imagine other possible constellations of space and action in this world as well as outside of it.

9 Georges Didi-Huberman, "Non-Knowledge of the Passer-By (04.06.2009)," in "Glimpses. Between Appearance and Disappearance," in *ZMK. Zeitschrift für Medien- und Kulturforschung* 7, no. 1 (2016), 112.

10 Pier Paolo Pasolini, "Il vuoto del potere" or "L'articolo delle lucciole," *Corriere della Sera* (February 1, 1975).

> Horizont. Wir sehen gänzlich verschiedene Dinge, je nachdem, ob wir unsere Sicht erweitern, um den sich immens und unbeweglich ausbreitenden *Horizont* zu erfassen, der weit von uns entfernt ist; oder ob wir unsere Aufmerksamkeit auf das *Bild* lenken, das vorbeizieht, klein und beweglich, nah bei uns in der Nacht. Das Bild ist tatsächlich ein kleines Schimmern, wie ein *Glühwürmchen* vergänglicher und sporadischer Ereignisse.[9]

In diesen Zeilen spricht Didi-Huberman nicht nur von der Instabilität der Bilder, sondern auch vom Glühwürmchen-Wissen als einem schwachen, aber doch widerständigen Licht. Er analysiert die kulturelle Krise mit einer Metapher, die er von Pier Paolo Pasolini übernommen hat. Dieser schrieb 1975 einen berühmten Artikel, der als *L'articolo delle lucciole* bekannt wurde.[10] Über Glühwürmchen zu sprechen ist so, wie über Erinnerungen und kulturgeschichtliche Werte zu reden, die im blendenden Licht des neokapitalistischen Systems beziehungsweise des »Neofaschismus der Konsumgesellschaft« verschwinden, wie er es formuliert hat.

Aber das ist wie gesagt ein Problem der Perspektive und Orientierung. Er geht davon aus, dass nicht die Glühwürmchen verschwinden, sondern dass unser desillusionierter Blick nicht mehr in der Lage sei, sie zu sehen; dass wir unfähig wären, sie noch zu erkennen in der Überfülle des Lichts und der Transparenz, die von unserer Gesellschaft auferlegt wird.

Jenseits der Tatsache, dass diese beiden männlichen Autoren möglicherweise Neuerungen feindlich gegenüberstehend in passiver, vielleicht sogar romantischer Nostalgie für eine verlorene, bessere Zeit schwelgen, sollten wir Ivana Frankes Einladung, uns »in die Dunkelheit zurückzuziehen« als eine Gelegenheit ansehen, unsere epistemologischen Paradigmen aufzubrechen, sie aktiv zu reflektieren, und uns andere mögliche Konstellationen des Raums und der Handlungen in dieser Welt und auch außerhalb von ihr vorzustellen.

9 Georges Didi-Huberman, »Non-Knowledge of the Passer-By (04.06.2009)«, in: »Glimpses. Between Appearance and Disappearance«, in: *ZMK. Zeitschrift für Medien- und Kulturforschung*, 7 (2016) Nr. 1, Hamburg: Felix Meiner Verlag, 2016, S. 112.

10 Pier Paolo Pasolini, »Il vuoto del potere« oder »L'articolo delle lucciole«, *Corriere della Sera*, 1. Februar 1975.

Zeichnungen der geometrischen Linienstrukturen der Ausstellungsobjekte in der Installation *Retreat into Darkness. Towards a Phenomenology of the Unknown.*

Drawings of geometric, linear structures of objects in the installation *Retreat into Darkness. Towards a Phenomenology of the Unknown.*

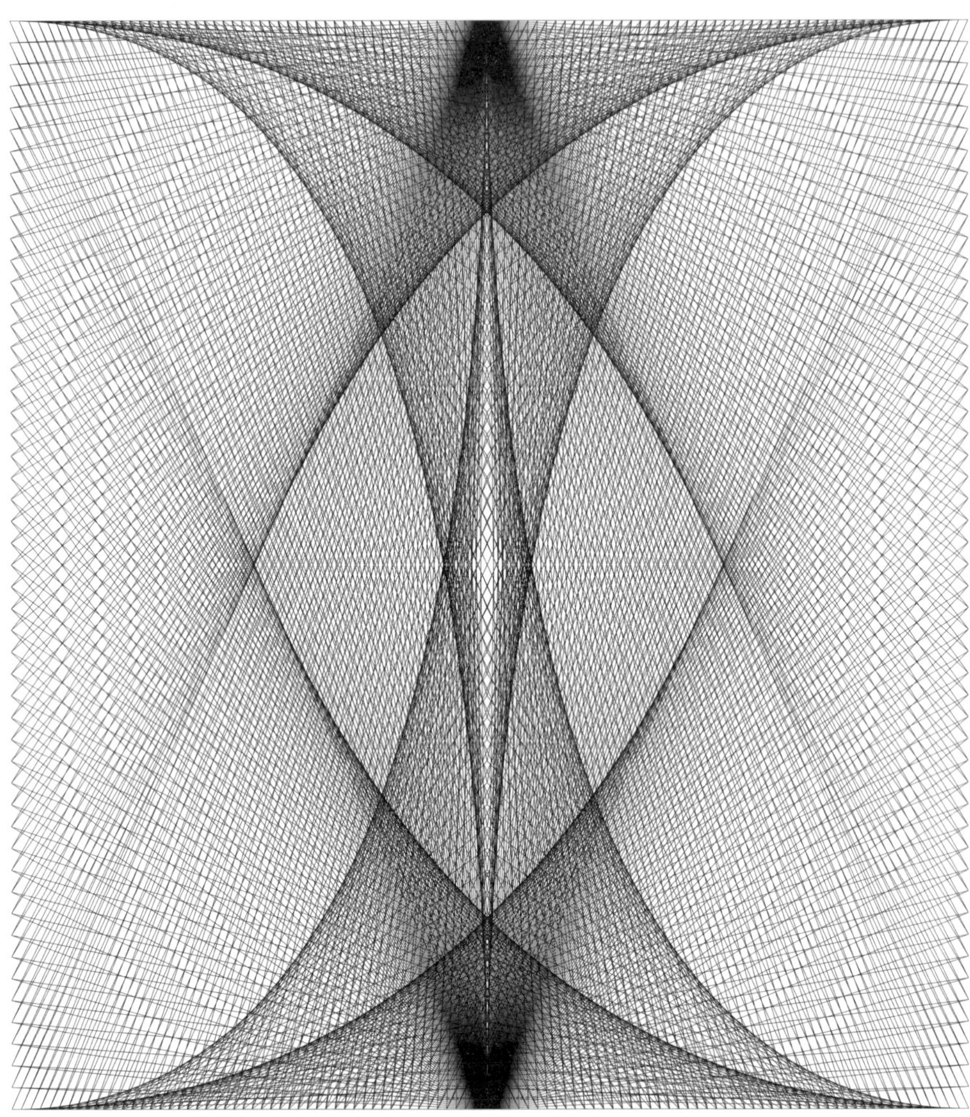

Monofilamentstruktur des zentralen Objektes, Vorderansicht.

Monofilament structure of central object, front view.

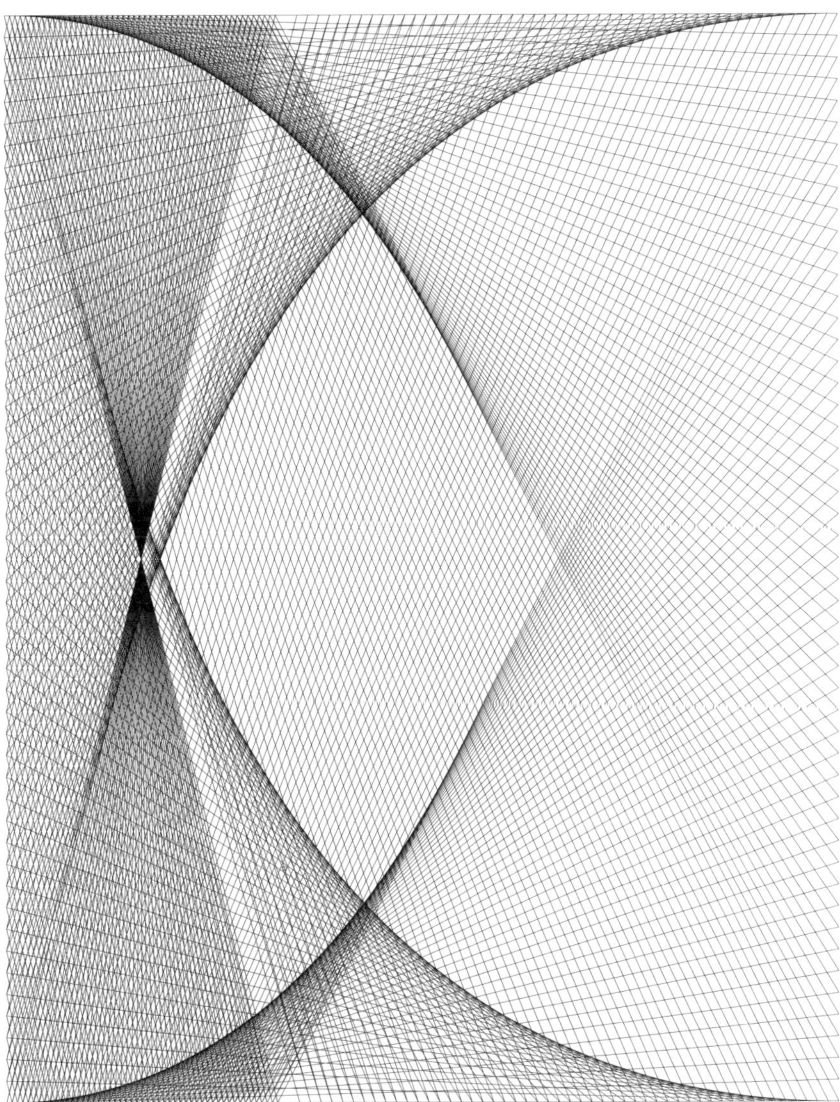

Monofilamentstruktur des zentralen Objektes, Seitenansicht.

Monofilament structure of central object, side view.

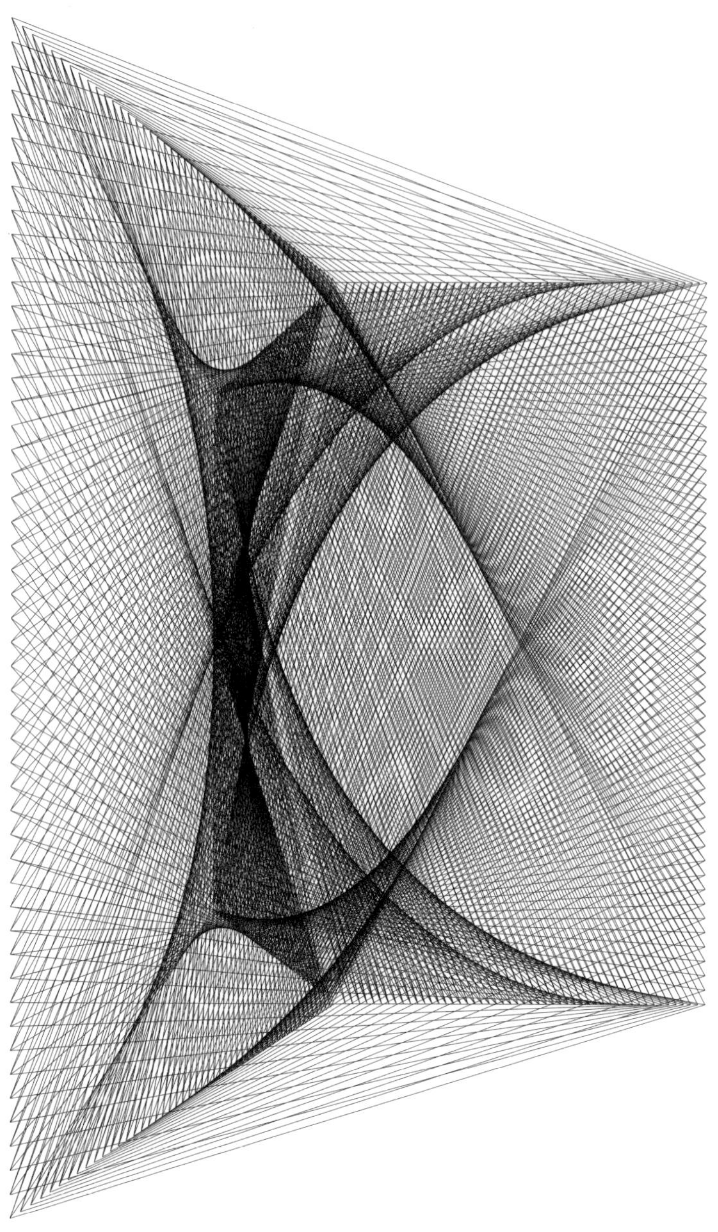

Monofilamentstruktur des zentralen Objektes, perspektivische Darstellung.

Monofilament structure of central object, perspective view.

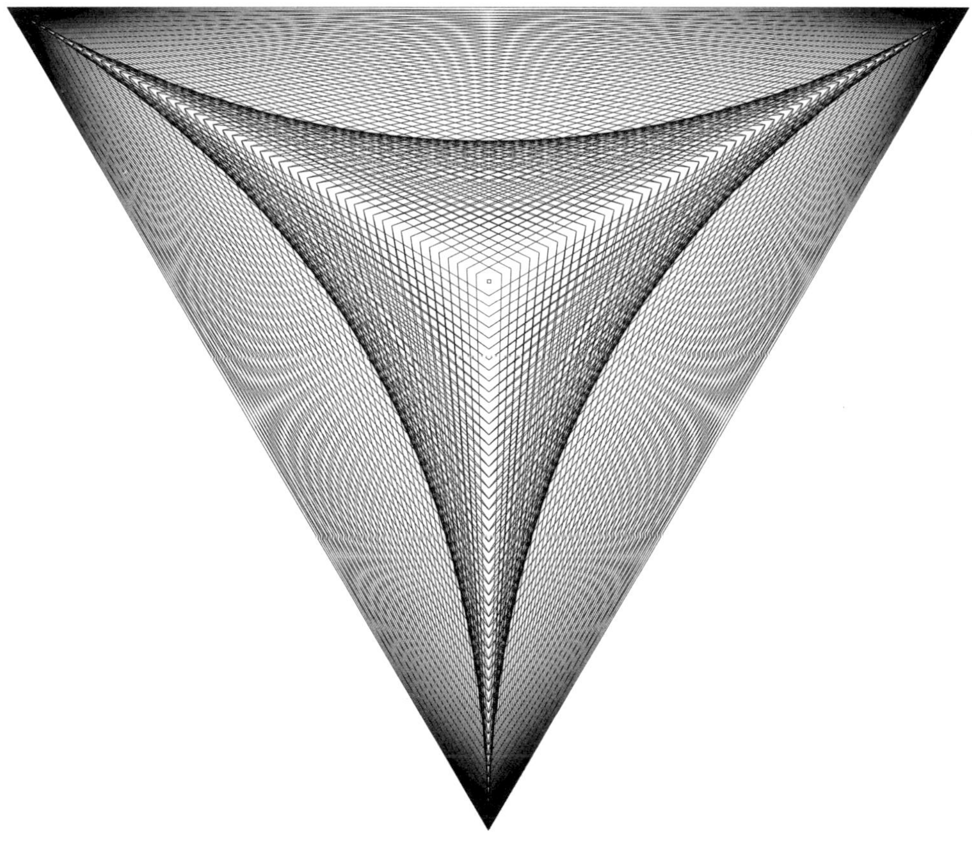

Monofilamentstruktur des zentralen Objektes, Draufsicht.

Monofilament structure of central object, top view.

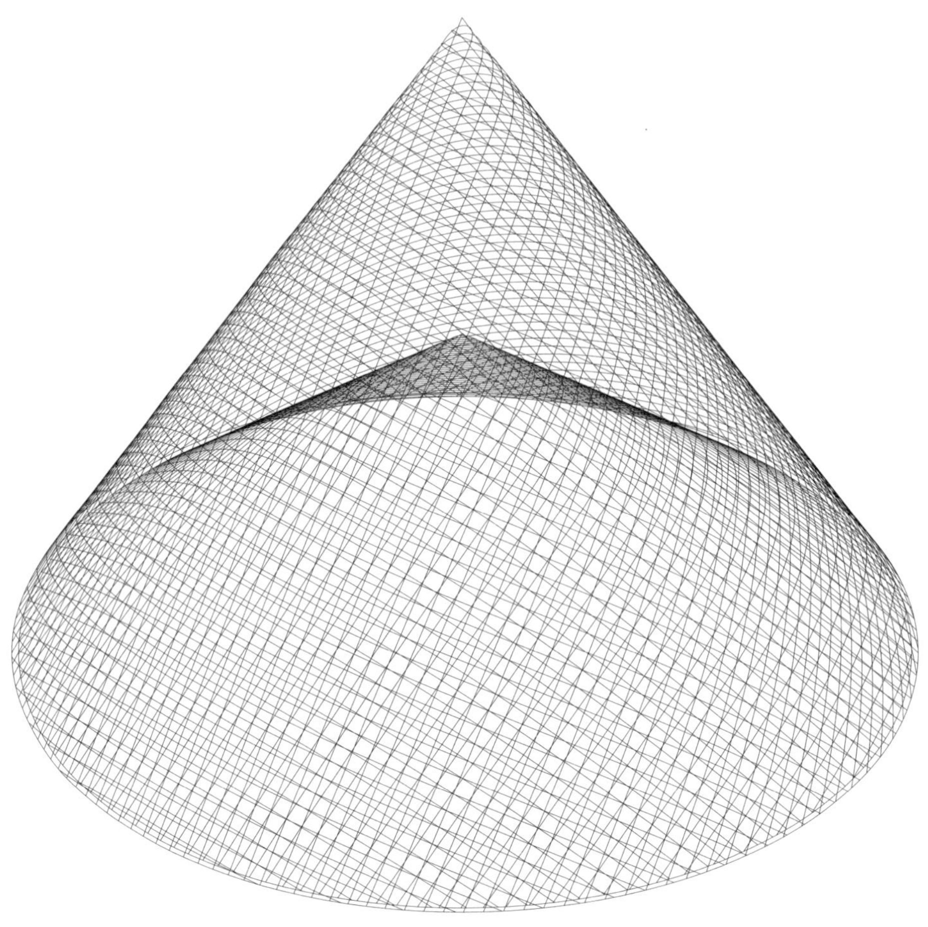

Monofilamentstruktur des großen Kegels, isometrische Ansicht.

Monofilament structure of large cone, isometric view.

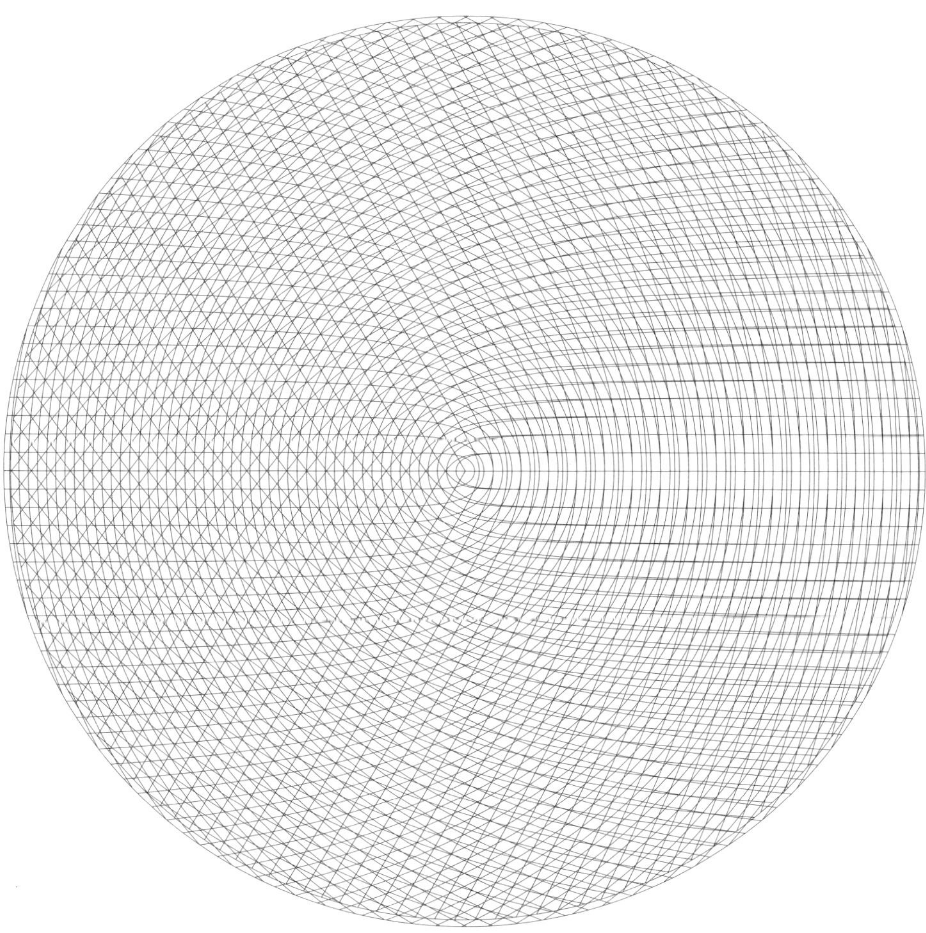

Monofilamentstruktur des großen Kegels, Draufsicht.

Monofilament structure of large cone, top view.

Entfernung Unbekannt

Distance Unknown

Jimena Canales

»Ihnen etwas zu zeigen, dass Sie noch *nie zuvor* gesehen haben; Sie sehen zu lassen, *wie Sie noch nie zuvor gesehen haben*. Zu verändern, was Sie *bisher gesehen haben*. Warum? Vielleicht hatten Sie einen zu engen Blick auf die Welt. Das könnte Sie auf einen bestimmten Weg gelenkt haben: Sie haben Vermutungen angestellt und voreilige Schlüsse gezogen. Diese Schlussfolgerungen sind nicht mehr gültig. Jetzt können Sie das Finale ihrer Lebensgeschichte verändern und dessen sonderbare Ursprünge neu bewerten.« So hat Ivana Franke mir ihr Werk erklärt. Es erinnert mich an die Worte des Philosophen Henri Bergson, der 1911 das Folgende zur Rolle der Philosophie geschrieben hat:

> [Sie] sollte der Theorie nach die Wahrnehmung erweitern und vervollständigen; in Wirklichkeit aber ist sie gezwungen, eine Fülle von Wahrnehmungen zu unterschlagen, damit diese oder jene unter ihnen repräsentativ für die anderen werden könne. – Aber nehmen wir einmal an, daß wir, anstatt zu versuchen, uns über die Wahrnehmung der Dinge zu erheben, tiefer in sie eindringen würden, um sie zu ergründen und zu erweitern. Nehmen wir einmal an, daß wir uns in sie einfühlen und so unsere direkte Schau der Dinge zu erweitern suchen: dann würden wir zu einer Philosophie kommen, in der nichts von den unmittelbaren Gegebenheiten der Sinne und des Bewußtseins geopfert würde. Keine Qualität, kein Aspekt des Wirklichen würde an die Stelle der übrigen treten unter dem Vorwand, sie erklären zu wollen.[1]

Wenn man diesen Maßstab anlegt, dann ist Ivana Franke zweifellos eine herausragende Künstler-Philosophin. Aber ihr Werk geht über Bergsons Philosophie hinaus und entfernt sich von den Standards der Phänomenologie. Als ich durch den Ausstellungsraum ging und erfolglos versuchte, mir darüber klar zu werden, was ich sah, erkannte ich, dass ich beim Nachdenken über das Konzept der »Distanz« den falschen Ansatz gewählt hatte. Distanz wäre nicht mehr das, was ich bis dahin gedacht hatte, es müsste etwas anderes, etwas Größeres werden.

Entfernung Unbekannt[2]

»Das ist ein kleiner Schritt für einen Menschen, aber ein riesiger Sprung für die Menschheit«, bemerkte Neil Armstrong, als er zum ersten Mal die Mondoberfläche betrat. Ein Schritt ist durchschnittlich immer ungefähr 74 cm lang, egal ob auf der Erde

1 Henri Bergson, »Die Wahrnehmung der Veränderung«, in: *Denken und schöpferisches Werden*, übers. von Leonore Kottje, Frankfurt am Main: Syndikat Autoren- und Verlagsgesellschaft, 1985, S. 153–154.

2 Teile dieses Beitrages wurden zunächst für den Vortrag »Precisely. Differentiating Accuracy, Precision, and Exactitude in the Sciences and Humanities« entwickelt, den die Autorin zusammen mit Markus Krajewski beim jährlichen Treffen der History of Science Society in Chicago im Jahr 2014 gehalten hat.

"To show you something you have *never seen;* to make you see *as you have never seen* before. To change what you *have seen so far.* Why? You might have observed the world too narrowly. This could have led you down a certain path: You have made assumptions and jumped to conclusions. Those conclusions are no longer valid. Now you can change the finale of your life story and reevaluate its curious origins." This is how Ivana Franke explained her work to me. It reminds me of the words of the philosopher Henri Bergson, writing about the role of philosophy in 1911:

> [It] should in theory extend and complete perception; it is obliged in fact to require that many perceptions stand aside so that some of them may become representative of the others.—But suppose that instead of trying to rise above our perception of things we were to plunge into it for the purpose of deepening it and widening it. Suppose that we were to insert our will into it, and that this will, expanding, were to expand our vision of things. We should obtain this time a philosophy where nothing in the data of the senses or consciousness would be sacrificed; no quality, no aspect of the real world would be substituted for the rest ostensibly to explain it.[1]

If judged by those standards, Ivana Franke is no doubt a superb artist-philosopher. However, her work takes me beyond Bergson's philosophy and away from standard phenomenology. As I walked around the exhibition space, trying unsuccessfully to determine what I was seeing, I realized that I had been thinking about the concept of "distance" in the wrong terms. Distance would no longer be what I had considered it up to then; it was to be something else, something more.

Distance Unknown[2]

"That's one small step for man, one giant leap for mankind," remarked Neil Armstrong, as he stepped on the surface of the moon for the first time. The average length of a stride on Earth remains fixed at approximately 74 cm, as on the moon's surface. Measurements of length are some of the sturdiest, uncontestable facts available to us. But what kind of facts are they? Identical lengths can sometimes appear to be strikingly different. The distance between the master's and the servant's

1 Henri Bergson, "The Creative Mind: The Perception of Change." *Key Writings*, ed. Keith Ansell Pearson and John Mullarkey (New York: Continuum, 2002), pp. 250–251.

2 Some of the themes in "Distance Unknown" were first developed for the lecture "Precisely. Differentiating Accuracy, Precision, and Exactitude in the Sciences and Humanities" delivered with Markus Krajewski at the annual History of Science Society meeting in Chicago (2014).

oder dem Mond. Längenmaße gehören zu den stabilsten und unanfechtbarsten Fakten, die wir haben. Doch was sind das für Fakten? Identische Längen wirken manchmal erstaunlich unterschiedlich. Die Entfernung zwischen dem Zimmer des Herrn und dem des Dieners oder zwischen West- und Ost-Jerusalem ist wesentlich größer, als der in Zahlen gemessene Abstand es aussagt.

Was ist Entfernung? Woher wissen wir etwas über Entfernungen? Was sagt uns dieses Wissen und wo ist es lückenhaft?

Lassen Sie die Reise zum Mond einmal außer Acht und stellen sich einen einfacheren Fall vor: Die Distanz zwischen Rom und Wien. Für den berühmten Psychologen Sigmund Freud wirkte die Entfernung zwischen den beiden Städten unendlich. Um die Jahrhundertwende entwickelte Freud eine Phobie, die ihn daran hinderte, Rom zu besuchen. Aber selbst wenn wir einräumen, dass für Freud in psychologischer Hinsicht die Entfernung zwischen Rom und Wien eine andere war als für uns, müssen wir festhalten, dass die tatsächlich gemessene Distanz zwischen den beiden Städten bei ungefähr 763 Kilometern liegt.

Erst nach Einführung des Katasters wurde begonnen, geografische Distanzen einheitlich in Bezug auf festgelegte Standards zu messen – ein Kontrollprojekt, das direkt mit den fiskalischen Interessen des modernen Staates zusammenhing. In der Zeit nach 1800 haben wir angefangen, räumliche Distanzen durchgängig in Kilometern zu messen. Die Standardisierung des Meters war ein langes, mühsames und umstrittenes Projekt, das von Napoleon unterstützt wurde. Es funktionierte, wenn auch mit Unterbrechungen, relativ gut im weiteren Verlauf des 19. Jahrhunderts, bis es schließlich der vorherrschende Standard für Maßeinheiten in Frankreich und darüber hinaus wurde. Andere Standardisierungsprojekte fanden weltweite Verbreitung und gipfelten schließlich im Internationalen Einheitensystem (SI), das heute allgemein gebräuchlich ist.[3]

Wir wurden von einer »Lawine gedruckter Zahlen« überrollt, die uns seit dem 19. Jahrhundert eine präzise Erfassung der Welt gestattet hat.[4] Der Wissenschaftler William Thomson, auch bekannt als Lord Kelvin, hat seine Bewunderung für die Quantifizierung in einem berühmten Satz ausgedrückt: »Ich sage oft, wenn man das, worüber man spricht, auch messen und in Zahlen ausdrücken kann, dann weiß man etwas darüber; aber wenn man es nicht messen und es nicht in Zahlen ausdrücken kann, dann ist das Wissen dürftig und unbefriedigend.«[5] Selbst in der Medizin, einem der letzten Bereiche, der erobert wurde, ist heute das »Verordnen nach Zahlen« vorherrschend.[6] Da immer mehr Fakten über das Universum akkumuliert werden, glauben einige Wissenschaftler, dass eine große vereinheitlichte Theorie (engl.: Grand Unified Theory: GUT) und eine Weltformel (engl.: Theory of Everything: TOE) in Reichweite seien.

3 Ken Alder, »A Revolution to Measure: The Political Economy of the Metric System in France«, in: *The Values of Precision*, hg. v. M. Norton Wise, Princeton: Princeton University Press, 1995.

4 Ian Hacking, »Biopower and the Avalanche of Numbers«, in: *Humanities and Society*, Nr. 5, 1983.

5 Aus einem Vortrag vor der Vereinigung der Bauingenieure, London (3. Mai 1883), veröffentlicht in: William Thomson, »Electrical Units of Measurement«, in: *Popular Lectures and Addresses*, London: 1891–1894 (1883), S. 80–81.

6 Jeremy A. Greene, *Prescribing by Numbers: Drugs and the Definition of Disease*, Baltimore: Johns Hopkins University Press, 2007.

room, or West and East Jerusalem, appears much greater than when their separation is simply expressed in numbers.

What is distance? How do we know distances? What does our knowledge about distances tell us, and what does it lack?

Let us forget about traveling to the moon and consider a simpler case: the distance between Rome and Vienna. For the famed psychologist Sigmund Freud, the distance between the two cities was infinite. At the turn of the century, Freud developed a phobia that prevented him from visiting Rome. If we admit that, psychologically, the distance between Rome and Vienna was different for Freud than it is for us, we must also acknowledge that the actual measured distance between the two cities remains fixed at approximately 763 kilometers.

Geographic spans began to be consistently measured by referring to fixed standards only after the introduction of the cadastre in a control project directly tied to the taxation interests of the modern state. We began to consistently measure spatial distances in terms of kilometers sometime after 1800. The standardization of the meter was a long, laborious, and contested project backed by Napoleon. It worked reasonably well, yet was only effective on-and-off for the rest of the nineteenth century until it finally became the dominant standard of measurement in France and elsewhere. Other standardization projects spread throughout the world and culminated with the International System of Units (SI) used today.[3]

An "avalanche of printed numbers" has been descending upon us, permitting us to grasp the world with precision, since the nineteenth century.[4] The scientist William Thomson, also known as Lord Kelvin, expressed his admiration for quantification in a famous phrase: "I often say that when you can measure what you are speaking about, and express it in numbers, you know something about it; but when you cannot measure it, when you cannot express it in numbers, your knowledge is of a meagre and unsatisfactory kind."[5] Today, even medicine, one of the last fields to be conquered, is characterized by "prescription by numbers."[6] Thanks to the progressive accumulation of facts about the universe, some scientists now believe that a GUT (Grand Unified Theory) and a TOE (Theory of Everything) are within sight.

Let us return to the moon. Were the steps taken there by Neil Armstrong comparable to those he took back on planet Earth? Have Rome and Vienna *always* been separated by 763 km? Although their distance was not always measured thus, and admitting that it took modern science many years to give us this number (which today can almost be obtained with the click of a mouse), it has always been the case. Or was the world itself a different place before we determined the distance between

3 Ken Alder, "A Revolution to Measure: The Political Economy of the Metric System in France," in *The Values of Precision*, ed. M. Norton Wise (Princeton: Princeton University Press, 1995).

4 Ian Hacking, "Biopower and the Avalanche of Numbers," *Humanities and Society* 5 (1983).

5 From a lecture at the Institution of Civil Engineers, London (May 3, 1883), published in William Thomson's "Electrical Units of Measurement," in Popular *Lectures and Addresses* (London: 1891–1894 (1883)), pp. 80–81.

6 Jeremy A. Greene, *Prescribing by Numbers: Drugs and the Definition of Disease* (Baltimore: Johns Hopkins University Press, 2007).

Lassen Sie uns zum Mond zurückkommen. Waren Neil Armstrongs Schritte auf dem Mond mit denen vergleichbar, die er auf dem Planeten Erde getan hat? Waren Rom und Wien *immer* 763 Kilometer voneinander entfernt? Obwohl die Entfernung nicht immer auf diese Weise gemessen wurde und man einräumen muss, dass die moderne Wissenschaft viele Jahre gebraucht hat, diese Zahl zu ermitteln (die heute praktisch nur einen Mausklick entfernt ist), war es immer so. Oder war die Welt selbst ein anderer Ort, bevor wir die Entfernung zwischen Rom und Wien auf diese Weise ermittelt haben? War die Welt tatsächlich, im Sinne von *wirklich,* anders? Wie sehr wird die Welt, wie sie ist, durch die Konzepte, Kategorien und Standards, die wir verwenden, repräsentiert?[7] Diese Fragen bringen immer wieder die alte, hartnäckige Debatte zwischen Idealisten und Empirikern auf die Tagesordnung. Gibt es einen Ausweg aus dieser Sackgasse?

Die lange Geschichte, der wir die Welt der präzisen, standardisierten Messungen und Aufzeichnungen verdanken, beeinflusst nicht nur unser Handeln, sondern auch unser Denken. Eine Neubewertung dieser Geschichte kann als eine Weise des Erinnerns und Aufzeichnens in einem weiteren Sinn angewendet werden: als eine Vervollständigung.

Zusätzlich zu physischen Entfernungen sind wir im Alltag mit anderen Formen der Distanzierung konfrontiert: die wichtigsten davon sind soziale und affektive Distanzen. Entfernung schmerzt. All diese Aspekte leisteten einen Beitrag zu Freuds Schwierigkeiten, nach Rom zu kommen und die legendäre Stadt zu erreichen. Dem Konzept der physischen Entfernung liegt eine weiter gefasste, allgemeinere Bedeutung der Entfernung zu Grunde, welche wiederum auch den psychologischen Distanzen zu Grunde liegt. Was aber hat Freuds psychologisches Trauma mit der physischen Distanz zwischen Rom und Wien zu tun?

Stellen Sie sich vor, ein/e Wissenschaftler/in beginnt, in Wien sorgfältig ein Maßband auszurollen. Nach ein paar Tagen wäre er oder sie kaum über den Stadtrand hinausgekommen. Warum klammern sich die exakten Wissenschaften so erfolgreich an das Merkmal der Genauigkeit, während andere (oft) den Vorwürfen ausgesetzt sind, ungenau, zufällig und manchmal überbordend zu sein?[8]

Versuchen wir, Freud dabei zu helfen, nach Rom zu kommen. Seine gequälte Seele versuchte, sich durch eine sorgsame Selbstanalyse zu heilen. Nach vielen Jahren harter Analysearbeit kam er zu dem Schluss, dass diese spezielle Phobie aus einer sehr viel allgemeineren Angst herrührte. Der britische Historiker Perry Anderson zitiert Freuds Traumdeutung: »*Hannibal* und *Rom* symbolisierten dem Jüngling den Gegensatz zwischen der Zähigkeit des Judentums und der Organisation der katholischen Kirche.« Und er fügt hinzu: »Der Euphemismus »Organisation« selbst zeugt

7 Bernhard Siegert, »The Map is the Territory«, in: *Radical Philosophy,* Nr. 169, 2011.

8 Markus Krajewski, »Genauigkeit. Zur Ausbildung einer epistemischen Tugend im langen 19. Jahrhundert«, in: *Berichte zur Wissenschaftsgeschichte,* 2016.

Rome and Vienna in this way? Was the world actually, meaning *really*, different? How much do the concepts, categories, and standards we use represent the world as it is?[7] These questions often take us back to the old, intractable debate between idealists and empiricists. Is there a way out of this impasse?

The long history that brought us the world of accurate standardized measurements and records affects not only how we act but how we think. Reevaluating this history can be used as a way of remembering and recording in a much broader sense, in terms of completing.

In addition to physical distances, in our everyday lives we are confronted with other types of distancing, most prominently social and affective distances. Distance hurts. In Freud's attempts to go to Rome, all of these aspects were involved in his difficulties trying to reach the fabled city. The concept of physical distance is undergirded by a broader, more general sense of distance—one that also upholds psychological distances. But what does Freud's psychological trauma have to do with the physical distance between Rome and Vienna?

Picture a scientist meticulously unrolling his or her tape ruler, starting in Vienna. After a couple of days, he or she will have reached not much farther than the city's outskirts. But why do the exact sciences cling so effectively to the attribute of exactitude, while the others must (frequently) submit themselves to accusations of imprecision, contingency, and sometimes excess?[8]

Let us try to help Freud reach Rome. The tortured soul tried to cure himself by embarking on a careful therapy of self-analysis. After many years of hard work, he determined that this particular phobia arose from a much more general fear. "To my youthful mind," he explained, "Hannibal and Rome symbolized the tenacity of Jewry and the organization of the Catholic Church—where the euphemism 'organization' itself continues to testify to the intimidating power and menace of the Vatican."[9] Psychoanalysis finally helped him reach Rome.

But what was it that was really preventing him from reaching the famed city? Sometime during the process of his own self-analysis, Freud forgot all about the measurable physical distance separating the two cities. His psychoanalytical method only went so far. Can we complement the psychoanalysis he founded with a *physicoanalysis?* His psychological traumas remained an obstacle to getting there, but they were clearly not the *only* problem. The 763 kilometers in between were part of the problem, too.

Freud's "Roman Phobia" was in no small part a technological phobia as well. It was "a particularly severe manifestation of a more general phobia, to which Freud was especially subject in

7 Bernhard Siegert, "The Map is the Territory," *Radical Philosophy* 169 (2011).

8 Markus Krajewski, "Genauigkeit. Zur Ausbildung einer epistemischen Tugend im langen 19. Jahrhundert," *Berichte zur Wissenschaftsgeschichte* (2016).

9 Sigmund Freud, cited in Perry Anderson, *Spectrum: From Right to Left in the World of Ideas* (Verso: London, 2005), p. 199.

weiterhin von der einschüchternden Macht und Bedrohung durch den Vatikan.«[9] Die Psychoanalyse half ihm schließlich, Rom zu erreichen.

Aber was hielt ihn wirklich davon ab, die legendäre Stadt zu erreichen? Irgendwo in diesem Prozess der Selbstanalyse vergaß Freud die messbare physische Entfernung zwischen den beiden Städten. Seine psychoanalytische Methode kam an ihre Grenze. Können wir die von ihm begründete Psychoanalyse durch eine *Physiko-Analyse* ergänzen? Seine psychologischen Traumata blieben ein Hindernis, um das Ziel zu erreichen. Aber sie waren eindeutig nicht das *einzige* Problem – die 763 Kilometer zwischen den Städten spielten auch eine Rolle.

Freuds »römische Phobie« war zu einem beachtlichen Teil auch eine Technophobie. Sie war »ein besonders schweres Symptom einer allgemeineren Phobie, unter welcher Freud besonders in seiner Jugend litt, und von der er auch nie vollständig geheilt wurde: der Angst vor dem Reisen, besonders dem Reisen mit dem Zug.«[10] Aber so, wie er die 763 km vergessen hat, so scheint er auch den Zug vergessen zu haben, der ihn dorthin bringen sollte. Während Freud um die Jahrhundertwende ein paar Tage gebraucht hätte, um nach Rom zu kommen, können wir heute von Wien nach Rom in weniger als einer Stunde reisen. Die Psychoanalyse vergisst nicht nur die physischen Entfernungen, sie vergisst auch die Technologien, die zu deren Überwindung benutzt werden und betrachtet diese nur in Bezug auf deren symbolische Macht.

In seinem Buch *Das Unbehagen in der Kultur* (1930) hat Freud den Nutzen der Eisenbahn und des Telefons mit einem einzigen Satz abgetan: »Gäbe es keine Eisenbahn, die die Entfernungen überwindet, so hätte das Kind die Vaterstadt nie verlassen, man brauchte kein Telephon, um seine Stimme zu hören.«[11] Das Schrumpfen der Zeit und des Raums durch die modernen Technologien ist eine oft beobachtete Eigenschaft der Moderne (siehe zum Beispiel Paul Valéry, Walter Benjamin und viele andere).[12] Dieses scheinbare Schrumpfen der Entfernungen hatte positive und negative Folgen. Freud hat insbesondere die negativen sehr eloquent beleuchtet. Technologien haben erst dann funktioniert, als etwas anderes, etwas noch Grundlegenderes, zerbrochen war. Lässt die Technologie also nur die Entfernungen schrumpfen, die sie zuvor erzeugt hat?

Aus einer philosophischen Sicht werden Entfernungen sehr schnell unklar. Der Philosoph Martin Heidegger hinterfragt die sonderbare Technologie der Brille in seinem Buch *Sein und Zeit* (1927): »Für den, der zum Beispiel eine Brille trägt, die abstandsmäßig so nahe ist, daß sie ihm auf der »Nase sitzt«, ist dieses gebrauchte Zeug umweltlich weiter entfernt als das Bild an der gegenüber befindlichen Wand«, erklärt Heidegger.[13] Später schrieb er in *Das Ding* (1950) in Bezug auf die weitverbreitete Annahme, dass die

9 Perry Anderson, *Spectrum: From Right to Left in the World of Ideas,* London: Verso 2005, S. 199. Zitiert nach: Sigmund Freud, *Traumdeutung,* 1900, in: *Gesammelte Werke Bd. 5,* Altenmünster: Jazzybee Verlag, 2016, S. 214.

10 Sebastiano Timpanaro, »Freud's ›Roman Phobia‹«, in: *New Left Review,* Nr. 147, September/Oktober 1984. Vgl.: *Freud's Rome-Phobia and Phantasy,* Konferenz in Rom (23.–24. Juni 2010), organisiert von Andreas Mayer in Zusammenarbeit mit der American Academy in Rom.

11 Sigmund Freud, *Das Unbehagen in der Kultur,* Berlin: Europäischer Kulturverlag, 2015, S. 30.

12 Paul Valéry, »La conquête de l'ubiquité«, in: *De la musique avant toute chose,* hg. v. Camille Bellaigue/Henri Massis/Paul Valéry, Paris: Editions du Tambourinaire, 1928; Walter Benjamin, »Das Kunstwerk im Zeitalter seiner technischen Reproduzierbarkeit«, in: *Illuminationen,* Frankfurt am Main: Suhrkamp, 1977.

13 Martin Heidegger, *Sein und Zeit,* Tübingen: May Niemeyer Verlag, 2006, S. 106.

his youth but of which he was never completely cured: a fear of travelling, and notably of travelling by train."[10] But just as he forgot about the 763 km, he also seems to have forgotten about the train that was to get him there. While, at the turn of the century, it would take Freud a couple of days to reach Rome,now we can get from Vienna to Rome in a little more than one hour. Psychoanalysis not only forgets about physical distances, it forgets about the technologies used to conquer them and considers them only in terms of their symbolic power.

Freud discounted the benefits of railways and telephones in a single sentence in his book *Civilization and Its Discontents* (1930): "If there had been no railway to conquer distances, my child would never have left his native town and I should need no telephone to hear his voice."[11] The shrinking of time and space due to modern technologies is a frequently acknowledged characteristic of modernity (as noted by Paul Valéry, Walter Benjamin, and many others.)[12] This ostensible shrinkage of distances has come with positive as well as negative consequences. Freud was particularly eloquent when elucidating the negative aftereffects. According to him, technologies only worked after something else, something more essential, had been broken. Does technology only shrink the distances it creates?

If considered philosophically, distances become fuzzier even more quickly. The philosopher Martin Heidegger in *Being and Time* (1927) questioned the curious technology of eyeglasses. "When, for instance, a man wears a pair of spectacles which are so close to him ... that they are 'sitting on his nose,' they are environmentally more remote from him than the picture on the opposite wall," he explained.[13] Later in *The Thing* (1950), he explained how "all distances in time and space are shrinking," referring to the widespread belief that technology is reducing global distances. But this shrinkage, he warned, is deceptive. As the far comes near, the near escapes farther away. Despite "the frantic abolition of all distances," this "brings no nearness; for nearness does not consist in shortness of distance."[14]

Consider other ways of measuring distance. Your height, for example. In the early nineteenth century, we would not have measured it using the same units as those used to express the distance between two cities. Now we do. What does that do to us? For one, it narrows our understanding of the self.

Consider temporal distance. How old are you? Our understanding of biological age in terms of the astronomically based calendar we use in our civil life is a particularly modern (and contested) practice. The question of how far Rome is from Vienna can be answered in temporal terms. It comprised many years of analysis for Freud, one day for his contemporaries who could hop on a train, and a few hours in our time.

10 Sebastiano Timpanaro, "Freud's 'Roman Phobia'," *New Left Review* 147 (September–October 1984). See also Freud's "Rome-Phobia and Phantasy, Conference in Rome, June 23–24, 2010, organized by Andreas Mayer in cooperation with the American Academy in Rome.

11 Sigmund Freud, *Civilization and Its Discontents* (New York: W. W. Norton, 1989), p. 40.

12 Paul Valéry, "La conquête de l'ubiquité," in *De la musique avant toute chose*, ed. Paul Valéry, Henri Massis, and Camille Bellaigue (Paris: Editions du Tambourinaire, 1928); Walter Benjamin, "The Work of Art in the Age of Mechanical Reproduction," in *Illuminations*, ed. Hannah Arendt (New York: Schocken, 1968).

13 Martin Heidegger, *Sein und Zeit* (1927), cited in Heidegger, *Being and Time*, trans. John Macquarrie and Edward Robinson (New York: Harper and Row, 1962), p. 141.

14 Martin Heidegger, "The Thing," in *The Craft Reader*, ed. Glenn Adamson (London: Bloomsbury Publishing, [1950] 2009).

Technologie globale Entfernungen verringert: »Alle Entfernungen in der Zeit und im Raum schrumpfen ein.« Aber er warnte, dass dieses Schrumpfen trügerisch sei. Während das weit Entfernte näher kam, entfloh das Nahe in die Ferne. Er stellte fest: »Allein das hastige Beseitigen aller Entfernungen bringt keine Nähe; denn Nähe besteht nicht im geringen Maß der Entfernung.«[14]

Denken Sie an andere Wege, eine Entfernung zu messen: zum Beispiel Ihre Größe. Im frühen 19. Jahrhundert wäre diese nicht mit den gleichen Maßeinheiten wie die Entfernung zwischen zwei Städten gemessen worden. Jetzt machen wir das. Was macht das mit uns? Zum einen begrenzt dies unser Selbstverständnis.

Denken Sie an eine zeitliche Distanz. Wie alt sind Sie? Unser Verständnis des biologischen Alters auf Basis des astronomischen Kalenders, den wir im zivilen Leben verwenden, ist eine besonders moderne (und umstrittene) Praxis. Die Frage, wie weit Rom von Wien entfernt ist, kann man in zeitlicher Hinsicht beantworten. Für Freud brauchte es viele Jahre der Analyse, für seine Zeitgenossen war es ein Tag mit dem Zug und für uns sind es ein paar Stunden.

Nachdem Sie sich eingehend mit Maßeinheiten für räumliche und zeitliche Distanzen beschäftigt haben, denken Sie an die Sinne. Können Sie sehen? Können Sie hören? Können Sie schmecken? Können Sie riechen? Diese Fragen werden Sie nur mit ja beantworten, weil sich während der Aufklärung eine bestimmte Ordnung der Sinne entwickelt hat, die sich danach durchgesetzt hat.[15] Sind Sie am Leben? Die Sichtweise, dass bestimmte Teile unseres Körpers leben (unser Protoplasma und unsere lebendigen Zellen) und die meisten anderen nicht (Haare, Nägel, DNA, tote Zellen, Enzyme, Fette, Lipide, Proteine, Codons, Nukleotide usw.), ist eng mit bestimmten technologischen Ordnungen verbunden.[16]

Nachdem Sie sich eingehend in die Sinne vertieft haben, denken Sie an die Gefühle. Sind Sie verliebt? Die Philosophin Simone Weil hat geschrieben: »Nur die können nicht getrennt werden, die sich nicht lieben.« Liebe ist die Voraussetzung der Trennung. Als Weil ins Exil nach New York City ging, stellte sie eindeutig fest, dass Distanz nur im Licht der Affektivität, oder eher im Mangel derselben, einen Sinn ergibt.[17] Entfernung kann schmerzen oder helfen. Unser Gefühl des Getrenntseins und der Nähe ist moralisch und ethisch.

Der Philosoph Bruno Latour fragt, ob man dem Menschen, den man liebt, einfach ein Zeichen oder eine Aufnahme geben kann, die sagt »Ich liebe dich« und dieser Person dann sagen, dass sie die Aufnahme anhören soll, wenn sie sich einsam fühlt oder wenn sie eine Bestätigung der Liebe braucht.[18] Wir könnten argumentieren, wie viele vor uns, dass einer Aufnahme einfach etwas fehlt. Sie wurde an der Schwelle der Moderne entwickelt und hatte eine ungeplante Konsequenz: ein Verlangen nach etwas anderem und eine Sehnsucht nach mehr – einer unbekannten Entfernung.[19]

14 Martin Heidegger, *Vorträge und Aufsätze*, Stuttgart: Klett-Cotta, 2009, S. 157.

15 »Die Bildung der 5 Sinne ist eine Arbeit der ganzen bisherigen Menschheitsgeschichte.« In: Karl Marx, *Ökonomisch-philosophische Manuskripte aus dem Jahr 1844*, hg. v. Barbara Zehnpfennig, Hamburg: Felix Meiner Verlag, 2005, S. 93.

16 Jimena Canales, »Dead and Alive: Micro-Cinematography between Physics and Biology«, *Configurations*, 23 (2015) Nr. 2, S. 235–251.

17 Zitiert nach: Palle Yourgrau, *Simone Weil*, London: Reaktion Books, 2011, S. 87; Francine du Plessix Gray, *Simone Weil*, New York: Viking, 2001, S. 180.

18 Bruno Latour, *Jubiler ou les tourments de la parole religieuse*, Paris: Les Empêcheurs de penser en rond / Le Seuil, 2002.

19 Jimena Canales, »Recording Devices«, in: *Companion to the History of Science*, Malden, Mass.: Wiley-Blackwell, 2015.

After carefully considering measurements of spatial and temporal distances, think about sensing. Do you see? Do your hear? Do you taste? Do you smell? Answering "yes" to these questions has been made possible by a specific regime of sensations that emerged during the Enlightenment and later became dominant.[15] Are you alive? The understanding that certain parts of our bodies are living (our protoplasm and living cells), while most others are not (hair, nails, DNA, dead cells, enzymes, fats, lipids, proteins, codons, nucleotides, etc.) is closely tied to specific technological regimes.[16]

After carefully considering sensing, think about feeling. Are you in love? "Those who do not love each other cannot be separated," wrote the philosopher Simone Weil. Love is a prerequisite of separation. When Weil was about to go into exile to New York City, she clearly noted how distance only made sense in light of affectivity—or rather, a lack thereof.[17] Distance can hurt, or it can help. Our sense of apartness and closeness is moral and ethical.

Can I, asks the philosopher Bruno Latour, simply give my lover a sign or a recording that says "I love you" and ask her to play it whenever she feels lonely or whenever she needs to be reassured about love?[18] Recordings, we could argue, as many have done before us, are simply missing something. They arrived on the doorstep of modernity with an unintended consequence: a desire for something else and a longing for more—a distance unknown.[19]

Technologies that permit us to record loving messages are similar to those that permit us to measure spatial differences: They are both, in essence, standardized recording systems. They are both equally unsatisfying on some level. We are used to thinking about measurements and records simplistically as a gain; let us now ask what it is that they lack.

Consider distances not only in terms of love, but in terms of hate. Intercontinental ballistic missiles (ICBM) can be seen as an extension of older pikes, knives, and telegraphs, which in turn can be understood as extensions of our nails, teeth, and voices.[20] One aim of war and peace is to manage the right amount of distance between two parties who can no longer get along.

We embody distances, although they are rarely considered in this way. Our bipedal constitution permits us to cover distances without necessitating complicated paraphernalia. Although we rarely cover distances solely by foot, we cannot fully disembody them either. Our first steps may have fanned our desire to go farther and faster and to travel by water and air. We fight distances by hugging and embracing those close to us, or running, throwing, and screaming. We develop complex information and communications technologies to stay "in touch" while away.

15 "The forming of the five senses is a labor of the entire history of the world down to the present." in Karl Marx, *Economic and Philosophic Manuscripts of 1844*, trans. Martin Milligan (New York: International Publishers, 1968).

16 Jimena Canales, "Dead and Alive: Micro-Cinematography between Physics and Biology," *Configurations* 23, No 2 (Spring 2015), pp. 235–251.

17 Cited in Palle Yourgrau, *Simone Weil* (London: Reaktion Books, 2011), p. 87; Francine du Plessix Gray, *Simone Weil* (New York: Viking, 2001), p. 180.

18 Bruno Latour, *Jubiler ou les tourments de la parole religieuse* (Paris: Les Empêcheurs de penser en rond / Le Seuil, 2002).

19 Jimena Canales, "Recording Devices," in *Companion to the History of Science* (Malden, Mass.: Wiley-Blackwell, 2015).

20 André Leroi-Gourhan, *Évolution et techniques*, 2 vols. (Paris: A. Michel, 1943–1945); André Leroi-Gourhan, *Le geste et la parole* (Paris: A. Michel, 1964).

Technologien, die uns erlauben, Liebesnachrichten aufzuzeichnen, sind ähnlich wie jene, die uns erlauben, räumliche Entfernungen zu messen: Beide sind im Grunde standardisierende Aufzeichnungssysteme. Beide sind auf einer bestimmten Ebene unbefriedigend. Wir sind es gewöhnt, Maße und Aufzeichnungen einfach nur als Gewinn zu betrachten; lassen Sie uns jetzt fragen, was ihnen fehlt.

Denken Sie an Distanzen nicht nur in Bezug auf Liebe, sondern auch auf Hass. Interkontinentalraketen (ICBM) können als Verlängerungen der alten Piken, Messer und Telegrafen verstanden werden, wobei diese wiederum Verlängerungen unserer Zähne, Nägel und Stimmen sind.[20] Eines der Ziele von Krieg und Frieden ist, die richtige Distanz zwischen zwei Parteien festzulegen, die nicht länger miteinander auskommen können.

Distanzen sind eng mit dem Körper verbunden, obwohl sie selten in dieser Weise betrachtet werden. Unser Körperbau als Zweifüßler erlaubt es uns, ohne eine komplizierte Ausrüstung Entfernung zu überwinden. Distanzen werden inzwischen nur selten zu Fuß überbrückt, aber man kann sie auch nicht ganz vom Körper abtrennen. Unsere ersten Schritte mögen unser Verlangen angefacht haben, weiter und schneller zu gehen und dann über Wasser und in der Luft zu reisen. Wir überwinden Entfernungen, indem wir die umarmen, die uns nahe stehen, oder indem wir rennen, etwas werfen oder schreien. Wir entwickeln komplexe Informations- und Kommunikationstechnologien, um »in Kontakt« zu bleiben, während wir weg sind.

Auch zeitliche Entfernungen sind mit dem Körper verbunden. Unser Sinn für die Zukunft und die Vergangenheit – beides weit von uns entfernt – ist sehr unterschiedlich, je nachdem, wie wichtig etwas für uns ist. Erwartungen entstehen, wenn es uns wichtig ist – und wenn nicht, vergessen wir es. Die »offizielle Geschichte« versucht, sich an unsere Erinnerung von Ereignissen anzupassen, weil der Kalender für uns nur durch Rituale und Traumata eine Bedeutung bekommt.

Räumliche Entfernungen beeinflussen zeitliche und andersherum. Banale und oft übersehene Details, wie etwas neben sich zu haben oder in der Nähe der dominanten Hand, könnten wichtige Auswirkungen darauf haben, was als nächstes passiert. Sie enthüllen die uns ansonsten unbekannte Zukunft, die darauf ausgelegt ist, einem wahrscheinlicheren Kurs zu folgen. Ein Ereignis könnte eintreten oder nicht, je nachdem, wie nah oder fern etwas oder jemand von uns ist.

Der Hauptgrund, warum Technologie Distanzen verändern kann, ist nicht deren oft bemerkte Fähigkeit, den Raum erobern oder flüchtige Phänomene festhalten zu können. Es liegt an ihren poetischen und prophetischen Qualitäten. Diese verändern unsere Erinnerungen und unsere Träume, verändern unsere

20 André Leroi-Gourhan, *Évolution et techniques,* 2 Bände, Paris: A. Michel, 1943–1945; André Leroi-Gourhan, *Le geste et la parole,* Paris: A. Michel, 1964.

We embody temporal distances as well. Our sense of the future and the past, both far from us, varies depending on how much we care about something. Expectations rise when we care, and forgetfulness sets in when we do not. "Official history" strives to match up with our memory of events because it is only through rituals and trauma that the calendar becomes meaningful to us.

Spatial distances affect temporal distances, and vice versa. Details as mundane and overlooked as when you have something next to you or close to your dominant hand may have important consequences for what happens next. They reveal a future, otherwise unknown to us, that is primed to follow a likely path. An event might or might not occur simply due to how close or how far something or someone is to us.

The main reason why technology can alter distances is not due to its often-noted power of conquering space or fixing fleeting phenomena, but to its poetic and prophetic qualities. These alter our memories and our dreams, change our expectations and desires, and direct our actions in certain directions.

To help Freud reach Rome—and to help ourselves attain similar goals—we need a new concept of distance and the technologies designed to conquer it. We need a new understanding that encompasses at least three entangled dimensions simultaneously: the psychological, the physical, and the philosophical. For lack of a better term, we may tentatively describe this new concept as *phyphipsycoanlytical*. We can use it to study how the concept of distance acts outside of, as much as within, ourselves, affecting how we understand interiority, intimacy, and identity (and their opposites). We could also employ it as a way of unsettling the very idea of what it means to know something in relation to art and science.

Erwartungen und Sehnsüchte und lenken unsere Handlungen in bestimmte Richtungen.

Um Freud zu helfen, Rom zu erreichen – und uns selbst, ähnliche Ziele zu verwirklichen – brauchen wir ein neues Konzept der Distanz und der Technologien, mit denen wir diese überwinden. Wir brauchen ein neues Verständnis, das mindestens drei miteinander verwobene Dimensionen umfasst: die psychologische, die physische und die philosophische. Da es noch keinen passenden Begriff gibt, könnten wir das neue Konzept vorläufig als *phyphipsychoanalytisch* beschreiben. Damit können wir erkennen, wie das Konzept der Entfernung außerhalb wie auch innerhalb von uns selbst wirkt, was wiederum einen Einfluss darauf hat, wie wir Innerlichkeit, Intimität und Identität (und auch deren Gegensätze) verstehen. Mit diesem Konzept könnten wir vielleicht sogar die Vorstellungen, was Wissen in Bezug auf die Kunst und die Wissenschaft bedeutet, ins Wanken bringen.

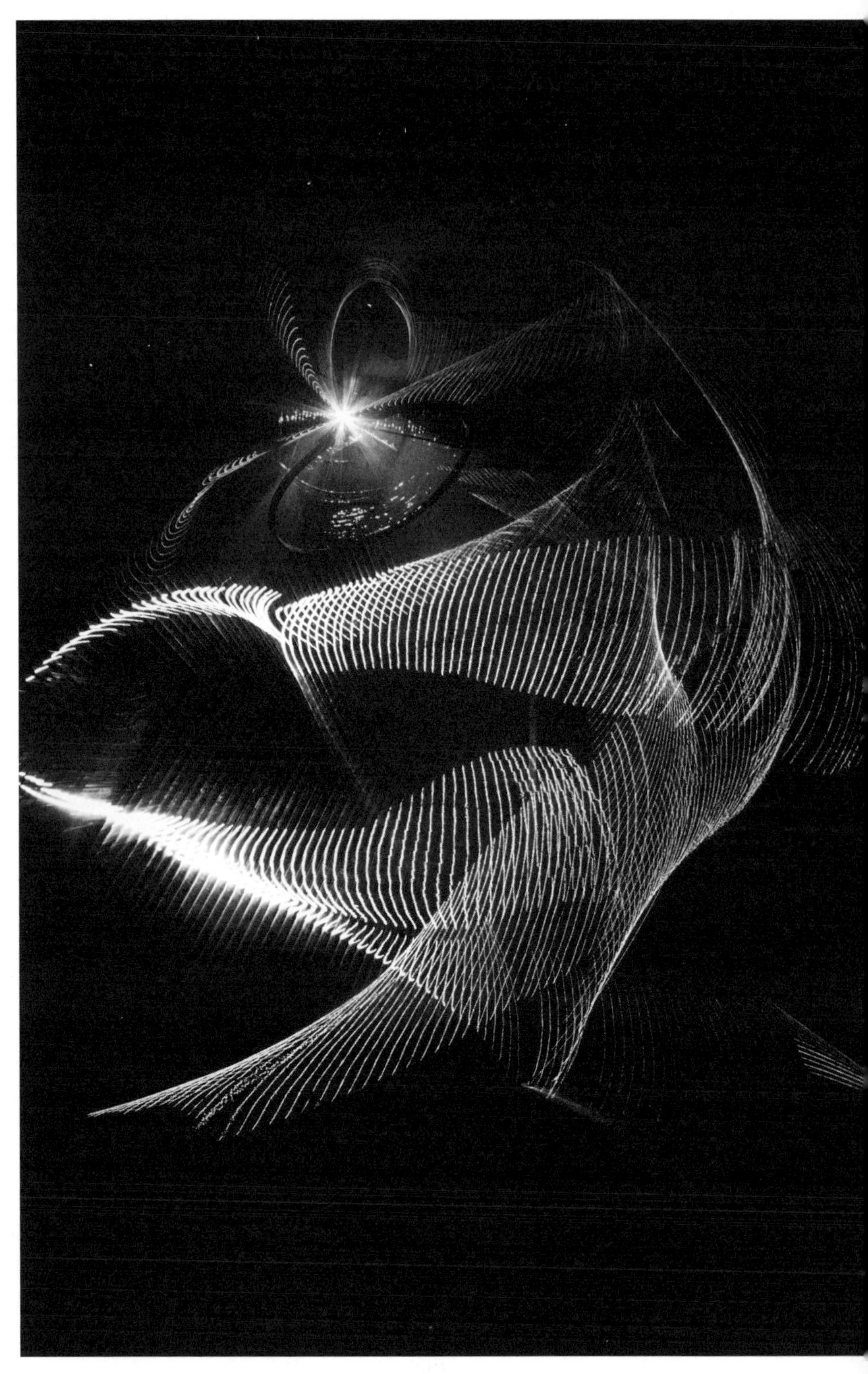

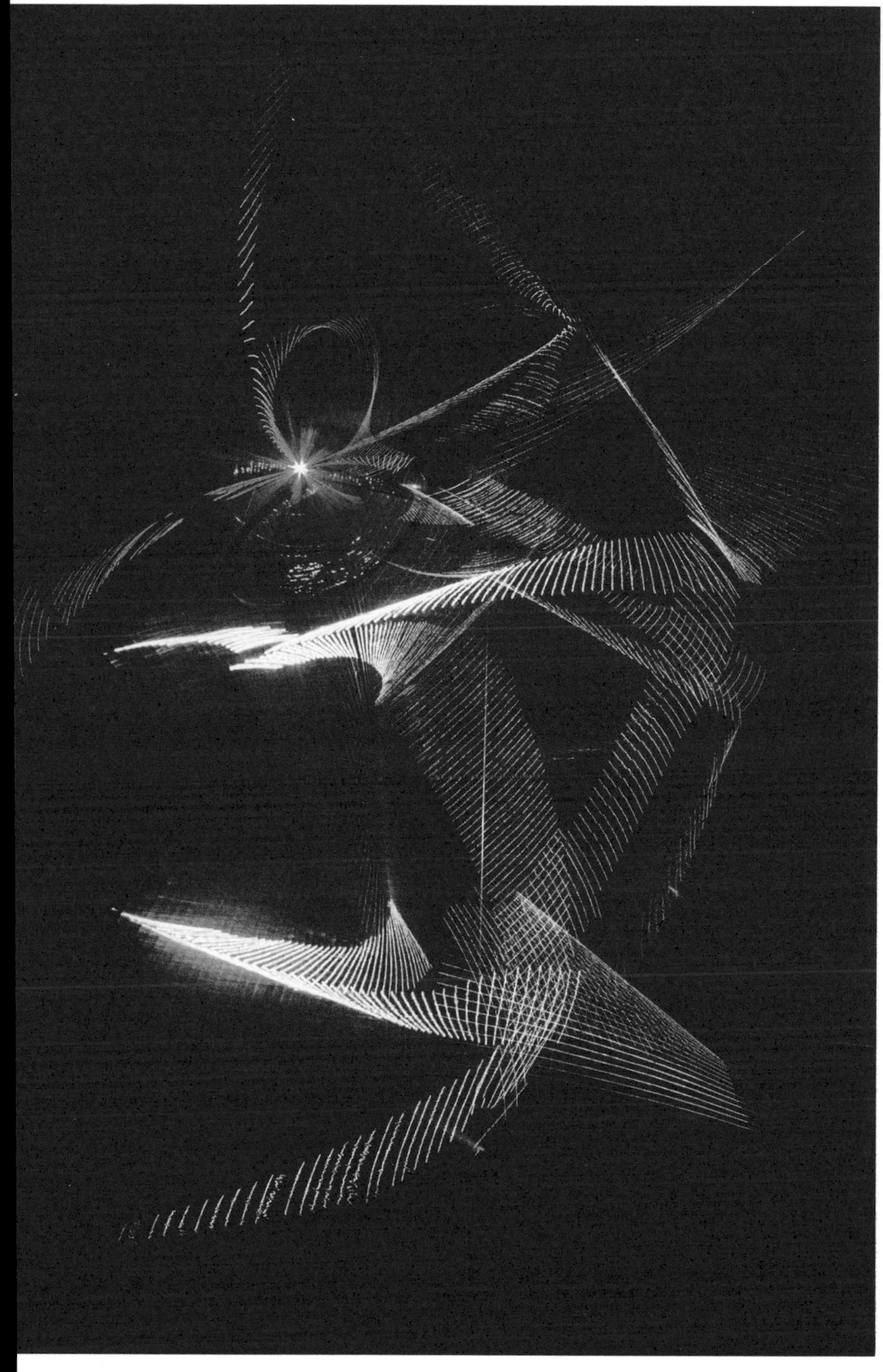

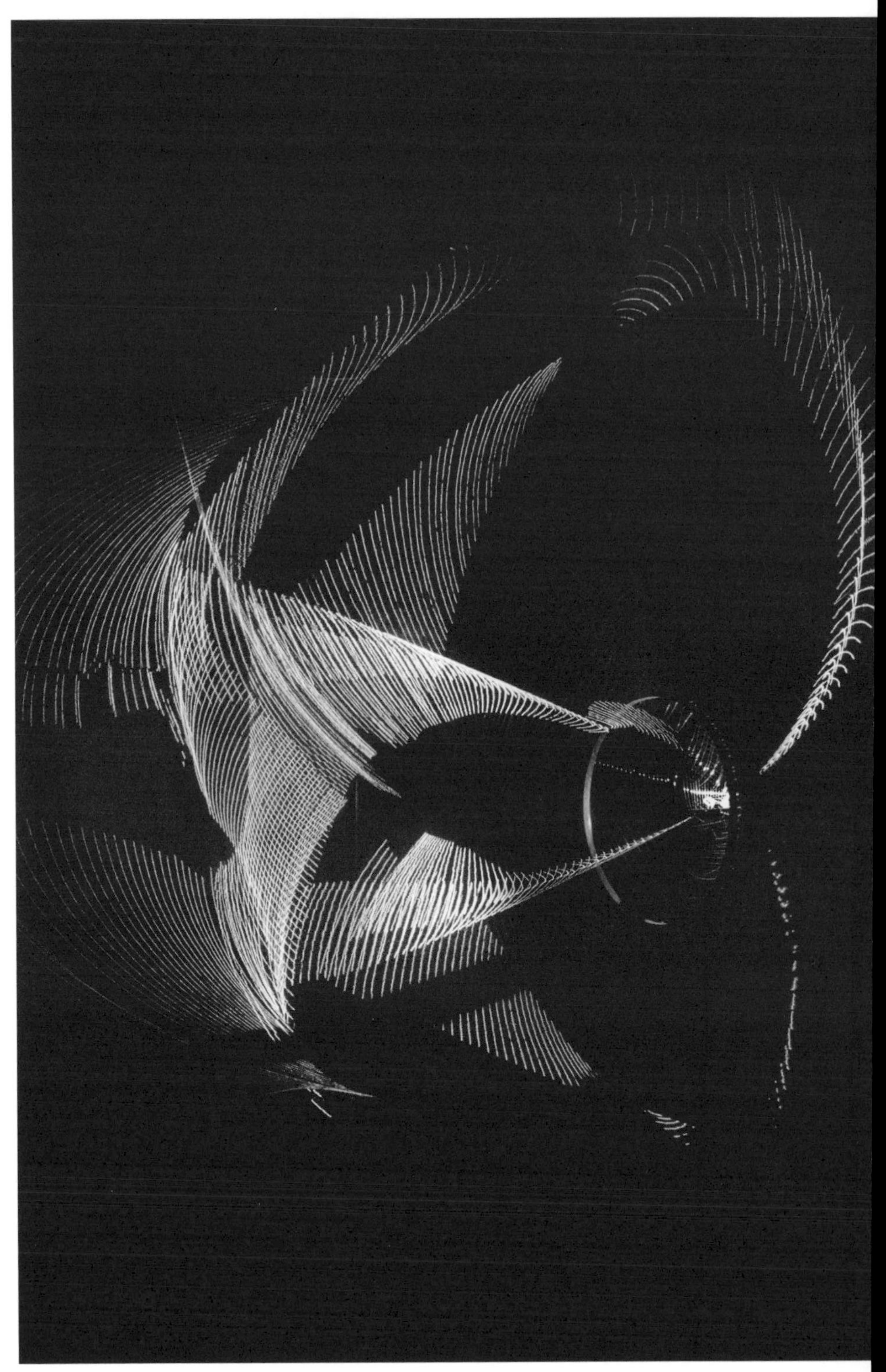

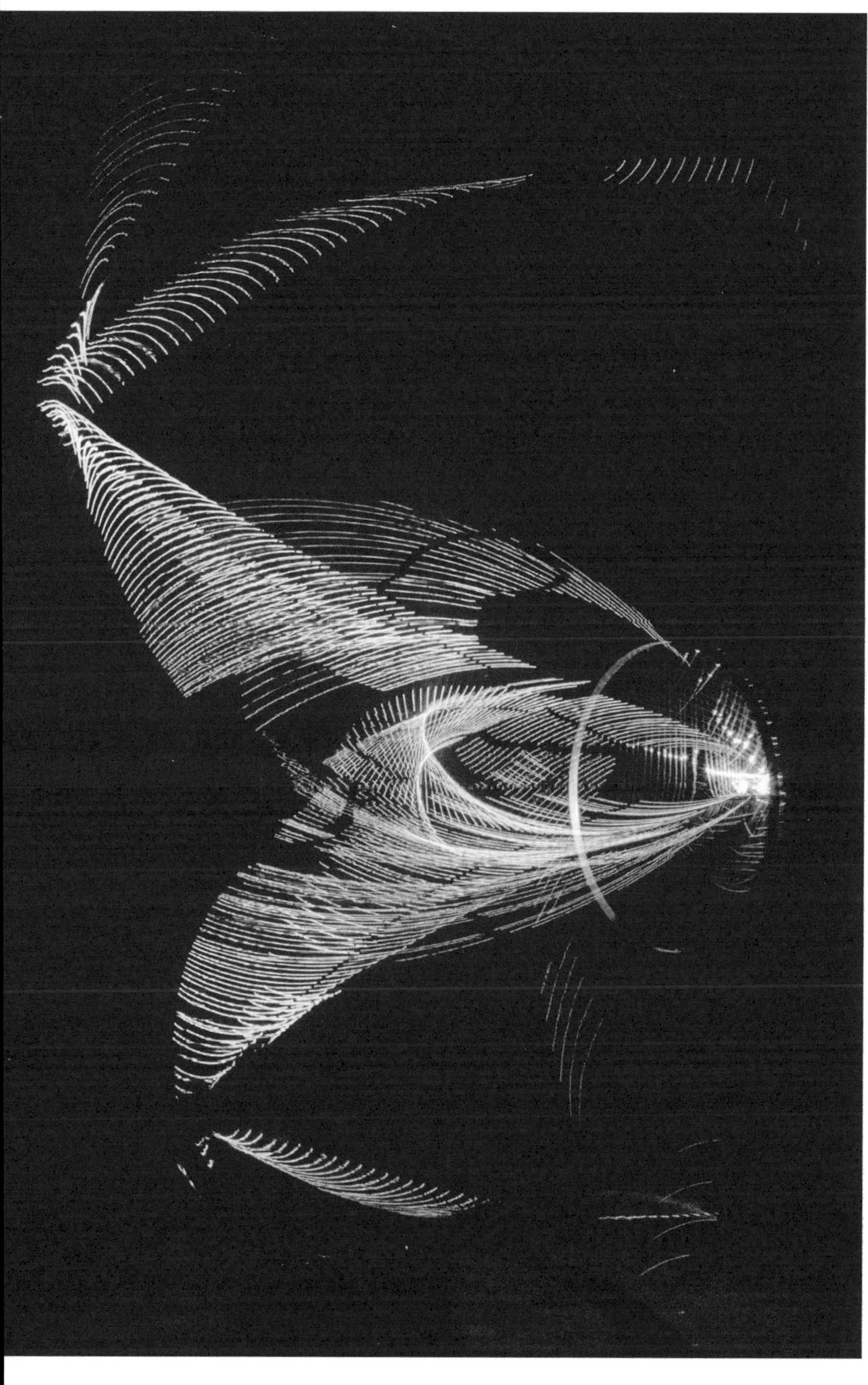

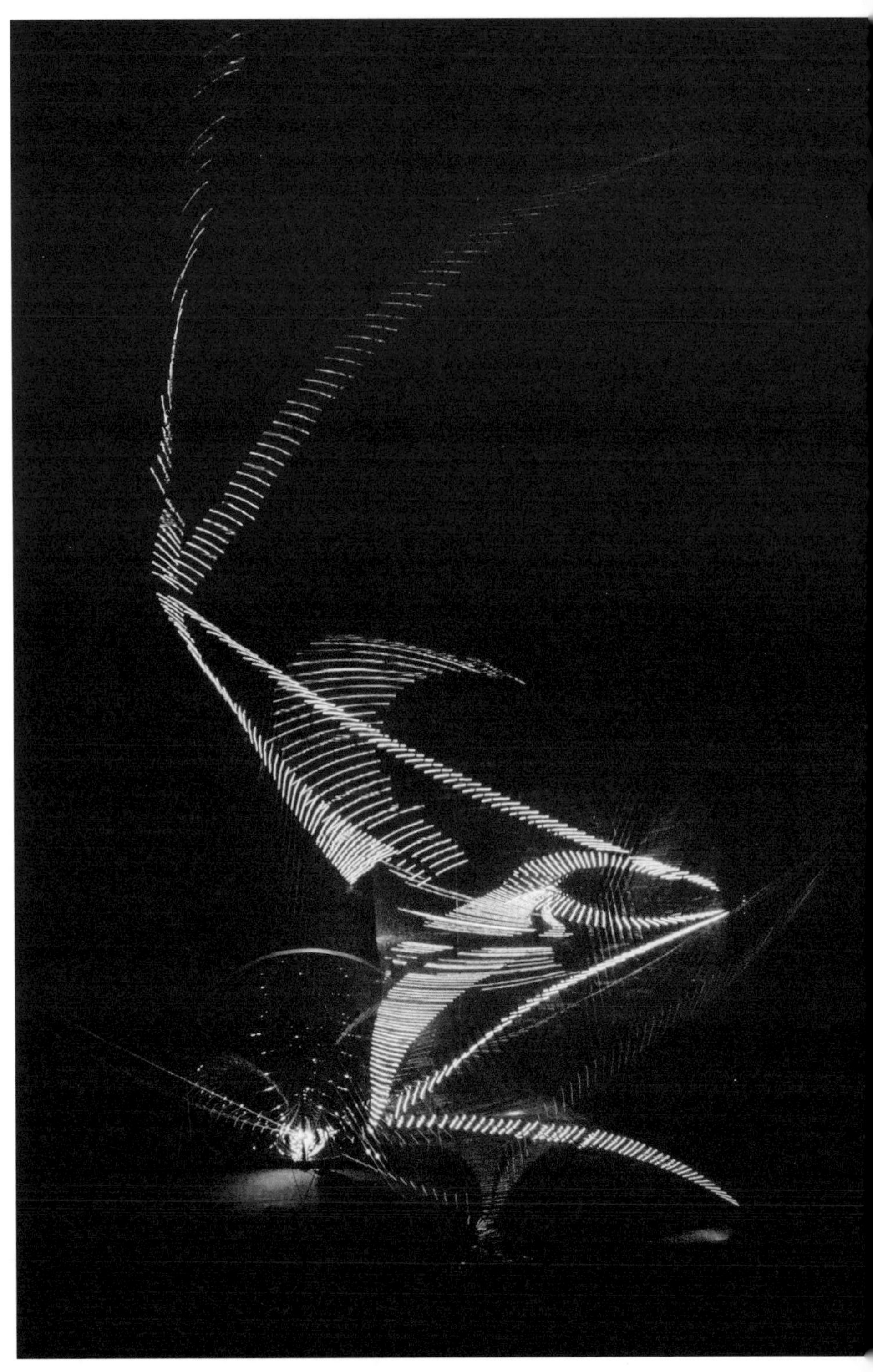

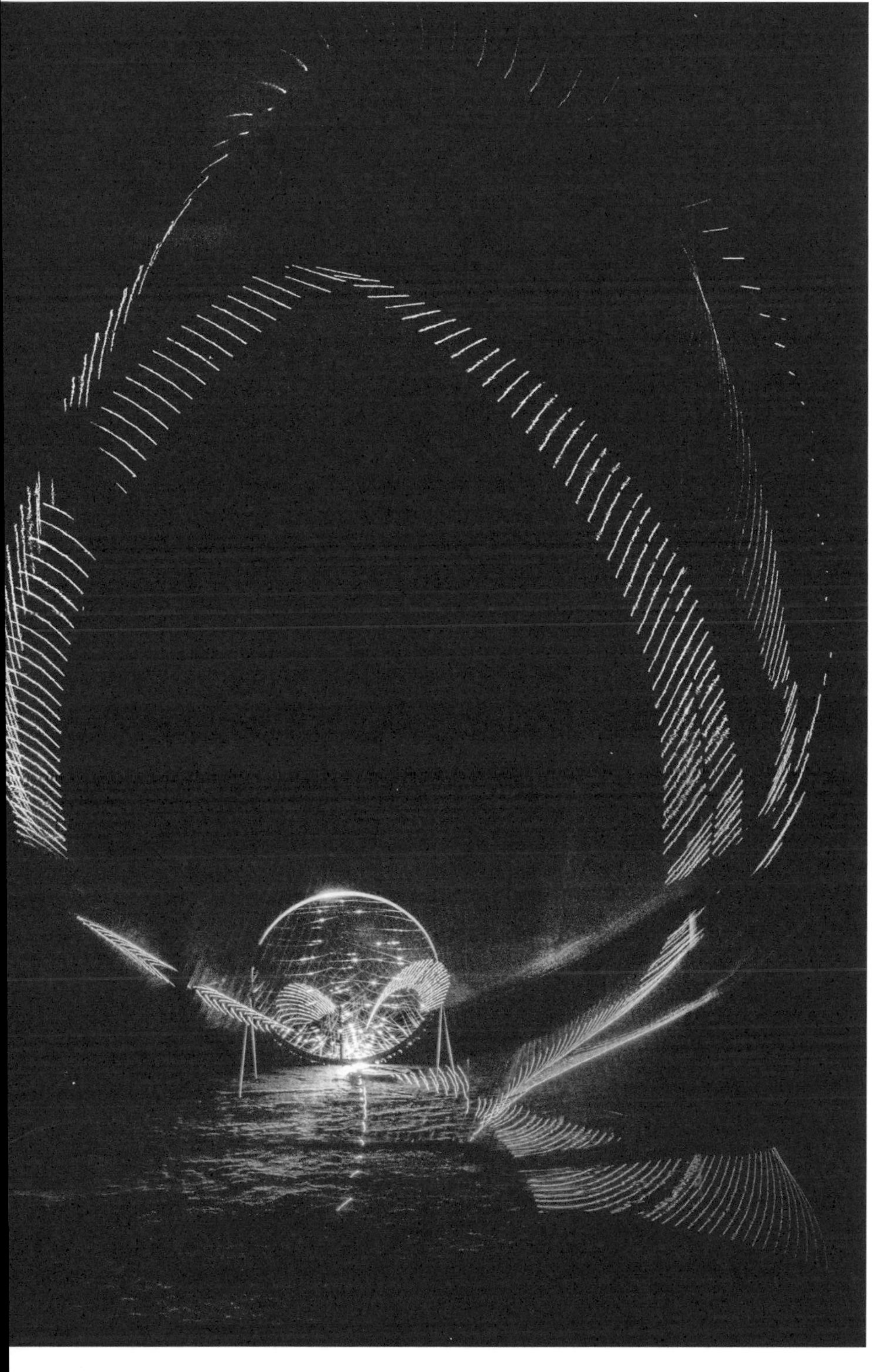

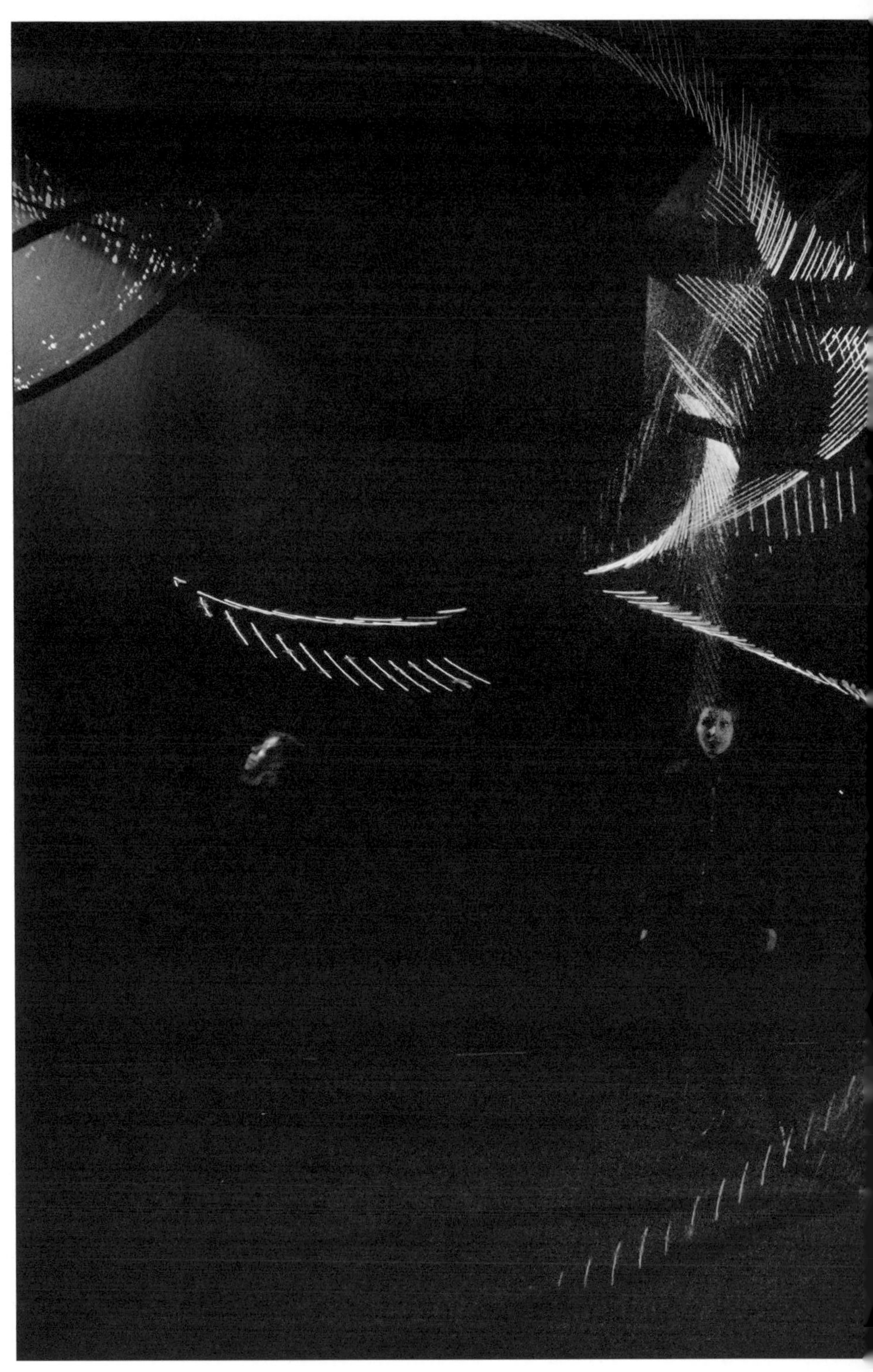

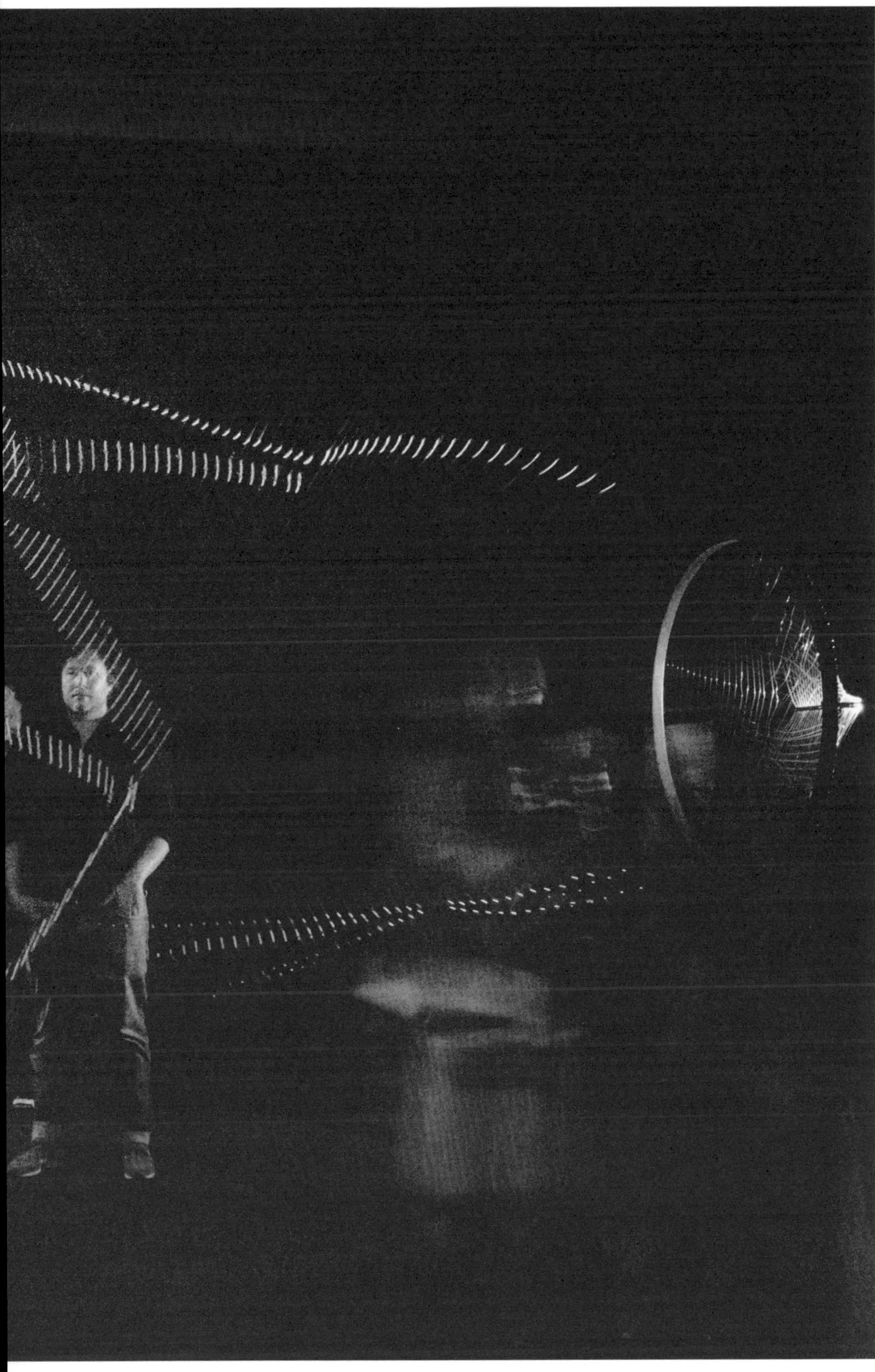

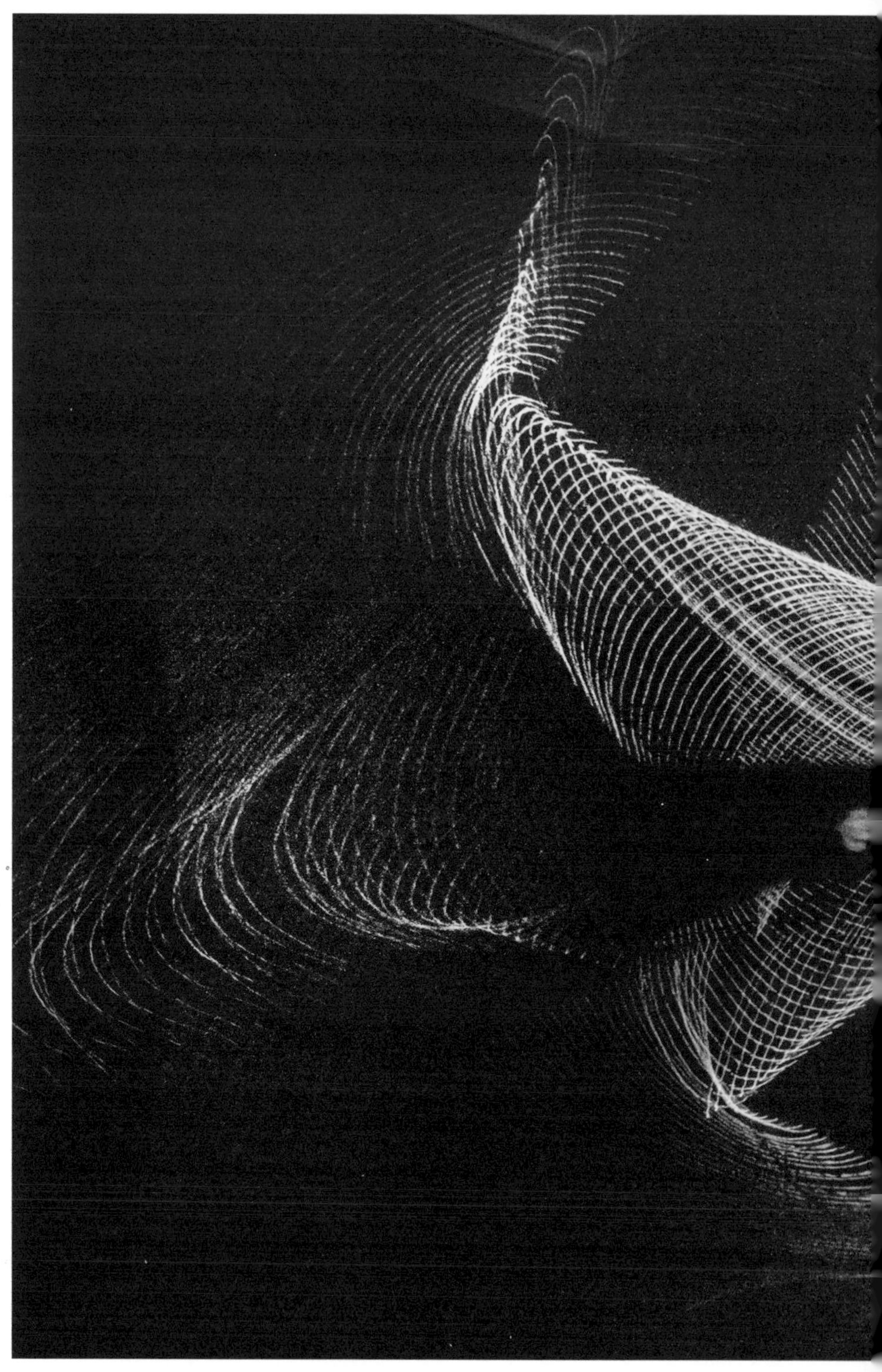

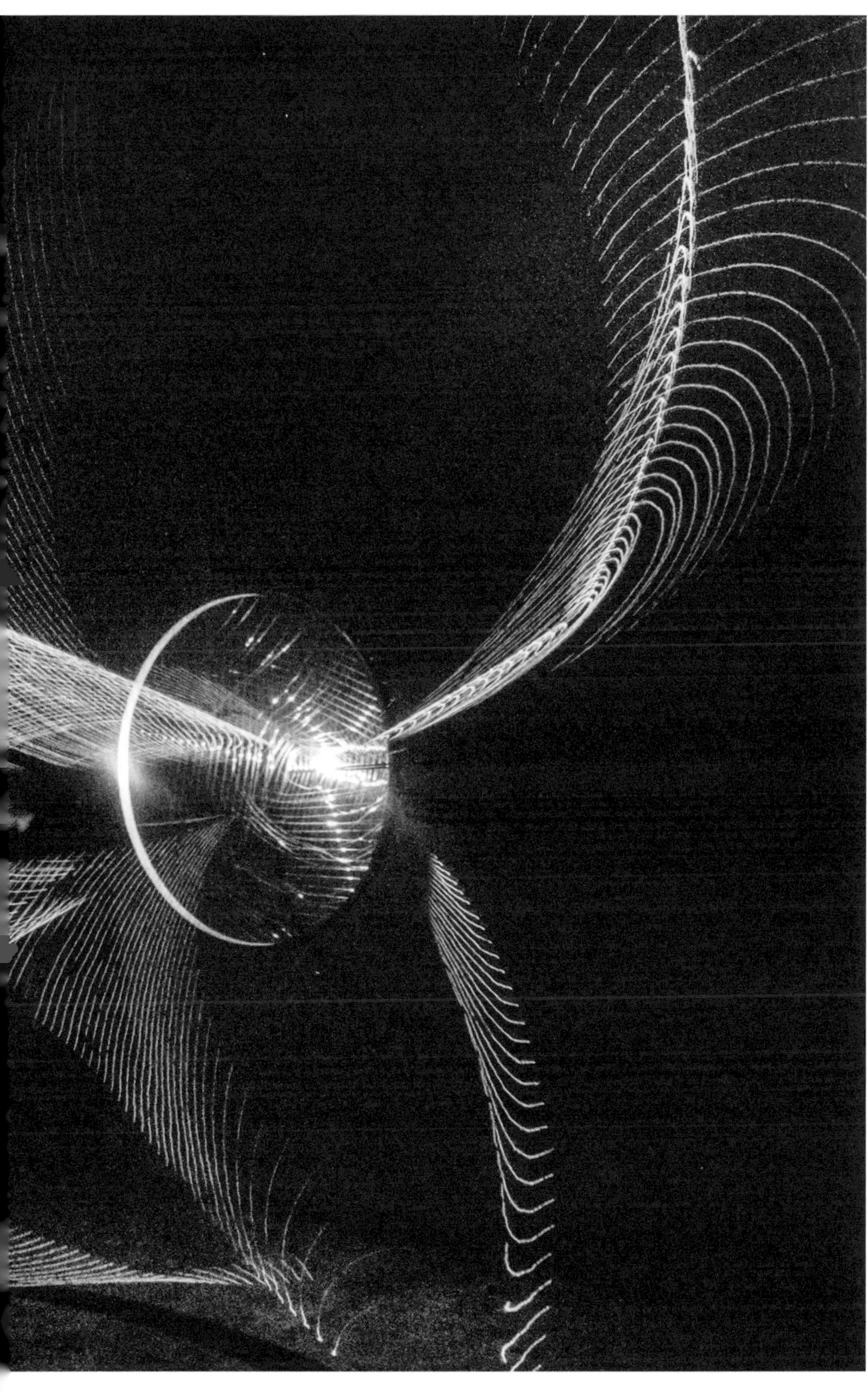

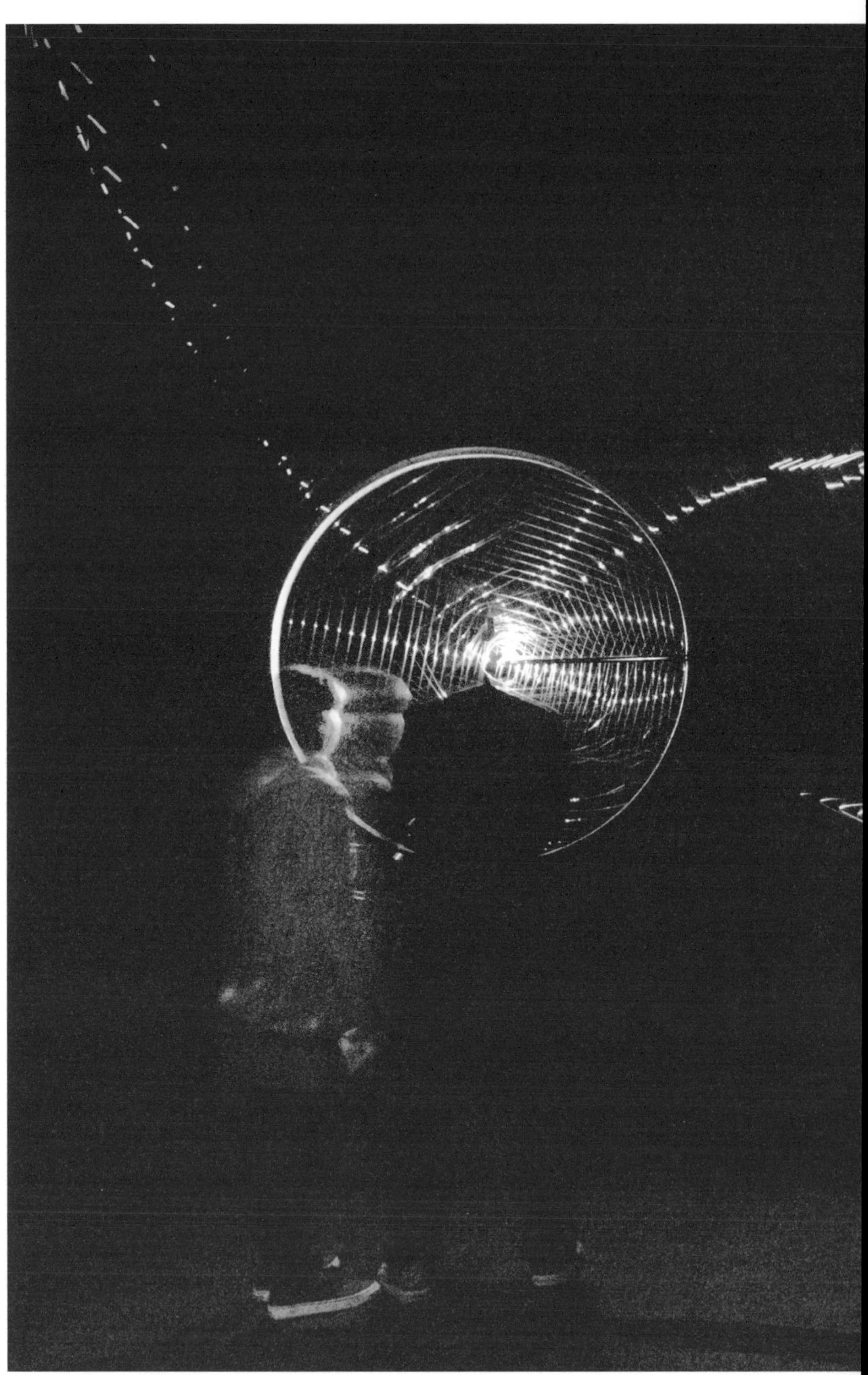

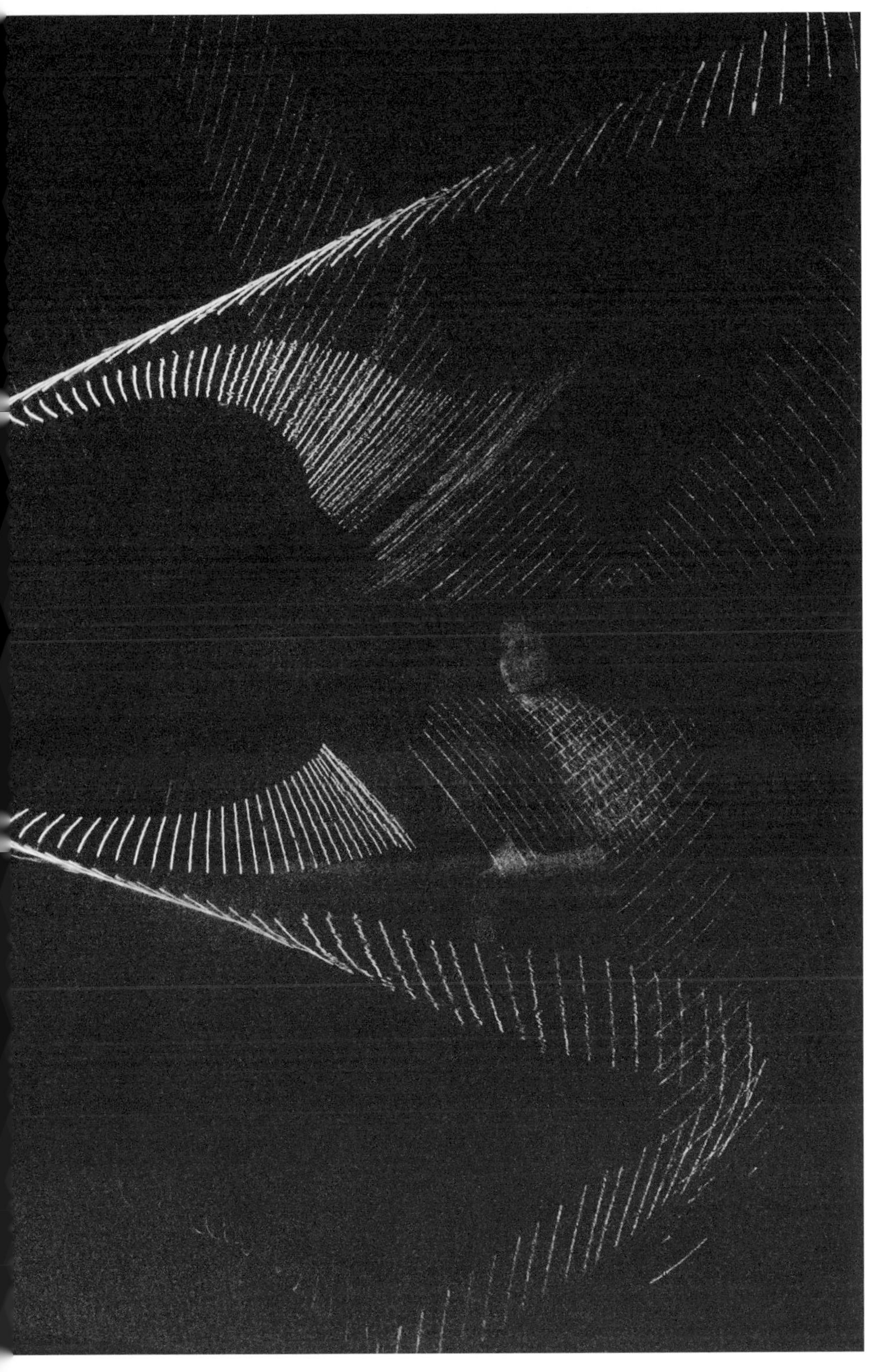

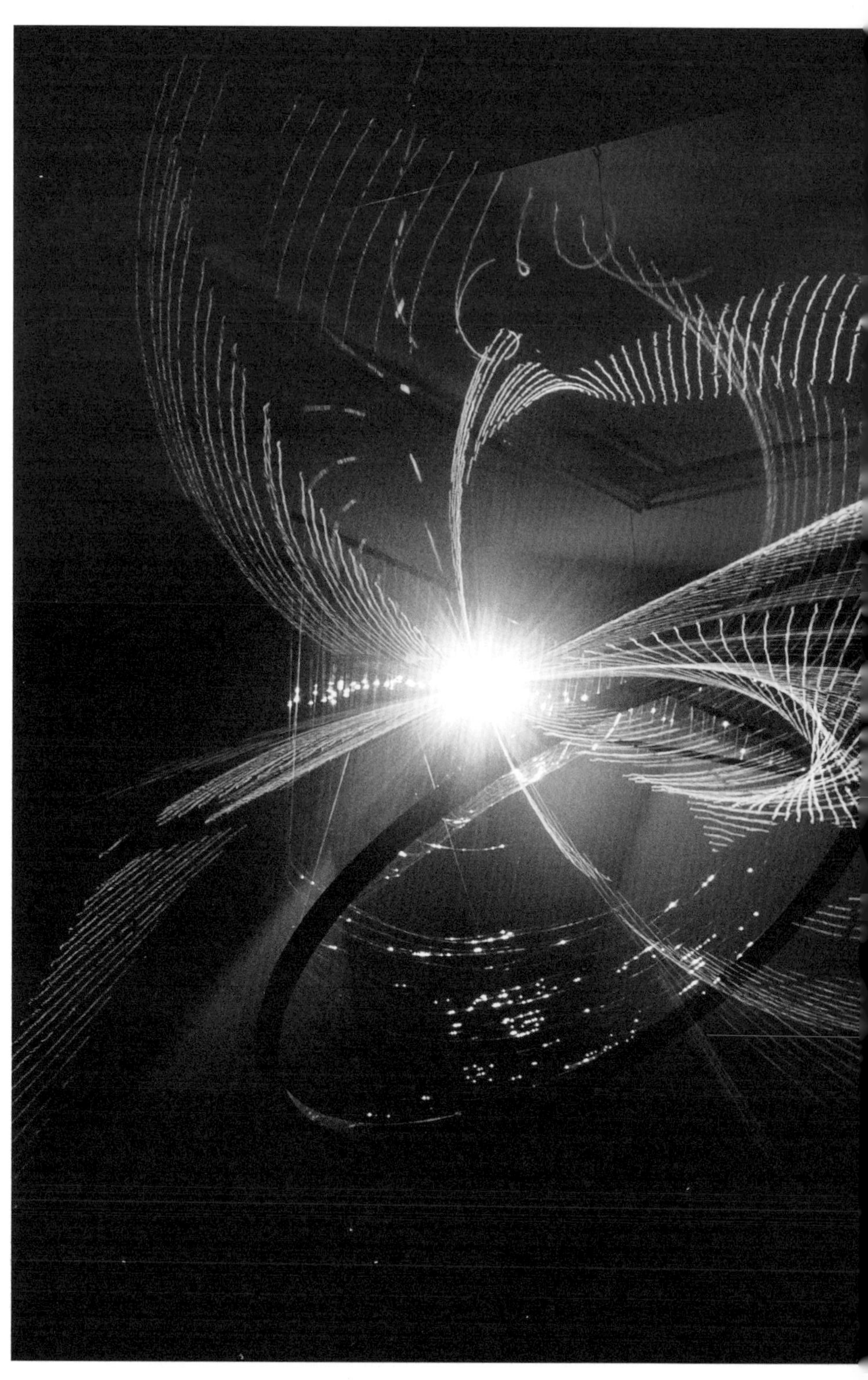

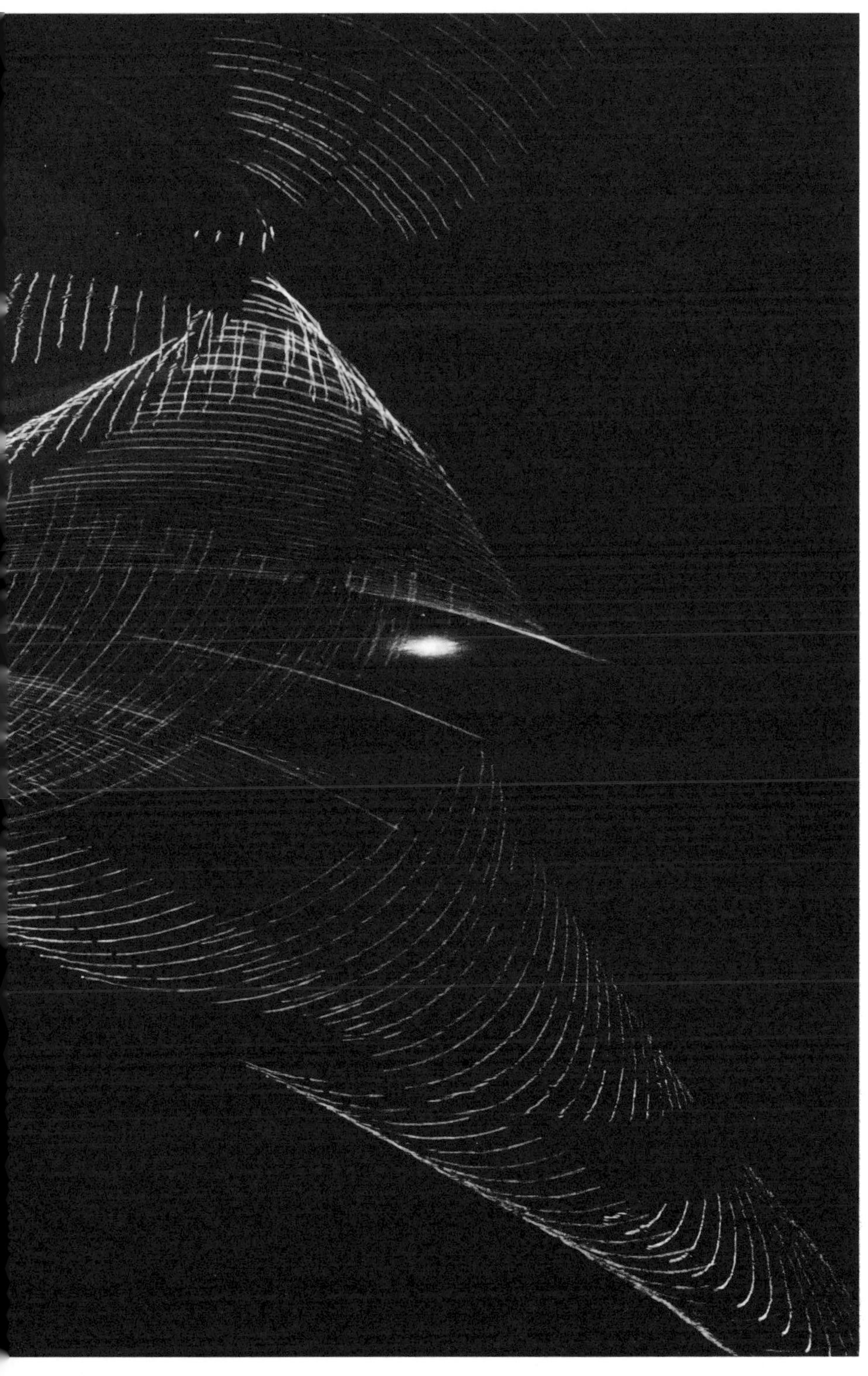

S. **pp.** 72–85:
Fotografien der Installation *Retreat into Darkness. Towards a Phenomenology of the Unknown,* aufgenommen mit einer langen Belichtungszeit (zwischen 60 und 120 Sekunden) als Studie zur räumlichen Geometrie. Durch die lange Belichtungszeit werden die Bewegungen der spiegelnden Glanzlichter in der Form von Linien sichtbar, die eine komplexe räumliche Struktur hervorbringen.
Photographs with a long exposure time of the installation *Retreat into Darkness. Towards a Phenomenology of the Unknown* as a study of spatial geometry (exposure time: 60–120 seconds). Through long exposure, the path of movement of the specular highlights becomes visible in the form of lines that create a complex spatial structure.

Kontrollierte Halluzinationen und die Phänomenologie der Präsenz

Controlled Hallucinations and the Phenomenology of Presence

Anil K. Seth

Die Beziehung zwischen Wahrnehmung und Realität ist eine der ältesten Problemstellungen der Psychologie und Philosophie. Auf den Alltag bezogen ist es einfach anzunehmen, dass die Wahrnehmung die Funktion habe, einige äußere Sachverhalte korrekt – »wahrhaftig« – wiederzugeben: zum Beispiel eine Welt gefüllt mit Dingen in verschiedenen Formen, Größen und Farben. Aber diese Mutmaßung ist natürlich irreführend. Basierend auf alteingeführten philosophischen Traditionen wies der Psychologe J. J. Gibson bereits in den 1970er-Jahren darauf hin, dass wir die Welt nicht unbedingt so wahrnehmen, »wie sie ist«, sondern in einer Art und Weise, die uns Handlungsmöglichkeiten aufzeigt. Dafür hat er den Begriff der »Affordanz« bzw. des »Angebotscharakters« geprägt.[1] Ein einfaches Beispiel dafür ist, dass unsere Wahrnehmung der Größe eines Objektes in unserer Reichweite von der (wahrgenommenen) Größe unserer Hände beeinflusst wird.[2] Wir nehmen also nicht Größe *an sich* wahr, sondern so etwas wie »Greifbarkeit«.

Gleichzeitig haben sowohl Wissenschaftler als auch Künstler schon lange erkannt, dass die Wahrnehmung und die Phänomenologie im gleichen Maße vom Beobachter wie vom Gegenstand der Beobachtung abhängen. William James, der Vater der modernen Psychologie, hat gesagt: »Während uns ein Teil der Wahrnehmung des Objekts durch unsere Sinne erreicht, kommt ein anderer Teil (und möglicherweise der größere) immer aus unserem eigenen Kopf«.[3] Für Georges Braque, einen Begründer des Kubismus, »existieren Objekte nicht [...] bzw. nur insofern, als eine enge Beziehung zwischen ihnen besteht und zwischen ihnen und mir«.[4] Die zeitgenössische Künstlerin Ivana Franke setzt sich sehr direkt mit diesen Ideen auseinander, indem sie mit Hilfe von Lichtinstallationen demonstriert, wie das Sehzentrum des Gehirns komplexe Objekte erkennt, wo es – in der realen Welt – gar keine gibt.

Beobachtungen wie diese, die repräsentativ für viele andere stehen, weisen darauf hin, dass es zwischen dem Inhalt unserer Sinneswahrnehmungen und den Entitäten in der äußeren Welt einen fundamentalen Mangel an Übereinstimmung beziehungsweise eine *nicht-Wahrhaftigkeit* gibt. Gleichzeitig erscheint uns die wahrgenommene Welt aber als »real«. Die Objekte, die wir wahrnehmen, wirken auf uns unmittelbar *als Objekte,* nicht als angebotsbezogene Repräsentationen von Objekten. Wenn ich in den Garten vor mir blicke, ist der Schuppen dort für mich ein reales Objekt in der Welt, mit einer Rückseite und Seitenwänden. Und ich bin mir bewusst, dass diese existieren, selbst wenn ich sie nicht direkt sehen kann, wobei dies nicht das Resultat einer eingehenden Reflexion über diese Wahrnehmungserfahrung ist, sondern unmittelbarer Teil der Wahrnehmung selbst.

Das Konzept der »Präsenz« ist eine Möglichkeit, diese Eigenschaft der alltäglichen Phänomenologie zu beschreiben.

1 James J. Gibson, *The Ecological Approach to Visual Perception,* Hillsdale, NJ: Lawrence Erlbaum, 1979.

2 Heinrich H.Bulthoff / Markus Leyrer / Sally A. Linkenauger / Betty J. Mohler, »Welcome to Wonderland: The Influence of the Size and Shape of a Virtual Hand on the Perceived Size and Shape of Virtual Objects«, in: *PLoS One,* 8 (2013) Nr. 7, e68594.

3 William James, *The Principles of Psychology,* New York: Henry Holt, 1890.

4 John Richardson (Hg.), *Georges Braque: An American Tribute,* New York: Public Education Association, 1964.

The relationship between perception and reality is one of the oldest questions in psychology and philosophy. In everyday life, it is easy to assume that the function of perception is to recover an accurate, "veridical" representation of some external state of affairs—for instance, of a world full of objects of different shapes, sizes, and colors. But this intuition is of course misleading. Back in the 1970s, and building on long-established traditions in philosophy, the psychologist J. J. Gibson pointed out that we perceive the world not so much "as it is," but in ways that reveal opportunities for action—what he called "affordances."[1] A simple example is that the perceived size of a reachable object is influenced by the (perceived) size of our hands,[2] so that our perceptual experience is not of size *per se*, but of something like "graspability."

At the same time, both scientists and artists have long recognized that perception and phenomenology depend as much on the observer as on what is observed. William James, the father of modern psychology, said, "Whilst part of what we perceive comes through our senses from the object before us, another part (and it may be the larger part) always comes out of our own head."[3] For Georges Braque, a founder of Cubism, "objects don't exist ... except insofar as a rapport exists between them, and between them and myself."[4] The contemporary artist Ivana Franke is exploring these ideas very directly, using light installations to demonstrate how the visual brain can infer complex objects where, in the world, no such objects exist.

1 James J. Gibson, *The Ecological Approach to Visual Perception* (Hillsdale, NJ: Lawrence Erlbaum, 1979.)

2 Heinrich H. Bulthoff / Markus Leyrer / Sally A. Linkenauger / Betty J. Mohler, "Welcome to Wonderland: The Influence of the Size and Shape of a Virtual Hand on the Perceived Size and Shape of Virtual Objects," *PLoS One* 8, no. 7 (2013): e68594.

3 William James, *The Principles of Psychology* (New York: Henry Holt, 1890).

4 John Richardson, (ed.). *Georges Braque: An American Tribute* (New York: Public Education Association, 1964).

Wahrnehmungsobjekte haben eine Präsenz, wenn sie als *tatsächlich existierend wahrgenommen werden* – als Teil der Welt anstelle einer Fiktion des Verstandes.[5] Ein verwandtes Konzept versteht die neurokognitiven Repräsentationen, die unseren sinnlichen Wahrnehmungen zu Grunde liegen, als *transparent:* das heißt, sie werden nicht *als* Repräsentationen wahrgenommen.[6] Und bezogen auf die Wahrnehmung der Dinge-in-der-Welt, können wir uns Präsenz als »Objekthaftigkeit« vorstellen – die Wahrnehmung, dass ein Objekt eine dreidimensionale Ausdehnung im Raum hat, mit einer »Rückseite und Seitenwänden«. Der Philosoph Alva Noë formuliert dies wie folgt:

> Wie ist es möglich – und ich bin der Meinung, dass dies der Fall ist –, dass wir beim Anblick einer Tomate in unserer Wahrnehmung auch ein Bewusstsein von dem Teil der Tomate haben, den wir genau genommen nicht wahrnehmen. Das ist das Rätsel der wahrnehmungsbezogenen Präsenz.[7]

Die Phänomenologie der Präsenz ist so allgegenwärtig, dass man sie einfach als gegeben annimmt. Es gibt jedoch erstaunliche Gegenbeispiele, die andeuten, dass dieser Aspekt der Phänomenologie, wie alle anderen auch, einer Erklärung bedarf. Dazu gehören auf einer sehr fundamentalen Ebene Nachbilder auf der Netzhaut – wie die nachklingende Helligkeit, wenn man zu lange in die Sonne geschaut hat. Andere Beispiele sind Halluzinationen, die *als Halluzinationen wahrgenommen werden* (also als nicht real empfunden werden) – wie es unter anderem beim Charles-Bonnet-Syndrom vorkommt.[8]

Bei dem relativ weit verbreiteten Phänomen der Synästhesie haben Menschen zusätzliche Sinneswahrnehmungen, die manchmal als sehr plastisch, aber selten als Teil der realen Welt wahrgenommen werden. Zum Beispiel nehmen die sogenannten »Projektoren« unter den Synästhetikern bei der Graphem-Farb-Synästhesie Farbphänomene wahr, wenn sie (farblose) Buchstaben sehen. Sie verwechseln dabei aber nicht die tatsächliche Farbe der Buchstaben mit deren synästhetischen Pendants.[9] Und in einigen (dissoziativen) psychiatrischen Störungen, wie z. B. der Depersonalisation und der Derealisation, haben Menschen das verstörende Gefühl eines allgemeinen Mangels an Präsenz. Sie erleben bei sich selbst oder der Welt (oder bei beidem) das Fehlen eines subjektiven Gefühls der Realität.[10] Diese Zustände sind oft schwierig zu diagnostizieren, weil sie mit dem Fehlen von etwas einhergehen, das an sich schon nicht einfach zu definieren ist.

Welche komplexen Vorgänge in den Schaltkreisen des Gehirns, die für die Wahrnehmung zuständig sind, könnten also die Phänomenologie der Präsenz untermauern? Die Beantwortung dieser Frage wird nicht nur unser Verständnis der normalen visuellen

5 Alva Noë / J. Kevin O'Regan, »A Sensorimotor Account of Vision and Visual Consciousness«, in: *Behavioral and Brain Sciences,* 24 (2001) Nr. 5, S. 939–973; Diskussion: S. 973–1031.

6 Thomas Metzinger, »Phenomenal Transparency and Cognitive Self-Reference«, in: *Phenomenology and the Cognitive Sciences,* 2 (2003) Nr. 4, S. 353–393.

7 Alva Noë, »Experience without the Head«, in: T. Gendler / A. Hawthorne (Hrsg.), *Perceptual experience,* NY: Clarendon / Oxford University Press, 2006, S. 411–434, hier: S. 414.

8 Dominic H. ffytche / Robert J. Howard / Alastair M. Santhouse, »Visual Hallucinatory Syndromes and the Anatomy of the Visual Brain«, in: *Brain: A Journal of Neurology,* Nr. 123, Teil 10, 2000, S. 2055–2064.

9 Anil K. Seth, »A Predictive Processing Theory of Sensorimotor Contingencies: Explaining the Puzzle of Perceptual Presence and Its Absence in Synesthesia«, in: *Cognitive Neuroscience,* 5 (2014) Nr. 2, S. 97–118.

10 Anthony S. David / Mauricio Sierra, »Depersonalization: A Selective Impairment of Self-Awareness«, in: *Consciousness and Cognition,* 20 (2011) Heft 1, S. 99–108.

These observations, which stand for many others, point to an essential lack of correspondence, or *non-veridicality*, between the contents of our perceptual experience and entities in the external world. Yet, at the same time, the experienced world "seems real." Objects within our experience appear to us directly *as objects*, not as affordance-related representations of objects. Looking out into the garden in front of me, the shed appears to me to be a real object, out there in the world, with a back and sides that I perceive as being there, even if I cannot directly see them. This is not a conclusion I reach after some amount of reasoning about my experience; it is directly given in the experience itself.

One way to describe this property of everyday phenomenology is with the concept of "presence." Perceptual objects have presence when they are *experienced as really existing*—as part of the world rather than as a fiction of the mind.[5] A related idea is that the neurocognitive representations that underlie our perceptual experiences are *transparent*—that is, they are not experienced *as* representations.[6] Furthermore, when applied to experiences of things-in-the-world, we can think of presence also as "objecthood"—the experience of an object as having a three-dimensional extension in space, as having a "back and sides." The philosopher Alva Noë puts it like this:

> How can it be true, as I think it is, that we are perceptually aware, when we look at a tomato, of the part of the tomato which, strictly speaking, we do not perceive. This is the puzzle of perceptual presence.[7]

The phenomenology of presence is so ubiquitous that it is easy to take it for granted. However, there are striking counterexamples that indicate that this aspect of phenomenology, like all others, requires some explanation. These counterexamples include, at a very simple level, retinal afterimages—like the persistent brightness experienced after looking for too long at the sun. Others include perceptual hallucinations that are *experienced as being hallucinations* (i.e., as being not real), as happens, for instance, in Charles Bonnet syndrome.[8]

In synesthesia, a relatively common phenomenon, people have additional perceptual experiences that, while sometimes very vivid, are rarely experienced as being part of the world. For example, in grapheme-color synesthesia, so-called "projector" synesthetes will experience color phenomena on seeing (achromatic) letters, but they will not confuse the real color of the letter with its synesthetic counterpart.[9] Furthermore, in some (dissociative) psychiatric conditions, like depersonalization and derealization, people can experience a distressing lack of

5 Alva Noë / J. Kevin O'Regan, "A Sensorimotor Account of Vision and Visual Consciousness." in *Behavioral and Brain Sciences* 24, no. 5 (2001): pp. 939–73; discussion pp. 973–1031.

6 Thomas Metzinger, "Phenomenal Transparency and Cognitive Self-Reference," *Phenomenology and the Cognitive Sciences* 2, no. 4 (2003): pp. 353–93.

7 Alva Noë, "Experience without the Head," in *Perceptual Experience*, ed. Tamar Szabo Gendler & John Hawthorne, (New York: Clarendon / Oxford University Press, 2006), pp. 411–34: p. 414.

8 Dominic H. ffytche / Robert J. Howard / Alastair M. Santhouse, "Visual Hallucinatory Syndromes and the Anatomy of the Visual Brain," *Brain: A Journal of Neurology* 123, part 10 (2000): pp. 2055–64.

9 Anil K. Seth, "A Predictive Processing Theory of Sensorimotor Contingencies: Explaining the Puzzle of Perceptual Presence and Its Absence in Synesthesia," *Cognitive Neuroscience* 5, no. 2 (2014): pp. 97–118.

Wahrnehmung erweitern, sie wird auch Aufschluss über die oben beschriebenen, ungewöhnlichen Situationen geben, in denen eine perzeptuelle Präsenz ausdrücklich fehlt.

Prädiktive (vorhersagende) Wahrnehmungsprozesse und unbewusste Schlussfolgerungen

In der kognitiven Neurowissenschaft erfreut sich die Vorstellung zunehmender Beliebtheit, dass Wahrnehmung eine Frage der Prädiktion (also des Vorhersagens) oder Schlussfolgerns ist.

Dabei handelt es sich bei der Idee eigentlich um ein sehr altes Konzept. Bereits im 19. Jahrhundert schlug der Physiologe und Psychologe Hermann von Helmholtz vor, dass das Gehirn eine *Vorhersagemaschine* sei, und dass das, was wir sehen, hören und fühlen, nichts anderes sei als ein Versuch des Gehirns, die Ursachen der Sinneseindrücke zu »deuten«.

Man kann es so betrachten: Das Gehirn ist in einem knöchernen Schädel gefangen und alles, was es empfängt, sind widersprüchliche und verrauschte Sinneseindrücke, die nur indirekt mit den Dingen in der Welt verbunden sind. Wahrnehmung muss deshalb ein Prozess der Interpretation sein, in dem unbestimmte Sinneseindrücke mit früheren Erfahrungen oder »Überzeugungen«, wie die Welt ist, kombiniert werden, damit das Gehirn eine optimale Hypothese der Ursachen dieser Sinneseindrücke entwickeln kann. Was wir sehen, sind die Versuche des Gehirns zu »deuten«, was da draußen ist.

Sowohl im Labor als auch im Alltag ist es einfach, Belege für vorhersagende Wahrnehmung zu finden. Wenn man an einem nebligen Morgen das Haus verlässt, in der Erwartung, eine Freundin an einer Bushaltestelle zu treffen, dann könnte es sein, dass wir diese Person so lange dort wahrnehmen, bis eine nähere Betrachtung ergibt, dass es eine andere Person ist. Gesichter in Wolken zu erkennen (ein Beispiel für etwas, das als Pareidolie bekannt ist), ist ein weiterer Beleg für den Einfluss unserer (unbewussten) Wahrnehmungsvorhersagen.

Abbildung 1 (Fig · 1) zeigt ein konkretes Beispiel. Vielleicht kennen Sie diese Illusion schon. Es geht hier allerdings keineswegs darum, einen »Fehler« in unserem Sehen aufzuzeigen, sondern zu demonstrieren, wie wirkmächtig die Vorhersagemaschine in unserem Gehirn tatsächlich sein kann. In diesem Bild, das auch »Adelsons Schachbrett« genannt wird, wirkt es, als hätten die Felder A und B sehr verschiedene Grauschattierungen, während sie in Wirklichkeit den exakt gleichen Farbton aufweisen. Sollten Sie

presence in a rather general sense, experiencing the self or the world (or both) as lacking in a subjective sense of reality.[10] These conditions are often difficult to diagnose because they involve the absence of something that seems, on the face of it, rather difficult to define in the first place.

So what in the complex operations of the brain's perceptual circuitry could underpin the phenomenology of presence? Answering this question will not only advance our understanding of normal visual experience, it will also shed light on the unusual situations, like those described above, where perceptual presence is specifically lacking.

Predictive Perception and Unconscious Inference

Our starting point is the notion, increasingly popular in cognitive neuroscience, that perception is a matter of prediction or inference.

This is actually a very old idea. Back in the nineteenth century, the physiologist and psychologist Hermann von Helmholtz proposed that the brain is a *prediction machine*, and that what we see, hear, and feel are nothing more than the brain's "best guesses" about the causes of its sensory inputs.

Think of it like this. The brain is locked inside a bony skull. All it receives are ambiguous and noisy sensory signals, which are only indirectly related to objects in the world. Perception must therefore be a process of inference in which indeterminate sensory signals are combined with prior expectations or "beliefs" about the way the world is in order to form the brain's optimal hypotheses of the causes of these sensory signals. What we see is the brain's "best guess" of what is out there.

It is easy to find examples of predictive perception both in the lab and in everyday life. Walking out on a foggy morning, if we expect to meet a friend at a bus stop, we may perceive her to be there, until closer inspection reveals a stranger. And when we see faces in clouds (an example of what is known as pareidolia), this again reveals the influence of our (unconscious) perceptual predictions.

Figure 1 provides a more specific example. You might have seen this illusion before, but instead of revealing a "flaw" in how we see, it actually shows how powerful the brain's predictive machinery can be. In this image, called Adelson's checkerboard, the patches A and B might look like very different shades of gray, but they are in fact the exact same shade. If you find this

10 Anthony S. David / Mauricio Sierra, "Depersonalization: A Selective Impairment of Self-Awareness," *Consciousness and Cognition* 20, no. 1 (2011): pp. 99–108.

Schwierigkeiten haben, das zu glauben, betrachten Sie bitte Abbildung 1B näher, die genau das gleiche Bild zeigt, mit dem Unterschied, dass zwei einfarbige, graue Balken die Felder A und B verbinden. So wird deutlich, dass A und B genau den gleichen Grauton haben.

Aber warum *sehen* sie dann verschieden *aus*? Das Gehirn greift hier auf sein tief in den Schaltkreisen des visuellen Kortex verankertes Vorwissen zurück, dass eine Fläche im Schatten dunkler wirkt. Deshalb sieht B für uns heller aus als es ist.

Dabei handelt es sich nicht um ein Versagen des visuellen Systems. Der Sinn des Sehens besteht nicht darin, einen genauen Lichtmesser abzugeben. Es geht eher darum, die handlungsrelevanten Ursachen der Sinneseindrücke aufzudecken, und genau das passiert hier.

→ Fig · 1 Adelsons Schachbrett. Die Felder A und B haben den gleichen Grauton. In 1A sehen sie sehr verschieden aus. In 1B wird die Übereinstimmung des Farbtons durch zwei einfarbige graue Balken verdeutlicht, die beide Felder verbinden. Quelle der Abbildung: Edward H. Adelson. Zur freien Verfügung für wissenschaftliche Zwecke.

Die Idee einer vorhersagenden Wahrnehmung stellt viele intuitive Vorstellungen über die Funktionsweise der Wahrnehmung in Frage. Die klassische Sicht auf die Wahrnehmung besagt, dass das Gehirn Sinneseindrücke von »unten-nach-oben« oder von »außen-nach-innen« verarbeitet: Sinneseindrücke werden durch Rezeptoren aufgenommen (zum Beispiel die Netzhaut), dringen dann tiefer ins Gehirn vor, wobei bei jedem Schritt zunehmend komplexere und abstraktere Verarbeitungsprozesse herangezogen werden. Ausgehend von dieser Sichtweise wird die perzeptuelle »Schwerarbeit« von diesen von »unten-nach-oben« gehenden neuronalen Verbindungen ausgeführt. Die helmholtzsche Sichtweise kehrt dies um und schlägt vor, dass die Signale aus der Außenwelt, die unser Gehirn erreichen, nur *Vorhersagefehler* übermitteln – also den Unterschied zwischen dem, was das Gehirn erwartet, und dem, was es empfängt, und zwar auf jeder Ebene des Prozesses. Der Inhalt der Wahrnehmung wird durch vorhersagende Wahrnehmungen übertragen, die in die *entgegengesetzte* Richtung fließen (also von »oben-nach-unten«), tief aus dem Gehirn nach außen zu den sensorischen Oberflächen.[11] Zur Wahrnehmung gehört die simultane Minimierung von Vorhersagefehlern über viele Verarbeitungsebenen hinweg innerhalb des Wahrnehmungssystems des Gehirns.

Nach dieser Sichtweise, die oft auch als »vorhersagendes Kodieren«[12] oder »vorhersagendes Verarbeiten«[13] bezeichnet wird, erscheint Wahrnehmung als eine *kontrollierte Halluzination,* in

11 Jakob Hohwy, *The Predictive Mind,* Oxford: Oxford University Press, 2013; Dana H. Ballard / Rajesh P. Rao, »Predictive Coding in the Visual Cortex: A Functional Interpretation of Some Extra-Classical Receptive-Field Effects«, in: *Nature Neuroscience,* 2 (1999) Nr. 1, S. 79–87.

12 Dana H. Ballard / Rajesh P. Rao, »Predictive Coding in the Visual Cortex: A Functional Interpretation of Some Extra-Classical Receptive-Field Effects«, a. a. O.

13 Andy Clark, »Whatever Next? Predictive Brains, Situated Agents, and the Future of Cognitive Science«, in: *Behavioral and Brain Sciences,* 36 (2013) Nr. 3, S. 181–204.

difficult to believe, look carefully at figure 1B, which shows exactly the same image but with the patches A and B joined by two single-colored gray bars. Now it should be very clear that A and B are actually the same shade of gray.

So why do they *look* different? What is happening is that the brain is using its prior knowledge, built deep into the circuitry of its visual cortex, that a cast shadow will dim the appearance of a surface. Therefore, we see B as lighter than it really is.

This is not a failure of the visual system. The purpose of vision is not to be an accurate light meter. It is, rather, to reveal the action-relevant causes of sensory signals, and this is exactly what is happening.

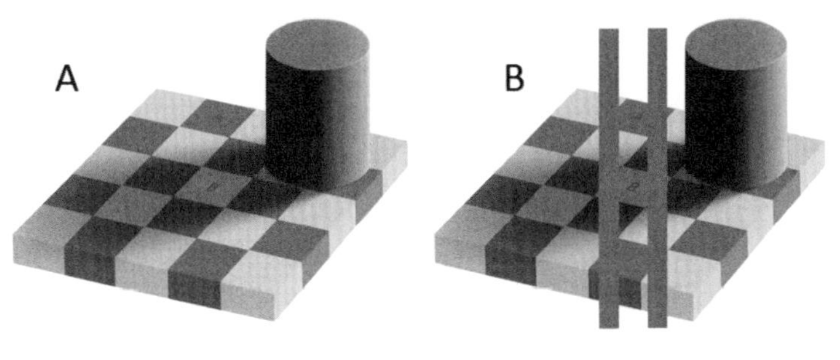

Fig · 1 Adelson's checkerboard. The squares A and B on the boards are the same shade of gray. In 1A they appear to be very different. In 1B the color equivalence is made explicit by solid uniform gray bars connecting the two squares. Image credit to Edward H. Adelson. Free use for academic purposes.

The idea of predictive perception overturns many intuitive ideas about how perception works. The classical view of perception is that the brain processes sensory information in a "bottom-up" or "outside-in" direction: Sensory signals enter through receptors (for example, the retina) and then progress deeper into the brain, with each stage recruiting increasingly sophisticated and abstract processing. In this view, the perceptual "heavy lifting" is done by these bottom-up connections. The Helmholtzian view inverts this framework, proposing that signals flowing into the brain from the outside world convey only *prediction errors*—the differences between what the brain expects and what it receives, at every level of processing. Perceptual content is carried by perceptual predictions flowing in the *opposite* (top-down) direction, from deep inside the brain out towards the sensory surfaces.[11] Perception involves the minimization of prediction error simultaneously across many levels of processing within the brain's perceptual systems.

11 Jakob Hohwy, *The Predictive Mind* (Oxford: Oxford University Press, 2013); Dana H. Ballard / Rajesh P. Rao, "Predictive Coding in the Visual Cortex: A Functional Interpretation of Some Extra-Classical Receptive-Field Effects," *Nature Neuroscience* 2, no. 1, (1999): pp. 79–87.

welcher die Hypothesen des Gehirns dauernd von den Sinneseindrücken, die aus der Welt und dem Körper eintreffen, im Zaum gehalten werden. »Eine Fantasie, die mit der Wirklichkeit zusammenfällt«, wie es der Psychologe Chris Frith so elegant formuliert hat.[14]

Kontrafaktische Vorhersagen und perzeptuelle Präsenz

Bisher hat uns das Konzept der vorhersagenden Wahrnehmung geholfen zu verstehen, *was* wir wahrnehmen: Das Gehirn sucht also nach der besten perzeptuellen Erklärung der Sinneseindrücke unter der Einbeziehung seiner Erwartungen über den wahrscheinlichen Zustand der Welt. Aber wie kann man dieses Konzept anwenden, um zu verstehen, *wie* wir wahrnehmen – in dem spezifischen Sinn einer Phänomenologie der Präsenz (oder Objekthaftigkeit), die alle unsere Wahrnehmungssituationen durchdringt? Präsenz an sich scheint nicht eine »Deutung« des Gehirns in einem unmittelbaren Sinn zu sein.

An dieser Stelle muss die Argumentation etwas detaillierter werden, aber es ist nicht zu kompliziert, wenn man es Schritt für Schritt durchgeht. Die wichtigste Erkenntnis ist die Rolle der Handlungen oder der Bewegungen für die Wahrnehmung. Wie ich bereits oben erwähnt habe, beinhaltet Wahrnehmung die Minimierung von Vorhersagefehlern als einen Prozess, bei welchem das Gehirn die »beste Annäherung« an die Deutung der Sinneswahrnehmungen entwickelt. Dies kann entweder durch das Aktualisieren der Vorhersagen des Gehirns passieren (zum Beispiel: »Ich dachte, ich hätte Peter gesehen, aber jetzt erkenne ich, dass es Paul ist«) oder indem es durch Handlungen die bestehenden Vorhersagen bestätigt (zum Beispiel: »Das ist nicht Peter, also schaue ich dort, wo Peter tatsächlich ist«). Dieser zweite Prozess wird auch *aktive Inferenz* (oder aktives Schlussfolgern) bezeichnet, weil es um mehr geht, als Wahrnehmungsvorhersagen passiv zu filtern.[15] Hierbei wird natürlich angenommen, dass sich alle diese Prozesse unbewusst vollziehen – und nur das Ergebnis Teil unserer bewussten Wahrnehmung wird.

Aktive Inferenz stellt einen deutlich höheren Anspruch an die Maschinerie der Wahrnehmungsvorhersagen. Ein System, das zur aktiven Inferenz in der Lage ist, muss nicht nur »Deutungen« über die Ursachen der aktuellen Sinneseindrücke abgeben können, es muss auch die Fähigkeit besitzen, sensorische Konsequenzen einer großen Bandbreite von Handlungen vorherzusagen. Damit die aktive Inferenz in dem gerade erwähnten Beispiel einen Nutzen ergibt, müsste das Gehirn vorhersagen, wie wahrscheinlich es

14 Chris D. Frith, *Making up the Mind: How the Brain Creates Our Mental World*, Malden, MA: Wiley-Blackwell, 2007.

15 Karl J. Friston, »The Free-Energy Principle: A Rough Guide to the Brain?«, in: *Trends in Cognitive Sciences*, 13 (2009) Nr. 7, S. 293–301.

In this view, which is often called "predictive coding"[12] or "predictive processing,"[13] perception is a *controlled hallucination* in which the brain's hypotheses are continually reined in by sensory signals arriving from the world and the body: "A fantasy that coincides with reality," as the psychologist Chris Frith eloquently put it.[14]

Counterfactual Predictions and Perceptual Presence

So far, the concept of predictive perception has helped us to understand *what* we perceive in terms of the brain seeking the best perceptual explanation of sensory data given its prior expectations about the likely state of the world. However, how can we use this framework to understand *how* we perceive in the specific sense of the phenomenology of presence (or objecthood) that permeates our perceptual scenes very generally? Presence itself does not seem to be a "best guess" by the brain in any straightforward sense.

Here is where the reasoning gets a bit more detailed, but it is simple enough if taken step-by-step. The key insight is the role of action or movement in perception. I mentioned above that perception involves the minimization of perceptual prediction errors as the process by which the brain reaches its "best guess" about the causes of sensory signals. This can be done either by updating the brain's predictions (e.g., "I thought I saw Peter, now I realize it is Paul") or by performing actions to confirm existing predictions (e.g., "This isn't Peter, so let me look over there, where Peter actually is"). The second process is called *active inference*, since it entails more than the passive filtering of perceptual predictions.[15] Remember, of course, that all these processes are assumed to take place unconsciously—with only the outcome forming part of our conscious perception.

Active inference makes a significant extra demand on the machinery of predictive perception. As well as making a "best guess" about the causes of current sensory signals, a system capable of active inference must also be capable of predicting the sensory consequences of a wide range of actions. In the example above, for active inference to be useful, the brain would need to be able to predict the likelihood of seeing Peter given the action of looking in a particular direction or moving to a different place. These are thus *conditional* or *counterfactual* predictions, because they are making predictions about possible, but not actual, sensory signals.

12 Ballard and Rao, "Predictive Coding in the Visual Cortex," pp. 79–87.

13 Andy Clark, "Whatever Next? Predictive Brains, Situated Agents, and the Future of Cognitive Science," *Behavioral and Brain Sciences* 36, no. 3 (2013): pp. 181–204.

14 Chris D. Frith, *Making up the Mind: How the Brain Creates Our Mental World*. (Malden, MA: Wiley-Blackwell, 2007).

15 Karl J. Friston, "The Free-Energy Principle: A Rough Guide to the Brain?" *Trends in Cognitive Sciences* 13, no. 7 (2009): pp. 293–301.

ist, Peter zu sehen, wenn man in eine bestimmte Richtung schaut oder sich an einen anderen Ort begibt. Es handelt sich um *konditionale* oder *kontrafaktische* Vorhersagen, weil sie Vorhersagen über mögliche und nicht tatsächliche Sinneseindrücke machen.

Glücklicherweise unterstützen die meisten theoretischen Anwendungen der Fehlerminimierung bei Vorhersagen ausdrücklich konditionale oder kontrafaktische Vorhersagen, weil sie mit sogenannten »generativen Modellen« arbeiten, die in einer sehr allgemeinen Weise die Dinge-in-der-Welt mit den von diesen hervorgerufenen Sinneseindrücken verknüpfen.[16] Für unsere Argumentation hier können wir diese Details jedoch zurückstellen und uns auf die phänomenologischen Auswirkungen der aktiven Inferenz konzentrieren.

An dieser Stelle soll es nun wieder um die Phänomenologie der Präsenz gehen. Eine Schlüsselerkenntnis in Noës Zitat (siehe oben) ist, dass Präsenz etwas damit zu tun hat, *sich der Teile eines Objektes bewusst zu sein, die unseren Sinnen nicht unmittelbar zugänglich sind* – zum Beispiel wenn man sich der Rückseite eines Objektes bewusst ist, auch wenn man nur Sinneseindrücke von der Vorderseite bekommt. In Bezug auf die vorhersagende Wahrnehmung passt dies ausgezeichnet zu der Annahme, dass das Gehirn in der Lage sei, ein reiches Repertoire an kontrafaktischen Vorhersagen über das Verhalten von Sinneseindrücken zu kodieren, die sich auf bestimmte Handlungen beziehen. Anders gesagt: ich erlange ein perzeptuelles Bewusstsein von der Rückseite einer Tomate (und damit profitiert die Tomate-als-Ganzes von der Phänomenologie der Präsenz und Objekthaftigkeit), wenn die Mechanismen der vorhersagenden Wahrnehmung in meinem Sehzentrum in der Lage sind, eine vielfältige Auswahl an Vorhersagen über die Sinneseindrücke zu machen, die ich erhalten *würde*, wenn ich diese oder jene Handlung *vollzöge* (in die Hand nehmen, umdrehen und so weiter).[17] Wenn diese Bedingungen erfüllt sind, nehme ich ein Objekt als *wirklich in der Welt existierend* wahr.

Diese Erklärung kommt Noës Vorstellungen tatsächlich sehr nahe, mit dem entscheidenden Unterschied, dass bei Noë Repräsentationen oder Wahrnehmungsmodelle keine Rolle spielen und er sich stattdessen auf ein mechanistisches und vages Konzept einer »enaktivistischen« Kognitionswissenschaft stützt.[18] Die Schlussfolgerung ist jedoch ähnlich: Die Interpretation von Sinneseindrücken *als von einem Objekt hervorgebracht* bedeutet nicht nur, dass diese in einer bestimmten Weise miteinander korrelieren; sie hängt auch davon ab, dass das Gehirn Vorhersagen über die »sensomotorischen Möglichkeiten«, die Sinneseindrücke mit Handlungen verknüpfen, kodiert hat.

Damit lassen sich nicht nur die normale Wahrnehmung von Präsenz und Objekthaftigkeit erklären, sondern auch Situationen, in denen es eine spezifische *Abwesenheit* von phänomenologischer

16 Rick A. Adams / Michael Breakspear / Karl J. Friston / Laurent Perrinet, »Perceptions as Hypotheses: Saccades as Experiments«, in: *Frontiers in Psychology*, 3 (2012), S. 151; Anil K. Seth, »A Predictive Processing Theory of Sensorimotor Contingencies: Explaining the Puzzle of Perceptual Presence and Its Absence in Synesthesia«, in: *Cognitive Neuroscience*, 5 (2014) Nr. 2, S. 97–118.

17 Anil K. Seth, »A Predictive Processing Theory of Sensorimotor Contingencies: Explaining the Puzzle of Perceptual Presence and Its Absence in Synesthesia«, a. a. O.

18 Alva Noë, »Experience without the Head«, in: T. Gendler / A. Hawthorne (Hrsg.), *Perceptual experience*, NY: Clarendon / Oxford University Press, 2006, S. 411–434.

Fortunately, most computational models of prediction error minimization explicitly support conditional or counterfactual predictions, since they involve so-called "generative models" that provide very general mappings between things-in-the-world and the sensory signals they induce.[16] For present purposes, however, we can set these details aside and focus on the phenomenological consequences of active inference.

This is where we return to the phenomenology of presence. A key insight in Noë's quote (above) is that presence has to do with *being aware of parts of an object that are not directly available to the senses*—for example, being aware of the back of an object, when only its front is providing immediate sensory input. In terms of predictive perception, this maps neatly onto the idea that the brain may encode a rich repertoire of counterfactual predictions about the behavior of sensory signals given specific actions. In other words, I become perceptually aware of the back of a tomato (and thus the tomato-as-a-whole benefits from the phenomenology of presence and objecthood) when the mechanisms of predictive perception in my visual brain are able to make a rich set of predictions about the sensory signals that I *would* encounter *were* I to do this-or-that action (picking it up, rotating it, and so on).[17] When these conditions are satisfied, I consciously experience an object as *really existing in the world.*

This explanation is, in fact, quite similar to Noë's own ideas, with the major difference that Noë excludes a role for representations or models in perception, relying instead on mechanistically vague concepts from "enactive" cognitive science.[18] The overall message is, however, similar: What it means to interpret sensory signals *as being caused by an object* is not only a matter of their being correlated in some way or another; it also depends on the brain encoding predictions about the "sensorimotor contingencies" linking sensory signals to actions.

As well as explaining normal experiences of presence and objecthood, occasions in which there is a specific *absence* of phenomenological presence can also be accounted for in this way.[19] For example, retinal afterimages and synesthetic concurrents do *not* behave in complex-but-predictable ways when particular actions are performed, and so would not be associated with vivid experiences of presence or objecthood. In fact, the positive experience of their "unreality" may be related to the violation of counterfactual predictions that would normally be associated with perceiving a patch of light or a color.

Any useful scientific concept should be able to make some clear experimental predictions. One prediction emerging from the set of ideas described here is that changing the repertoire of action-related counterfactual predictions should change the

16 Rick A. Adams / Michael Breakspear / Karl J. Friston / Laurent Perrinet, "Perceptions as Hypotheses: Saccades as Experiments," *Frontiers in Psychology* 3 (2012): p. 151; Seth, Anil K., "A Predictive Processing Theory of Sensorimotor Contingencies: Explaining the Puzzle of Perceptual Presence and Its Absence in Synesthesia," *Cognitive Neuroscience* 5, no. 2 (2014): pp. 97–118.

17 Seth, "A Predictive Processing Theory of Sensorimotor Contingencies," pp. 97–118.

18 Noë, "Experience without the Head," p. 414.

19 Seth, "A Predictive Processing Theory of Sensorimotor Contingencies," pp. 97–118.

Präsenz gibt.[19] Zum Beispiel verhalten sich Nachbilder auf der Netzhaut und synästhetische Zusatzempfindungen (Concurrents) *nicht* in komplexer, jedoch in vorhersagbarer Weise in Bezug auf Handlungen, und ließen sich somit auch nicht mit plastischen Erfahrungen von Präsenz oder Objekthaftigkeit assoziieren. Tatsächlich könnte die positive Erfahrung ihrer »Irrealität« mit dem Übergehen der kontrafaktischen Vorhersagen zu tun haben, die normalerweise mit der Wahrnehmung eines Licht- oder Farbflecks assoziiert werden.

Jedes anwendbare wissenschaftliche Konzept sollte in der Lage sein, klare experimentelle Vorhersagen zu treffen. Aus den hier beschriebenen Vorstellungen lässt sich ableiten, dass ein verändertes Repertoire an handlungsbezogenen, kontrafaktischen Vorhersagen auch das Level der wahrgenommenen Präsenz oder »Objekthaftigkeit« verändern sollte. Obwohl sie diese These nicht direkt einer Prüfung unterziehen, belegen einige alltägliche Beobachtungen diese Vermutung: Ein Beispiel wäre die Wahrnehmung eines einfarbig blauen Himmels, dem eine starke Phänomenologie der Objekthaftigkeit fehlt und der auch nicht auf vielfältige Weise auf vom Beobachter zu unternehmende Handlungen bezogen werden kann (abgesehen davon, die Augen zu schließen).

→ Fig · 2 Die experimentelle Anordnung einer Augmented Reality Studie, die untersucht, in welcher Weise die Wahrnehmung von »Präsenz« und »Objekthaftigkeit« davon abhängt, ob man (kontrafaktische) Vorhersagen über die Folgen einer Handlung in Bezug auf objektbezogene Sinneseindrücke machen kann. Quelle der Abbildung: Keisuke Suzuki (Sackler Centre for Consciousness Science).

Um diese Annahmen über Präsenz in einer direkteren Weise in einem wissenschaftlichen Experiment zu untersuchen, verwenden wir aktuell im Labor eine innovative Versuchsanordnung, die mit erweiterter Realität (Augmented Reality, AR) arbeitet. In unserem Experiment (siehe Fig · 2) sehen Probanden über ein Head-Mounted-Display (eine Art Brille) neuartige dreidimensionale Objekte, die in die reale Welt hineinprojiziert werden. Wichtig ist, dass sie mit den Objekten interagieren können, indem sie einen AR Marker (ein Schild mit einem Erkennungscode) bewegen. Bei einer Variante verhält sich das Objekt wie ein normales Objekt – man sieht zum Beispiel seine Rückseite, wenn man es um 180 Grad dreht. Bei einer zweiten Variante zeigt das Objekt immer dieselbe Seite, egal welche Handlungen ausgeführt werden – so wie der Mond nur eine Seite zeigt, während er um die Erde kreist. Bei einer dritten Variante reagiert das virtuelle Objekt zufällig, wenn Handlungen ausgeführt werden, was die Bildung verlässlicher kontrafaktischer Vorhersagen verhindert. Unsere Hypothese war, dass die erste Variante – die informative kontrafaktische Vorhersagen unterstützt –

19 Anil K. Seth, »A Predictive Processing Theory of Sensorimotor Contingencies: Explaining the Puzzle of Perceptual Presence and Its Absence in Synesthesia«, in: *Cognitive Neuroscience,* 5 (2014) Nr. 2, S. 97–118.

level of experienced presence or objecthood. Some everyday observations are consistent with this, although they do not directly test it. For instance, the perceptual experience of a uniform blue sky lacks a strong phenomenology of objecthood and also lacks a rich dependency on any actions an observer might make (besides closing one's eyes).

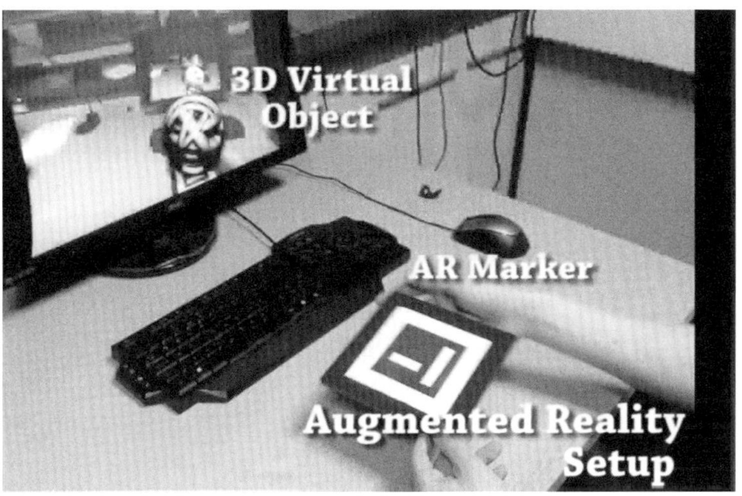

Fig · 2 Experimental setup for an augmented reality study investigating how experiences of "presence" and "objecthood" depend on the ability to make (counterfactual) predictions about the effects of action on object-related sensory signals. Image courtesy of Keisuke Suzuki (Sackler Centre for Consciousness Science).

In an effort to test these ideas about presence more directly, ongoing work in our laboratory is making use of an innovative augmented reality set-up. In our experiment (see Fig · 2), volunteers view novel three-dimensional objects superimposed into the real world through a head-mounted display. Importantly, they are able to interact with the virtual objects by rotating a marker. In one condition, the object behaves as a normal object would—for example, revealing its back when rotated 180 degrees. In a second condition, the object always shows the same face no matter what actions are made—much as the moon only ever shows one face as it orbits the Earth. Finally, in a third condition, the virtual object behaves rather randomly as actions are performed, preventing the formation of any reliable counterfactual predictions. We predicted that only the first condition, which supports informative counterfactual predictions, would lead to vivid experiences of objecthood and presence. While data collection is still ongoing, the results so far are promising.

plastische Erfahrungen von Objekthaftigkeit und Präsenz hervorbringen würde. Wir sind noch dabei die Daten zu sammeln, aber bisher sehen die Ergebnisse schon sehr vielversprechend aus.

Welche Resultate die Daten aus dieser speziellen Studie auch hervorbringen werden, sie sind ein nützliches Beispiel dafür, wie man aus Erkenntnissen zur Phänomenologie des Alltags, die sowohl für Wissenschaftler als auch Künstler interessant sind, Theorien über Mechanismen des Gehirns entwickeln kann, die dann im Labor wieder einer strengen Untersuchung unterzogen werden können. Wissenschaft und Kunst erscheinen hier, so wie sie sollten, als gleichwertige Partner in einem Versuch, die Natur der menschlichen Wahrnehmung in all ihrer Vertrautheit und Rätselhaftigkeit zu verstehen.

Whichever way the data from this particular study turn out, it serves as a useful example of how insights into everyday phenomenology, which are of equal interest to scientists and artists, can be formalized into theories about brain mechanisms, which themselves can be rigorously tested in the laboratory. Science and art emerge here, as they should, as equal partners in the attempt to better understand the nature of human experience in all its familiarity and in all its mystery.

Annäherung an
eine Phänomenologie
des Unbekannten

Towards a Phenomenology
of the Unknown

Bilge Sayim & Ivana Franke

Das Erlebnis von etwas vollkommen »Unbekanntem« assoziieren wir häufig mit Kindheitserinnerungen – bizarre Träume, tiefe Wälder, dunkle Nächte, alles Beispiele für etwas Unbekanntes mit einem Beiklang von Geheimnis und Angst; etwas, über das wir rein gar nichts wissen. Aber selbstverständlich machen wir nicht nur in unserer Kindheit Erfahrungen mit dem Unbekannten. Seltsame Lichterscheinungen am Himmel, Geräusche ohne erkennbare Quelle oder das Gefühl berührt zu werden, obwohl niemand in der Nähe ist, sind ebenfalls Beispiele, die dem Erlebnis von etwas durchweg Unbekanntem nahe kommen – es könnte alles Mögliche sein. Es könnte gefährlich sein. In solchen Situationen sind unsere Sinne geschärft, wir sind äußerst wachsam und häufig neugierig. Und wir sind uns nicht ganz sicher, ob unsere Wahrnehmung korrekt ist. Diese Art von Erfahrung widerspricht unserer vorgefassten Vorstellung der Realität. Was wir wahrnehmen, scheint völlig unerklärlich zu sein.

Die Installation *Retreat into Darkness. Towards a Phenomenology of the Unknown (Rückzug in die Dunkelheit. Annäherung an eine Phänomenologie des Unbekannten)* erzeugt eine Situation, die Erfahrungen hervorrufen kann, welche dieser Art der Erfahrung des »Unbekannten« ähneln. Bevor wir die zugrundeliegenden Prinzipien der Installation erläutern und darlegen, wie diese von Betrachtern erfahren wird, möchten wir einige Schlüsselprinzipien der visuellen Wahrnehmung einführen, die wichtig sind, um die Phänomenologie unseres »Rückzugs in die Dunkelheit« zu verstehen. Wir werden zeigen, wie die Wahrnehmung von Lichtreflexionen (Glanzlichtern) als »Objekte« unsere Sehgewohnheiten in Frage stellt und wie die Ausstellung uns in ungewöhnliche Wahrnehmungswelten versetzt, in welchen die normale Objektkategorisierung fehlschlägt. Schließlich werden wir einen näheren Blick auf unseren Wahrnehmungsprozess werfen und wie sich dieser verhält, wenn wir mit etwas phänomenologisch Unbekanntem konfrontiert sind.[1]

In den meisten Alltagssituationen sehen und interagieren wir mit Objekten in der Außenwelt als Mitgliedern einer Kategorie. So sehen wir zum Beispiel einen bestimmten Baum normalerweise einfach nur als einen weiteren, gewöhnlichen Baum. Die speziellen Eigenschaften, wie das Farbmuster, die Oberflächenstruktur und dergleichen, werden oft gar nicht bemerkt. Diese Wahrnehmung von Objekten als Mitglieder von eher breiten Kategorien ist sinnvoll und dient als Abkürzung, um schnell die wesentlichen Eigenschaften des Objekts zu erkennen.[2] Um sich in einer komplexen Umwelt zurechtzufinden, ist eine schnelle Kategorisierung nicht nur wünschenswert, sondern notwendig. Von der Einzigartigkeit des Sehens eines bestimmten Objekts zu einem bestimmten Zeitpunkt – genau genommen sehen oder erleben wir niemals genau dasselbe zweimal – wird in der Regel nicht Notiz genommen.

1 Es gilt zu beachten, dass individuelle, kulturelle, stimmungs- und erfahrungsabhängige Unterschiede auf vielen Wahrnehmungsebenen die Erfahrungen modulieren, die wir hier zu beschreiben versuchen. Der Einfachheit halber arbeiten wir mit den nötigen Verallgemeinerungen und versuchen, eine Reihe typischer Beziehungen zwischen »äußeren« und wahrgenommenen Räumen zu skizzieren.

2 Es sei angemerkt, dass die Wahrnehmung nicht immer kategorial ist, wir nehmen Eigenschaften auch als Kontinuum wahr, und oft gibt es eine Mischung aus kategorialer und nicht-kategorialer Wahrnehmung.

Experiencing an "unknown" is often associated with memories from our childhood: the unknown of dreams, deep forests, or the night—the unknown with its connotations of mystery and fear; something about which we have utterly no idea what it could be. However, experiencing the unknown is not constrained to our childhood. For example, similar experiences can be triggered by a strange light in the sky, a sound with no plausible source, or the feeling of being touched, although no one is around. It could be anything; it could be dangerous. Our senses are sharpened, and we are highly alert, and curious. We are not certain if what we perceive is accurate. This type of experience does not fit into our preconceived idea of reality; what we perceive appears entirely inexplicable.

The installation *Retreat into Darkness. Towards a Phenomenology of the Unknown* creates a situation that may evoke similar experiences of this type of "unknown." Before we describe the underlying principles of the installation and how it is experienced by observers, we will introduce key principles of visual perception that are important for understanding the phenomenology of our "retreat into darkness." We will see how perceiving light reflections (highlights) as "objects" challenges our usual way of seeing, and how the exhibition takes us into unusual perceptual worlds where ordinary object categorization collapses. We will also take a closer look at our perceptual process itself as it manifests when confronted with an unknown phenomenon.[1]

In most everyday situations, we see and act on individual objects in the external world in a categorical fashion. For example, a tree is usually seen as just another tree. Details of its color pattern, surface structure, and other features often go unnoticed. Such perception of objects as members of rather broad categories is useful and serves as a shortcut for quickly extracting the object's essential features.[2] To accomplish tasks such as navigation in complex cluttered environments, rapid categorization is not only desirable, it is necessary. The ultimate uniqueness that accompanies seeing a particular object at a particular point in time—strictly speaking, we never see or experience exactly the same thing twice—therefore often goes unnoticed.

1 Note that individual, cultural, mood- and exposure-dependent variations on many levels of perception modulate the experiences we attempt to capture here. For simplicity's sake, we will accept the necessary generalizations and attempt to outline a number of characteristic relations between "external" and perceived spaces.

2 Note that not all perception is categorical—we also perceive features on continuums, and often there is a mixture of categorical and non-categorical perception.

In einigen Situationen ist die Kategorisierung schwierig, zum Beispiel wenn man etwas aus einer großen Entfernung, im Nebel, oder nur für eine kurze Zeit sieht. In solchen Momenten verharren wir in einem Zustand der Unklarheit, in dem wir nicht sicher sind, was wir sehen.[3] Dieser Mangel an Klarheit wird meistens nicht mit mysteriösen oder angstbesetzten Gefühlen in Verbindung gebracht, sondern als Zustand erfahren, in dem bestimmte, detaillierte visuelle Informationen einfach fehlen, um das (normalerweise ganz gewöhnliche) Objekt richtig zu erkennen. Erfahrungen in völliger Dunkelheit können allerdings den Erfahrungen des oben beschriebenen Unbekannten recht nahe kommen; und Dunkelheit ist in der Tat ein wichtiger Faktor in dieser Installation.

Um zu verstehen, was man in der Installation sieht und erlebt, müssen wir uns aber zunächst die Natur von Glanzlichtern beziehungsweise Reflexionen anschauen. Glanzlichter treten auf, wenn Licht von einer glänzenden (nicht-Lambertschen) Oberfläche reflektiert wird. Glanzlichter mit starken Intensitätsspitzen entstehen insbesondere dann, wenn das Licht im gleichen Winkel reflektiert wird, in dem es auf die Oberfläche trifft (in Relation zur Oberflächennormalen). Obwohl Glanzlichter überall in unserer Umwelt vorkommen, schenken wir ihnen in der Regel wenig Beachtung. Unser visuelles System verarbeitet und benutzt Glanzlichter allerdings fortwährend, beispielsweise um Rückschlüsse auf die Eigenschaften eines Materials vorzunehmen. Glanzlichter haben eine Reihe bemerkenswerter Eigenschaften. So hängen sie zum Beispiel von der Position der Lichtquelle in Relation zum Betrachter und der reflektierenden Oberfläche ab und sind nur von einer begrenzten Anzahl an Blickwinkeln aus sichtbar. Wichtig ist, dass Glanzlichter von Bewegung abhängen. Wenn sich das Objekt oder der Betrachter bewegen, dann verbleiben die Glanzlichter nicht an einer Stelle der Oberfläche, sondern ändern ihre Position auf dem Objekt. Durch diese Eigenschaft unterscheiden sie sich stark von anderen visuellen Merkmalen wie Farbe, Helligkeit, oder Textur, die sich nicht relativ zur Oberfläche bewegen, sondern dem Objekt »anhaften«. Glanzlichter sind der zweite wichtige Faktor, der in der Installation eingesetzt wird.

Der ungefähr 8 × 10 × 5 m große Ausstellungsraum der Schering Stiftung war völlig dunkel und mit schwarz gestrichenen Wänden und einem schwarzen Teppichboden ausgestattet. Zusätzlich wurde im Eingangsbereich ein Verdunklungsvorhang installiert, der verhinderte, dass beim Eintreten der Besucher Licht in den Raum eindringen konnte. Drei LED-Leuchten mit einer geringen Lichtstärke wurden an verschiedenen Standorten und in verschiedenen Höhen platziert und unterschiedlich ausgerichtet: eine am Boden, eine auf Augenhöhe und eine in der Nähe der Decke. Damit die Lichtquellen möglichst nicht zur Orientierung dienen konnten, wurden sie unterschiedlich und ohne offensichtliche

3 Ein verwandtes Phänomen tritt auf, wenn man ein Kippbild sieht, bei dem das visuelle System zwischen verschiedenen Interpretationen desselben Bildes hin und her schwankt.

In some situations, categorization is difficult—for example, when viewing something at a large distance, in fog, or for a very short time—and we remain in a state of vagueness in which it is unclear what we see.[3] This lack of clarity is most often not associated with any feelings of mystery or fear, but simply shows that some detailed visual information is missing to be able to see the (ordinary) object properly. Experiences in extreme darkness, however, may come close to the experiences of the unknown described above, and darkness is one of the important factors employed in the installation.

To understand what is perceived and experienced in the installation, we need first to introduce highlights. Highlights occur when light is reflected from shiny (non-Lambertian) surfaces. In particular, a specular highlight occurs when the light is reflected at an angle that is the same as the angle of incidence (relative to the surface normal). Although highlights are ubiquitous in our environment, we usually do not pay much attention to them. Our visual system, however, makes use of highlights all the time—for instance, to infer material properties. Highlights have a number of notable features. For example, they depend on the location of the light source relative to the observer and the reflecting surface, and they are only visible from a limited number of vantage points. More importantly, highlights are motion dependent. When the object or the observer moves, the highlights do not stick to the surface of the object, but move across it. This makes them very different from other visual features, such as color, lightness, or texture, which do not move relative to the surface structure, but are "attached" to the object. Along with darkness, highlights are the second important factor employed in the installation.

The Schering Stiftung's exhibition space, which is approximately 8 × 10 × 5 meters, was completely dark. The walls were painted black, the floor was covered with black carpet, and an additional entrance space with a blackout curtain was built to prevent light from leaking in when visitors entered the room. Three low intensity LED lights were placed in different locations and heights and oriented in different directions—on the floor, at eye level, and near the ceiling. The lights were arranged without obvious alignment in order to reduce the possibility of serving as a means of orientation. The lack of contextual information due to the darkness ensured that estimates of the location of the lights were very difficult. As most visual cues used for navigation were absent and no reliable landmarks were present, the sense of space and direction was significantly reduced.

3 A related phenomenon occurs when viewing bistable images in which the visual system switches between different interpretations of the same visual input.

Systematik ausgerichtet. Da wegen der Dunkelheit kontextuelle Informationen größtenteils fehlten, war es sehr schwierig, die Positionen der Lichtquellen zu lokalisieren. Weil die meisten visuellen Hinweise fehlten, um sich im Raum zurechtzufinden, und es keine verlässlichen Orientierungspunkte gab, waren das Raumgefühl und der Orientierungssinn erheblich eingeschränkt.

→ 1. Perspektivische Zeichnung der Installation. 2. Installationsansicht mit eingeschalteter Raumbeleuchtung. 3. Installationsansicht auf einer überbelichteten Fotografie.

Vor den LED-Leuchten befanden sich Metallkonstruktionen mit kegelförmigen Netzen aus Monofilament (feine Kunststofffäden), deren Grundflächen auf die Mitte des Raumes gerichtet waren. Ein großer, dreidimensionaler Metallrahmen (der grob einer Drehtür ähnelte) mit komplexen Gewebestrukturen aus Monofilamentfäden hing in der Mitte des Raumes und drehte sich langsam. Das Licht der LED-Lampen wurde von diesen Monofilamentstrukturen reflektiert, was starke, spiegelnde Glanzlichter an zahlreichen Positionen der Fäden produzierte, während andere Teile der Fäden unsichtbar blieben. Abhängig von der Position der Lichtquellen und dem Standpunkt der Betrachter erzeugte die Geometrie der Monofilamentstrukturen zusammen mit deren Drehbewegung komplexe, sich bewegende »Raumzeichnungen«. Die komplexe, geometrische Struktur wurde entwickelt, um zu verhindern, dass wiederkehrende Muster erkannt werden und um die Wahrnehmung sich permanent verändernder und unregelmäßiger Konfigurationen zu ermöglichen.

Beim Betreten des Raums sind die Besucher zunächst mit Dunkelheit konfrontiert. Wegen des schwachen Lichts wird das Nachtsehen aktiviert und man sieht nichts außer einigen wenigen, winzigen Lichtern an unbestimmten Positionen im Raum. Da die Dunkeladaptation der Augen Zeit in Anspruch nimmt, braucht es mehrere Minuten, bevor weitere schwache Lichtpunkte und Linien, die sich im Raum bewegen, entdeckt werden, und es dauert bis zu zwanzig Minuten, bevor man den ganzen Raum sehen kann. Während der Adaptation haben die Betrachter genug Zeit, die verschiedenen Grade der Sichtbarkeit zu erleben und zugleich die sich einstellenden Veränderungen zu bemerken. Wenn sich die Augen einmal an die Dunkelheit angepasst haben, hat man das Gefühl, den Raum und die geometrischen Strukturen recht gut zu sehen, insbesondere relativ zu den ersten im Raum verbrachten Minuten.

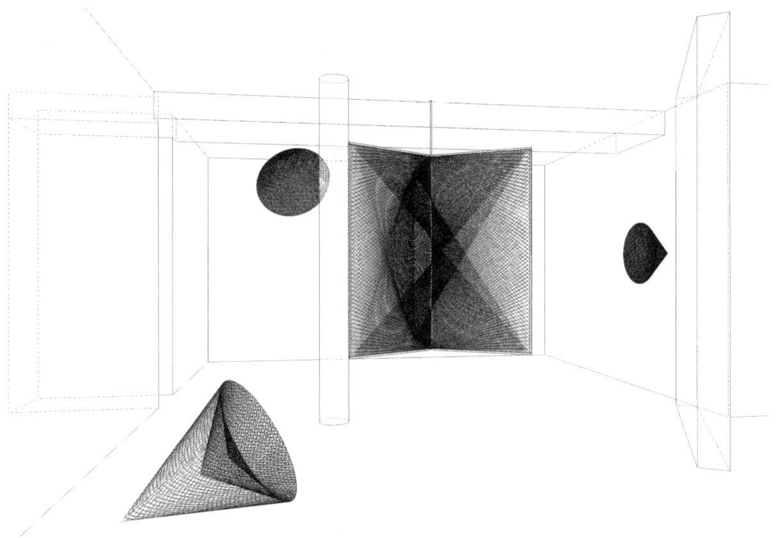

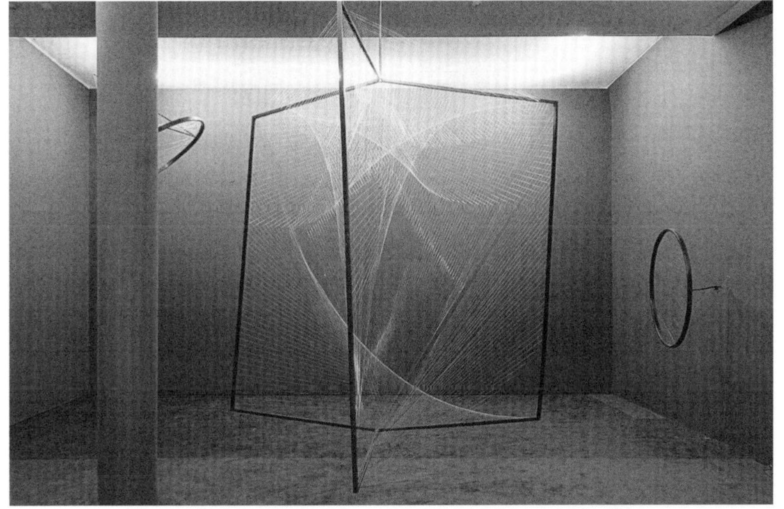

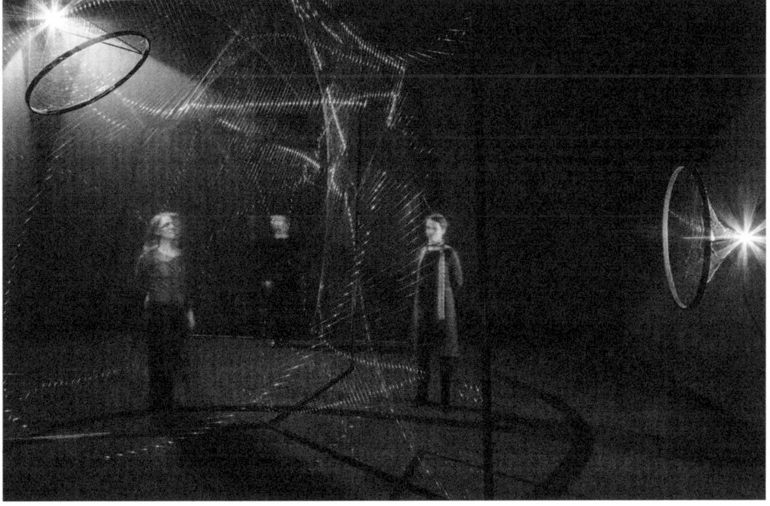

1. Perspective drawing of the installation. 2. Installation view with ambient lights on.
3. Installation view in an overexposed photograph.

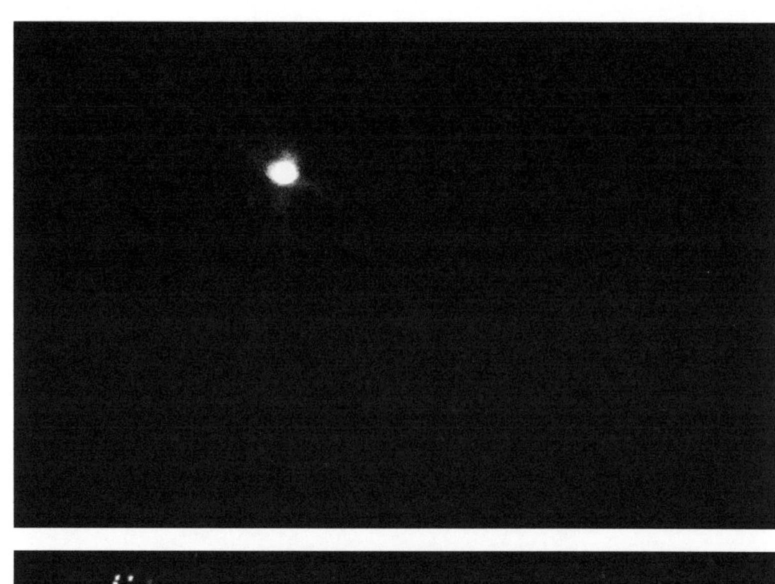

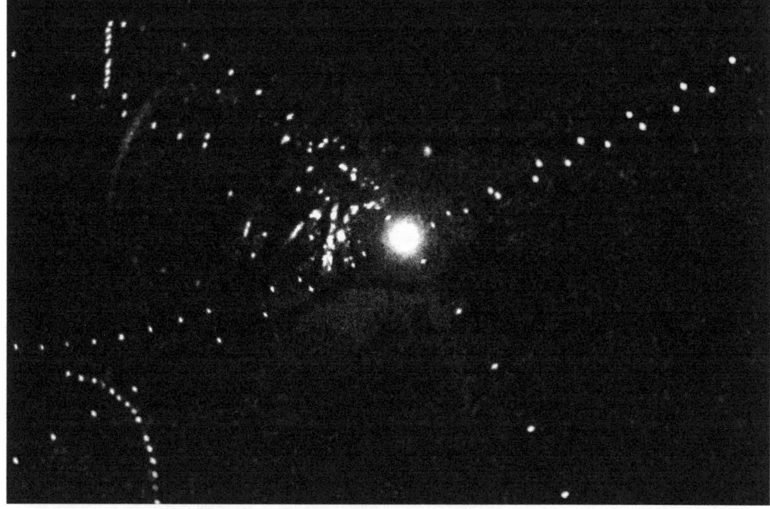

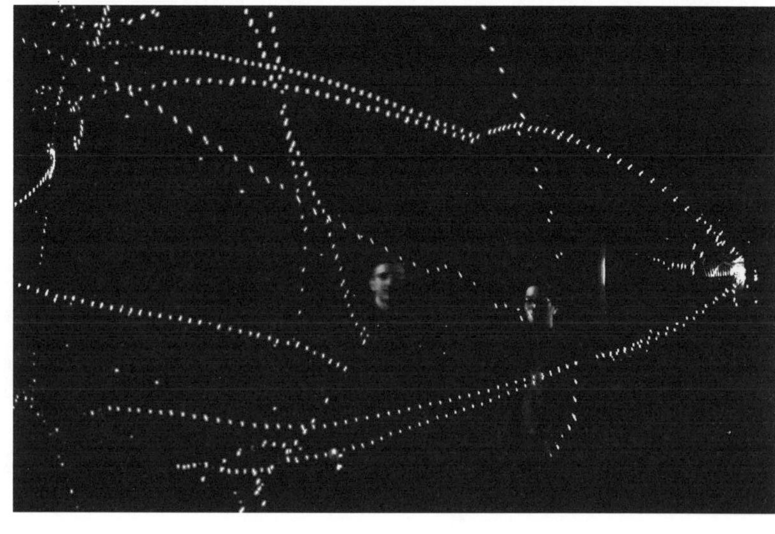

Installationsansicht direkt nach dem Eintreten in den Raum und nach einigen Minuten Dunkeladaptation (Illustration).

In front of the LEDs were metal structures with monofilament nets forming conical shapes with their bases pointing towards the center of the room. A large three-dimensional metal frame interwoven with complex monofilament string structures was suspended in the middle of the room and was slowly rotating. The light from the LEDs was reflected from the monofilament structures, producing strong specular highlights in numerous locations on the strings, while other parts of the strings were invisible. Depending on the position of the light sources and the position of the viewers, the geometry of the monofilament structures, together with their rotational movement, created complex, moving "spatial drawings." The geometry was developed with a high level of complexity to prevent the recognition of its repeating pattern, and it seemed to produce different, ever-changing, irregular configurations.

When entering the room, visitors first encounter darkness. Due to the low light level, the scotopic visual system is activated, and nothing is seen except for a few tiny lights in indefinite positions in space. Because the dark adaptation of the eyes takes time, several minutes are needed before faint appearances of more light points and lines moving in the space are detected, and it takes up to 20 minutes to see the entire space. During adaptation, observers have enough time to experience different levels of visibility, while noticing changes at the same time. Once the eyes have adapted to the darkness, it feels like one can see the space and the geometric structures quite well, not least because of how the appearance contrasts with the first few minutes of the experience.

← Installation view, as it appears on entering the space and after several minutes of adaptation (illustration).

While the light points seem to be individual entities, somewhat reminiscent of fireflies floating through space, they also combine and group flexibly into larger wholes, forming strings that appear and disappear in counterintuitive ways. The points and the string structures move on their own as well as relative to the observers' movements. The coming and going of the configurations is unlike any ordinary object. One wonders: "What is this? Is it alive? Are these configurations reacting to me?" Not seeing anything but the light points makes it difficult to detect what processes could be governing their coordinated dance. Something puzzling and strange is happening. It is difficult to understand what is going on, and at times it might seem like one is seeing "impossible configurations." There is simply no category of real world objects in which these unknown objects would fit.

Die Lichtpunkte scheinen einzelne Objekte zu sein, die entfernt an durch den Raum schwebende Glühwürmchen erinnern. Die einzelnen Punkte verbinden und gruppieren sich zu größeren Einheiten und bilden Ketten, welche auf eine Art und Weise erscheinen und wieder verschwinden, die unserer Intuition widerspricht. Die Punkte und auch die Kettenstrukturen bewegen sich von selbst und verändern sich, wenn die Betrachter ihre Position verändern. Das Kommen und Gehen der Konfigurationen verläuft anders als bei einem gewöhnlichen Objekt. »Was ist es? Ist es lebendig? Reagieren diese Konfigurationen auf mich?« Da man nichts außer den Lichtpunkten sieht, ist es schwierig auszumachen, welche Prozesse deren koordinierten »Tanz« steuern. Etwas Verwirrendes und Seltsames geschieht, es ist schwierig zu verstehen, was vor sich geht und manchmal erscheint es, als sähe man »unmögliche Konfigurationen«. Es steht einfach keine Kategorie in der »realen Welt« zur Verfügung, in die man diese unbekannten Objekte einordnen könnte.

→ Installationsansichten, auf denen die Reflexionen als bewegte Formen erscheinen.

In welcher Weise nehmen die Betrachter nun diese »unmöglichen Konfigurationen« aus spiegelnden Glanzlichtern genau wahr? Inwiefern unterscheiden sich die Erfahrungen, wenn sich die Betrachter an das schwache Lichtniveau der Installation angepasst (beziehungsweise nicht angepasst) haben? Um diese und ähnliche Fragen zu untersuchen, haben wir eine Studie durchgeführt, in der wir 14 Teilnehmer baten zu berichten, was sie erlebt haben und Zeichnungen der Erscheinungen im Raum anzufertigen. Zu diesem Zweck entwickelten wir einen Fragebogen zur Untersuchung der Erfahrungen, Gedanken und Assoziationen der Teilnehmer. Die Teilnehmer verbrachten zuerst nur drei Minuten im Ausstellungsraum, damit sie nicht vollständig an die Dunkelheit adaptierten. Nach einer Pause verbrachten sie 20 Minuten in der Ausstellung und konnten so weitere Grade der Sichtbarkeit in der Installation erleben. Wir baten die Teilnehmer, ihre Erfahrungen zu beobachten und auf die Unterschiede innerhalb und zwischen den beiden Durchgängen zu achten. Der Fragebogen wurde jeweils nach den beiden Durchgängen ausgefüllt.

Um sicherzustellen, dass die Antworten verschiedene psychologische Dimensionen umfassen und um die Reaktionen der Teilnehmer so wenig wie möglich einzuschränken, gab es mehrere Fragen, zu denen die Teilnehmer ihre Gefühle, Gedanken und Assoziationen *frei* beschreiben konnten. Um das Gesamtmuster der Erfahrungen besser einschätzen zu können, haben wir die

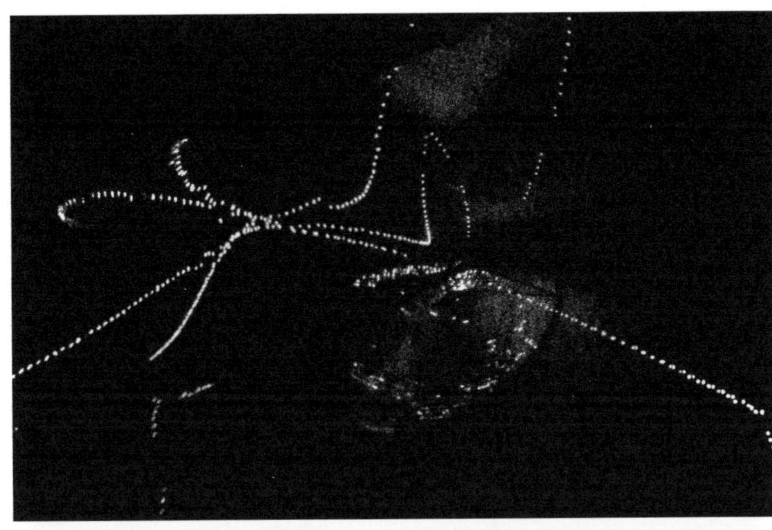

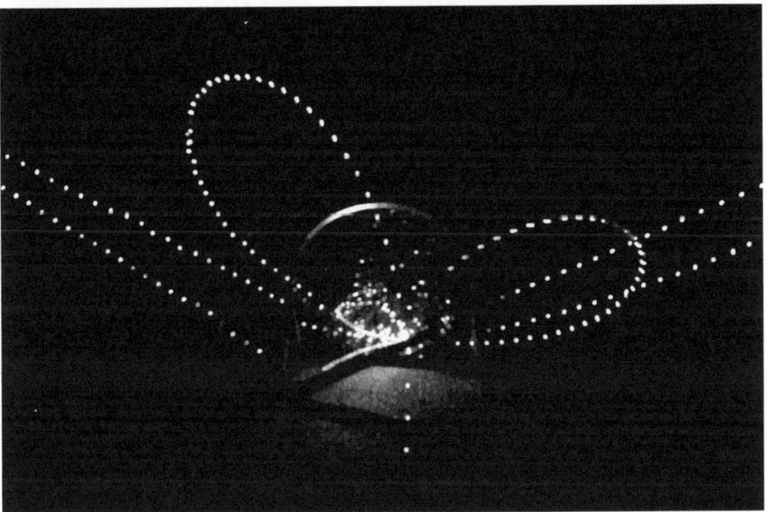

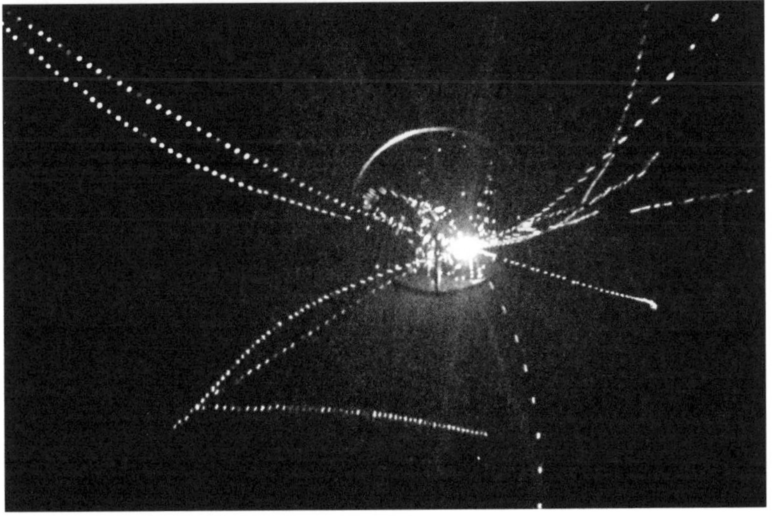

Installation views, appearing as animate shapes.

Antworten im Hinblick auf die zentralen Themen kategorisiert und untersucht, wie häufig diese bei den Teilnehmern insgesamt auftraten.

Es war wenig überraschend, dass die Mehrheit der Teilnehmer in irgendeiner Weise Helligkeit, Dunkelheit und Sichtbarkeit erwähnten. Während etwas mehr als die Hälfte der Teilnehmer Dunkelheit beziehungsweise das Fehlen von Licht bei dem 3-minütigen Durchgang erwähnten (»[Ich sah] fast völlige Dunkelheit«), berichteten knapp 80 % über den 20-minütigen Durchgang, dass sie Licht gesehen hatten (»Ich habe Licht wahrgenommen«, »Ich habe mich von Licht umgeben gefühlt«). Die eigene Beobachtung, mehr und mehr zu sehen ging damit einher, die Installation besser zu verstehen: Etwa zwei Drittel der Teilnehmer berichteten, dass sie diese nun besser nachvollziehen konnten. Allerdings bezogen sich die meisten der Antworten, in denen von einem besseren Verständnis der Installation die Rede war, darauf, dass die Betrachter mehr von der eigentlichen Konstruktion gesehen hätten, zum Beispiel Schnüre statt einfach nur Lichtpunkte oder die sich drehende Rahmenkonstruktion, und nicht darauf, dass sie besser verstanden hätten, wie die eigene visuelle Erfahrung durch die Konstruktion hervorgebracht wurde. Mehrere Teilnehmer berichteten, dass sie Veränderungen der Strukturen als Folge der eigenen Bewegungen bemerkten, oft von einem Staunen begleitet (»Kleinste Bewegung von mir – auch mit dem Kopf – führt zu erstaunlichen Strukturveränderungen der Girlanden-Beziehungen«). In einer ähnlichen Weise wurde die Beziehung zwischen der eigenen Bewegung und den Veränderungen der Struktur als verwirrend und schwer verständlich beschrieben (»Überraschend war dann die Feststellung, dass sich das ganze System veränderte, wenn ich nur den Kopf bewegte. Ich versuchte, mir die Ursache dafür zu erklären – ohne Erfolg«). Außerdem wurde berichtet, dass die Strukturen lebendig erschienen: »Ich fühlte, dass die Strukturen mich anschauten, meinen Bewegungen folgten.«

Über den zweiten Durchgang (nach der Adaptation an die Dunkelheit) berichteten die Teilnehmer nicht nur häufig, dass sie mehr verstanden hätten, sondern auch, dass die Erfahrung beruhigend und freudvoll war (»Ich habe das ruhige und meditative Gefühl von Lichtern genossen, die sich im Raum bewegen«). Obwohl die Erfahrung von Ruhe fast genauso oft bezogen auf den 3-minütigen wie den 20-minütigen Durchgang beschrieben wurde, empfanden eine Reihe von Teilnehmern den ersteren als unbehaglich (»Meine anfängliche Neugierde verwandelte sich nach und nach in eine leichte Paranoia und Angst«). Die Angst und Unbehaglichkeit wurden wahrscheinlich zum Teil durch die Dunkelheit und die Notwendigkeit ausgelöst, sich im Dunkeln zu bewegen und zurechtzufinden, und vermutlich auch durch die Präsenz von etwas Unerklärlichem in einer unbekannten

How exactly do people perceive these "impossible configurations" of specular highlights? To what extent do the experiences differ when viewers are adapted (or not) to the low light levels in the installation space? In order to better explore these and similar questions, we conducted a study in which we asked 14 participants to report what they experienced and to make drawings of the shapes in the space. For this purpose, we developed a questionnaire inquiring about participants' experiences, thoughts, and associations. Participants first spent only three minutes in the exhibition space to ensure that they did not fully adapt to the darkness. After a break, they then spent 20 minutes in the exhibition in order to experience the installation with a larger range of visibility levels. We asked participants to monitor their experiences and to pay attention to differences within and between the sessions. After each session, they completed the questionnaire.

Because we wanted to ensure that we received responses for several psychological dimensions, while also constraining participants' responses as little as possible, we included several questions in which participants were able to freely report what they felt and thought, and what associations they had. To get a better idea of the overall pattern of experiences, we categorized the responses in regard to their apparent central meaning and looked at their occurrence rate among all participants.

Unsurprisingly, the majority of participants mentioned brightness or darkness and visibility in some way. While a little more than half of the participants mentioned the darkness and/or a lack of light during the 3-minute session ("[I saw] almost complete darkness"), almost 80 % reported that they saw light in the 20-minute session ("I perceived light," "I felt surrounded by light"). The increased visibility went hand in hand with a better general comprehension of the installation, according to two-thirds of the participants. However, most of the responses implying greater comprehension referred to having seen more of the actual structure—for example, seeing strings instead of just light points, or seeing the rotating frame structure—and not to a better understanding of how their visual experience is caused by the structure. Several participants reported that they noticed changes in the structures as a consequence of their own movement, something that was often accompanied by surprise ("Kleinste Bewegung von mir—auch mit dem Kopf—führt zu erstaunlichen Strukturveränderungen der Girlanden-Beziehungen" / "Smallest movement, even just my head, causes stunning changes in the garland-like structures"). Others also reported that the relation of their own motion to changes in the structures was puzzling and difficult to understand ("Überraschend war dann die Feststellung, dass sich das ganze System veränderte,

Entfernung, das sich von selbst bewegte, dessen Bewegung auf die der Betrachter reagierte und das manchem lebendig erschien.

Auf die Frage nach den Gedanken und Assoziationen wurden am häufigsten der »Weltraum«, das »Universum« und die »Sterne« genannt. Teilnehmer berichteten zum Beispiel: »Wunderbare Lichtformen, als wäre man inmitten von Sternen, die aus dem All kommen«; oder: »Als wäre man an einem friedlichen Ort im Weltraum«. Bemerkenswert ist, wie diese Aussagen das Gefühl der Teilnehmer festhalten, Teil des Raums zu sein und sich also nicht als eindeutig außerhalb der Installation, sondern eher als »in der Mitte« und »innerhalb« dieses »Universums« zu befinden. Das legt die Annahme nahe, dass die Teilnehmer bis zu einem gewissen Grad ihre Seh- und Denkgewohnheiten hinter sich gelassen haben, was auch durch den erhöhten Grad der Selbstreflexion unterstrichen wird. Mehr als zwei Drittel der Teilnehmer berichteten beim ersten Durchgang von einem erhöhten Maß an Selbstreflexion und Eigenwahrnehmung. Beim zweiten Durchgang war dieser Anteil wesentlich geringer, wahrscheinlich, weil die Teilnehmer sich jetzt stärker auf die sich langsam abzeichnenden Details der verschiedenen Strukturen und des Raums konzentrierten.

Damit man einen besseren Eindruck der Erfahrungen der einzelnen Teilnehmer erhält, lassen wir im Folgenden deren Zitate und Zeichnungen für sich selbst sprechen. Wir werden sehen, dass Angst und Paranoia, Sterne und das Universum sowie Fragen und Spekulationen darüber, was diese Wahrnehmungen hervorgerufen haben könnte, wiederkehrende Themen in den Erfahrungsberichten der Teilnehmer sind, und dass ihre Erfahrungen idiosynkratische Interpretationen und Assoziationen des Unbekannten beinhalteten und manchmal in Halluzinationen gipfelten.

wenn ich nur den Kopf bewegte. Ich versuchte, mir die Ursache dafür zu erklären—ohne Erfolg" / "I was surprised when I realized that the whole system changed when I only moved my head. I tried to find out why, but was unsuccessful"). Moreover, it was reported that the structures were animate: "I felt the structures were looking at me, following my movements."

In the second, dark-adapted session, participants not only frequently reported that they had an increased comprehension, but also that the experience was calming and joyful ("I enjoyed a calm and meditative feeling of lights moving in the space"). By contrast, although the experience of calm was reported in the 3-minute session almost as often as in the 20-minute session, the former was discomforting for a number of participants ("My initial curiosity gradually succumbed to a mild level of paranoia and anxiety"). Such fear and discomfort were caused not only by the darkness and the need to move around and navigate in the dark, but presumably also by the presence of something unexplainable at an unclear distance that moved on its own and in response to the motion of observers, and sometimes even appeared alive.

When asked about their thoughts and associations, what most often came to mind was "outer space," the "universe," and "stars." For example, participants reported "wonderful light forms, like being in the middle of lights coming from space," and "like being in a peaceful place inside the universe." These reports capture how the participants were immersed in the space and did not experience themselves as clearly outside of the installation, but rather as "in the middle of" and "inside" the "universe." Taken together, we may assume that the participants' habitual way of seeing and thinking changed to some extent, which is supported by the high rate of increased self-reflection: Over two-thirds of the participants reported increased levels of self-reflection and self-awareness in the first session. In the second session, the rate was much lower, possibly because participants focused more strongly on the slowly emerging details of the different structures and the room.

To provide a better idea about individual participants' experiences, we will now let their quotes and drawings tell their own tales. As we will see, fear and paranoia, stars and the universe, and questions and speculations about causes of their perception are recurrent themes in the participants' experiences, sometimes culminating in hallucinations and sometimes yielding idiosyncratic interpretations of and associations with unknowns.

»Während der ersten drei Minuten habe ich so gut wie nichts gesehen, obwohl mir auffiel, dass in den letzten 30 Sekunden der Raum tatsächlich dunkler zu werden schien. Ich habe bemerkt, dass meine anderen Sinne extrem geschärft waren und dass mich das leiseste Geräusch in Alarmbereitschaft versetzt hat.«

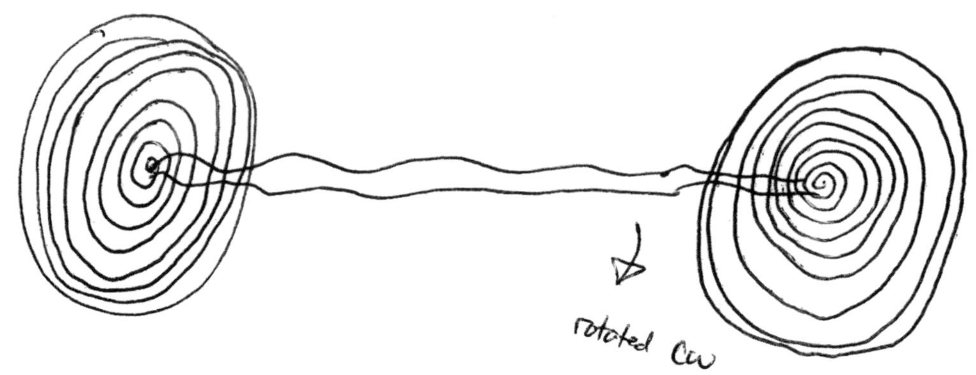

»Ich begann, ausgehend vom Licht an der linken Seite, einen geschlängelten Lichtstrahl zu sehen, der mit Gewissheit vorher nicht da gewesen war. Ungefähr 30 bis 45 Sekunden nachdem ich die erste Linie gesehen hatte, tauchte von demselben Licht eine zweite Linie auf und schien den Raum zwischen sich selbst und der zweiten Linie rechts von mir zu durchqueren.«

»Meine anfängliche Neugier verwandelte sich nach und nach in eine leichte Paranoia und Angst, als wir den Punkt im Raum erreichten, an dem die große sich drehende Konstruktion stand. Ich meinte, Schatten und auch helle Farbblitze zu sehen. Erst als ich in den zweiten Teil des Raums gegangen bin, habe ich begonnen, die wirklichen visuellen Halluzinationen von Schatten und Lichtwellen zu sehen.«

»Nachdem ich die von den spiegelartigen Strukturen ausgehenden Lichtwellen gesehen hatte, wurde die Paranoia und Angst durch eine Faszination und die Erkenntnis abgelöst, dass meine Stäbchenzellen komplett übernommen hatten und diese visuelle Informationen auf einer Ebene verarbeiteten, die ich aus meinem täglichen Leben nicht gewohnt war.«

"During the first three minutes, I didn't really see anything, although I noticed that the room actually seemed to become even darker during last 30 seconds. I noticed that my other senses were extremely heightened and the smallest auditory cue put me on edge."

"I started to see a squiggly ray of light emitting from the light on the left, which had certainly not been there before. Approximately 30 seconds–45 seconds after seeing the first line, a second line appeared from the same light and seemed to traverse the space between itself and the second light on my right."

"My initial curiosity gradually succumbed to a mild paranoia and anxiety as we reached a point in the room where the large rotating structure stood. I thought I saw shadows as well as bright sparks of color. It wasn't until after walking to the second part of the room that I began to experience real visual hallucinations of shadows and light waves."

"Upon seeing waves of light emanating from the mirror-like structures, the anxiety and paranoia were replaced by fascination and the understanding that my rod cells had completely taken over and were processing visual information on a level I was not accustomed to during day-to-day life."

»Ich stand in einem dunklen Raum, das vorhandene Licht half mir nicht, mich zu orientieren, ganz im Gegenteil: es war verwirrend. [Ich sah] fast völlige Dunkelheit. [Ich sah] elektrostatische Ladungen auf dem Metallgestell in der Mitte (mehrere Male).«

»[Ich dachte an] Zeitreisen durch abgelegene Teile des Universums. Bei der Betrachtung der Lichtmuster habe ich an den Film *Interstellar* gedacht. Der Raum war größer als vorher.«

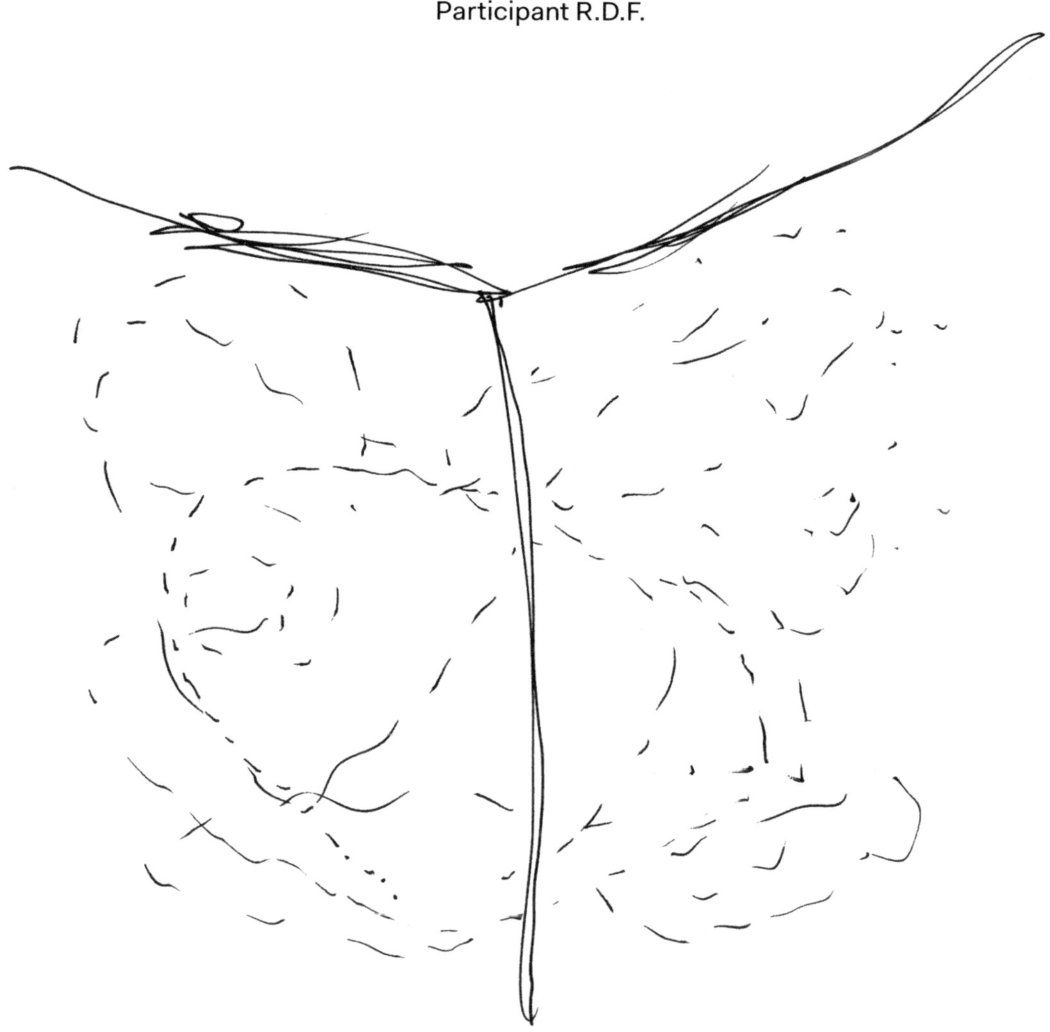

"I was standing in a dark room. The light present didn't help me orientate myself. Quite the opposite, it was confusing. [I saw] almost complete darkness. [I saw] electrostatic current from the metal frame in the middle (multiple times)."

"[I thought about] time travel through remote parts of the universe. The movie *Interstellar* came to my mind, watching the light patterns. The room was bigger than before."

»Da gab es ein sich drehendes Objekt in der Mitte des Raums, das Formen und eine spinnennetzartige Umgebung erzeugte. Traumfänger. Oder besser gesagt: Gedankenfänger. Schmetterlingsförmige Lichtfäden. Der Himmel voller Sterne. Eine Wiese mit Glühwürmchen.«

»Ich sah etwas, das mich an eine Sternenexplosion oder Ausdehnung erinnerte, etwas wie einen Sternennebel. Es sah auch gleichzeitig wie ein Auge und ein Spinnennetz aus. Es drehte sich, erzeugte andere Gestalten und Formen, wie den Himmel oder eine Sternenkonstellation.«

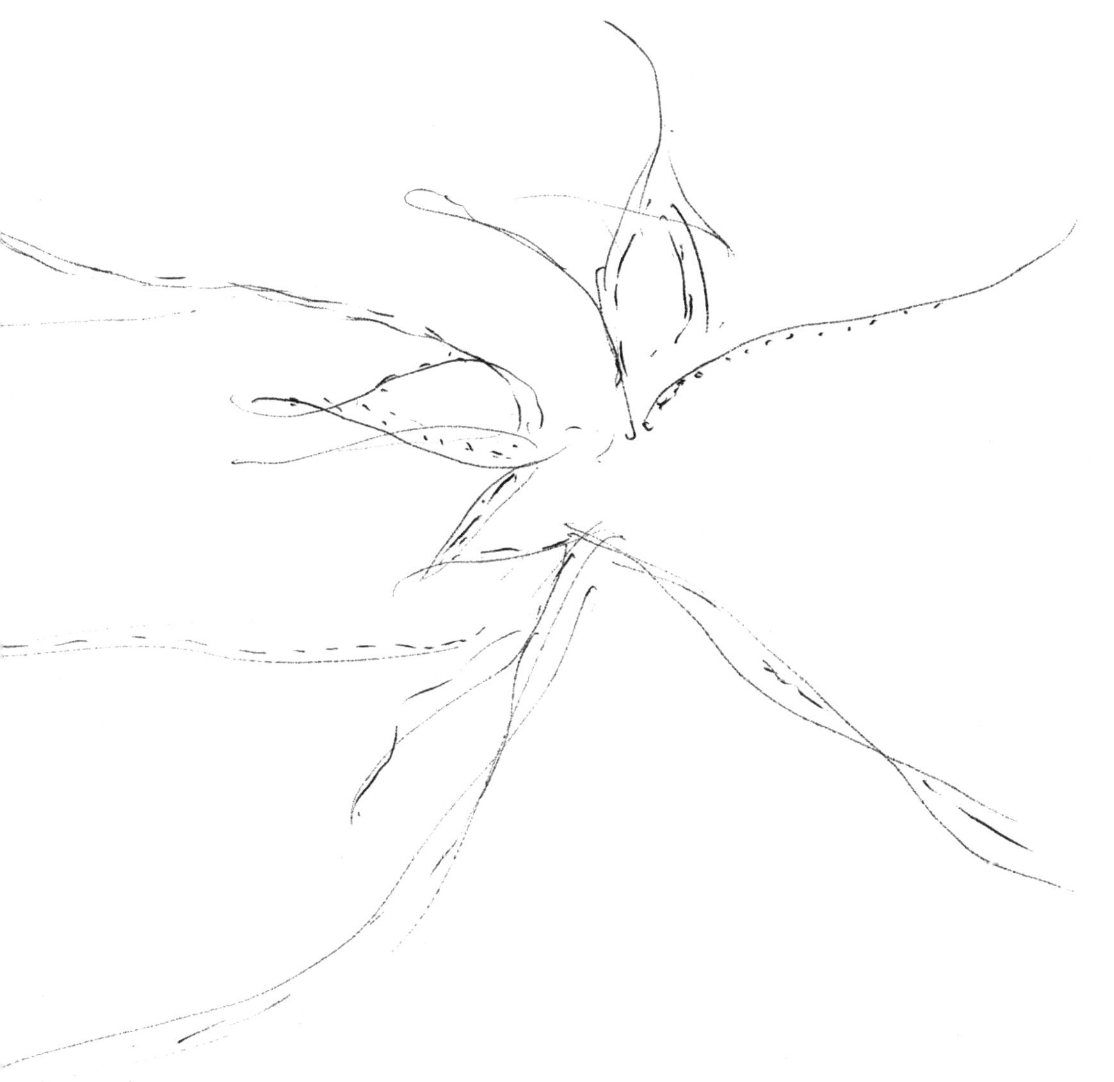

"There was a rotary object in the center of the room, creating shapes and a spider-like environment. Dream catcher, or better yet thought catcher. Butterfly shaped strings of light. Sky full of stars. Meadow with fireflies."

"I saw something reminding me of a star burst or expansion, something like a nebula. Also it looked like an eye and a spider web at the same time. It was rotating, creating other shapes and forms, like a sky or starry constellation."

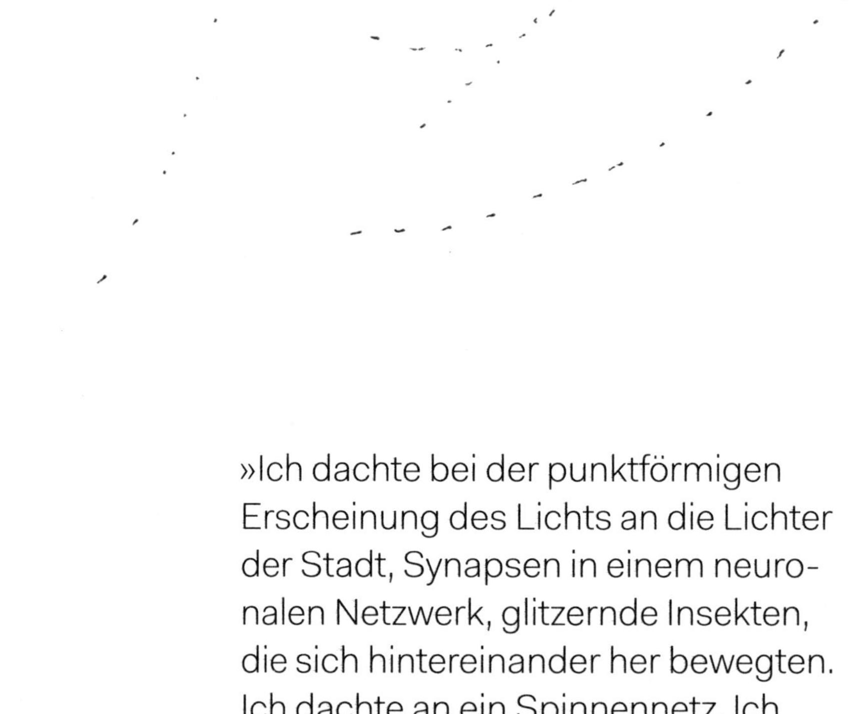

BILGE SAYIM & IVANA FRANKE

»Ich dachte bei der punktförmigen Erscheinung des Lichts an die Lichter der Stadt, Synapsen in einem neuronalen Netzwerk, glitzernde Insekten, die sich hintereinander her bewegten. Ich dachte an ein Spinnennetz. Ich dachte an Netzwerke, an Neuronen, weil ich Neurowissenschaftler bin.«

»Ich fing an, das Licht zu betrachten, das von oben kam und konnte nicht aufhören hinzuschauen. Ich war wie gebannt von ihm.«

"I thought about how the dotted appearance of light reminded me of city lights, synapses in a neuronal network, or sparkling insects moving one after the other. I thought about a spider web. I thought about networks, about neurons, because I am a neuroscientist."

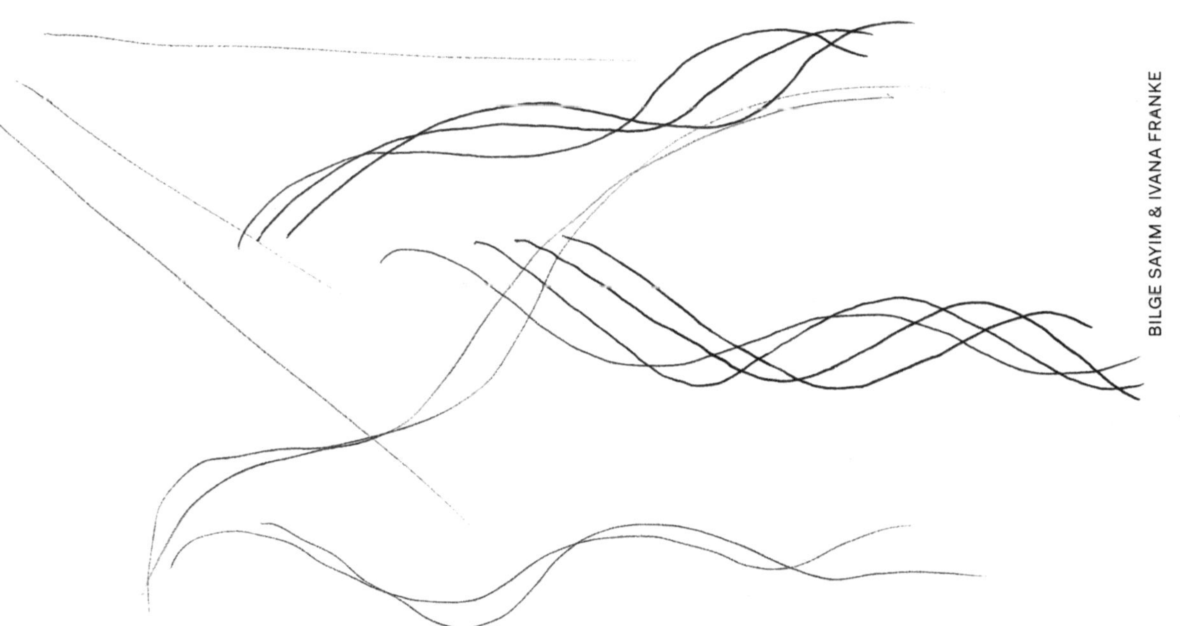

BILGE SAYIM & IVANA FRANKE

"I started watching the light coming from above and I couldn't stop watching. I was kind of kidnapped by it."

»Ich beschäftige mich komplett mit dem Sammeln von Informationen. Wo sind Menschen? Was für eine Art Geräusch? Die Sinne...Fühlen, Hören, Sehen. Was passiert in meinem Kopf? Warum?«

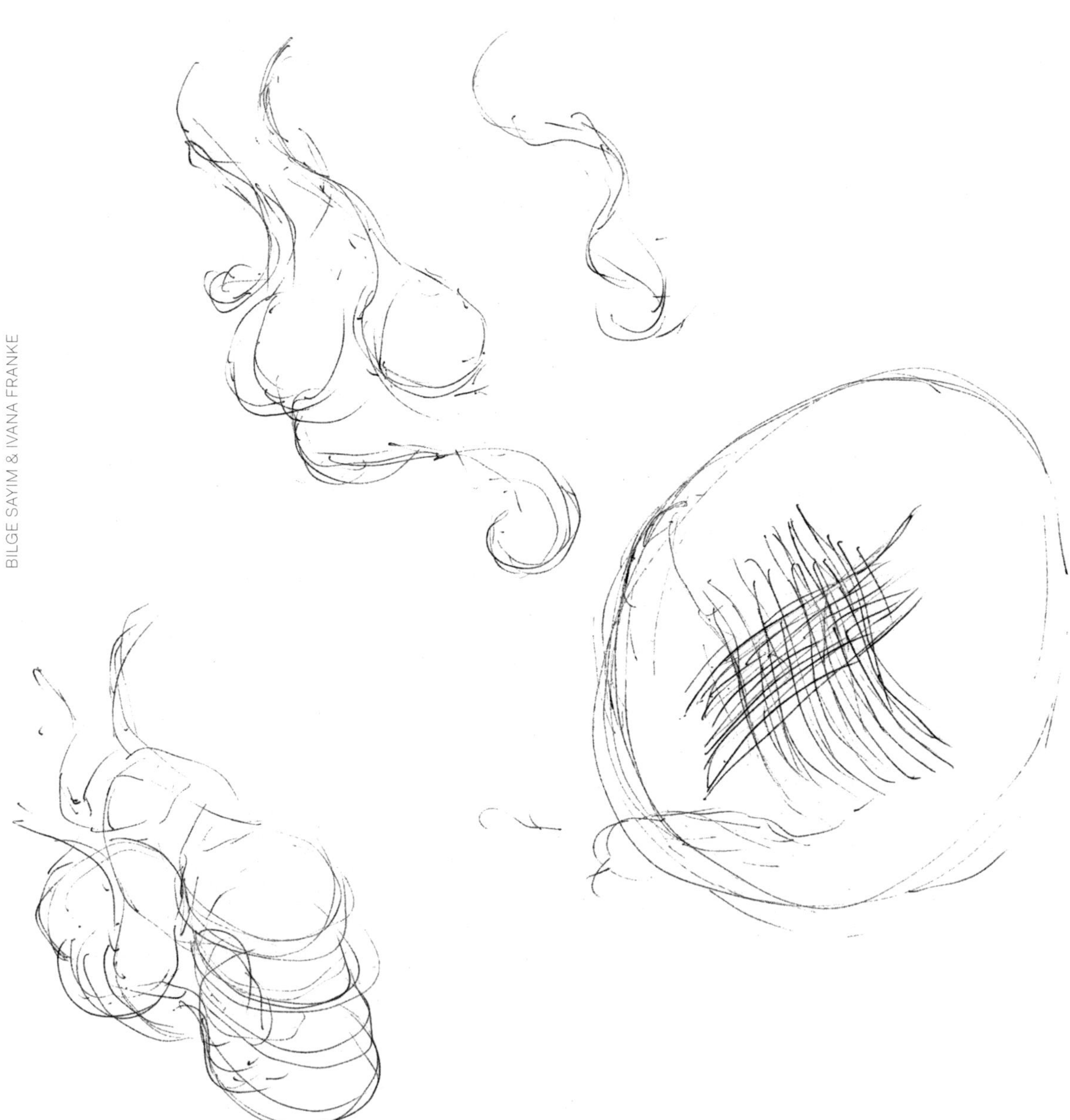

“I’m all occupied with collecting information. Where are the people? What kind of sound [is this]? Senses ... feeling, hearing, seeing. What is occurring in my mind? Why?”

»Gegen Ende wirkte es etwas unwirklich.«

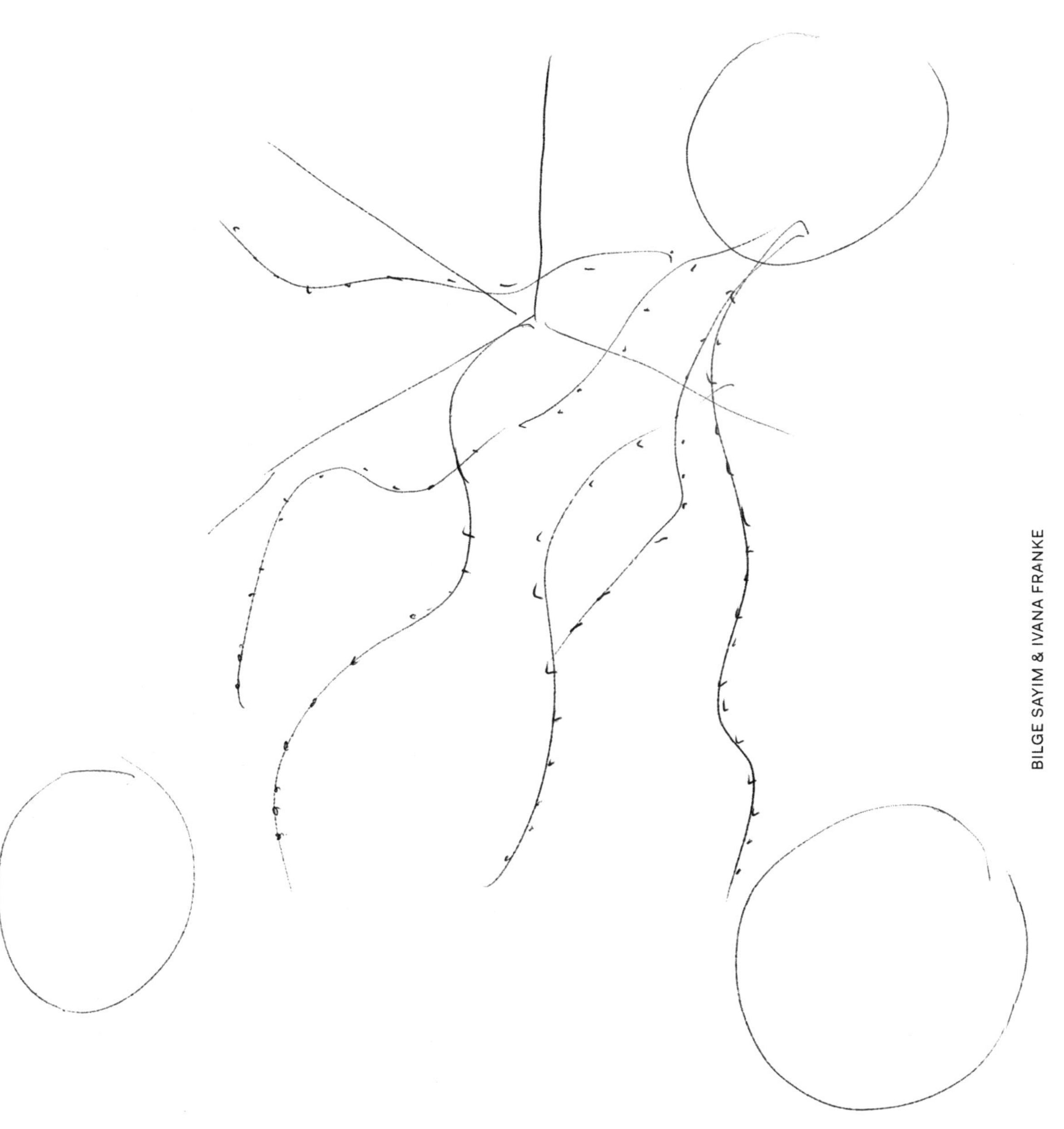

"Towards the end, it seemed somewhat unreal."

Was würden Sie sehen? Was würden Sie erleben? Es gibt viele verschiedene Weisen, die Installation zu sehen und zu erfahren: als Halluzination, Universum und neuronale Netzwerke. Die Bandbreite reicht vom Außergewöhnlichen über das Langweilige bis zum Psychedelischen (»Ich fühlte mich, als wäre ich high, wie bei einem psychedelischen Erlebnis«). Generell hängen die eigenen Erfahrungen nicht nur von allgemeinen kulturellen und individuellen Unterschieden ab, sondern auch von der eigenen aktuellen Stimmung und wie aktiviert und aufnahmebereit man ist. Der langsame Rhythmus der visuellen Bewegung an einem stillen und dunklen Ort wurde manchmal als meditativ und beruhigend empfunden, manchmal als ermüdend. Wegen der geringen äußeren Stimulierung gab es häufig eine Konzentration auf Details und ein erhöhtes Bewusstsein der Wahrnehmung selbst. Ohne äußere Ablenkungen wurde es einfacher, sich selbst als Beobachter zu erleben und es erschien bisweilen sogar möglich, einen Einblick in die konstruktive Natur der Wahrnehmung zu erhalten.

Die »unmöglichen Objekte«, die wir in der Installation sehen, unterscheiden sich von allen anderen, gewöhnlichen Objekten und stellen unsere Sehgewohnheiten in Frage. Insbesondere verhindert die Installation eine angemessene kategoriale Wahrnehmung, indem ein visueller Input erzeugt wird, der sich durch eine reduzierte Auswahl an potentiell korrespondierenden Kategorien in der Außenwelt auszeichnet. Die Linien, die sich langsam annähern und wieder verschwinden, erscheinen mehrdeutig, fremd, unbekannt, unwirklich, gespenstisch – weil sie eben anders als jede andere Objektkategorie sind, mit der wir normalerweise zu tun haben. Obwohl es in der Natur vorkommt, dass wir (fast) nur Glanzlichter wahrnehmen, zum Beispiel wenn man lediglich die Reflexionen auf einer Wasseroberfläche sieht, aber das Wasser selbst praktisch unsichtbar ist, gibt es normalerweise ausreichend kontextuelle Faktoren, die uns über den Reiz informieren, auf dem unsere Wahrnehmungserfahrung beruht, so dass wir das Objekt korrekt kategorisieren können und wir uns dann mit der Erklärung auf der Basis des identifizierten physischen Objekts zufrieden geben. Wenn man andererseits versucht, sich begreiflich zu machen, was in der Installation passiert, muss unser gewohnter Ansatz scheitern, unsere Wahrnehmungen in Bezug auf das zu erklären, was »Außen« und nicht was »Innen« ist. Selbst wenn man langsam beginnt, die Monofilamentstrukturen zu erkennen, bleiben die Ursachen unserer phänomenologischen Eindrücke schwer fassbar. Unser visuelles System scheint nicht darauf ausgerichtet zu sein, Glanzlichter als eigene Objekte zu interpretieren.

Umgeben von einem endlosen Strom visueller Informationen in unserem Alltag erleben wir selten – wenn überhaupt – eine sensorische Auszeit. Völlige Dunkelheit ist selten und besonders ungewöhnlich ist es, sich in extremer Dunkelheit fortzubewegen

What would you have seen? What would you have experienced? There were many different ways of seeing and experiencing the installation, including as hallucinations, the universe, and neural networks, ranging from extraordinary and boring to psychedelic ("I also felt like I was high, as in a psychedelic experience"). In general, our experiences depend not only on general cultural and individual differences, but also on our current mood, energy level, and receptiveness. The slow rhythm of visual movement in a quiet and dark space was at times experienced as meditative and calming, and other times as tiresome. As there was very little external stimulation, attention to detail and a heightened awareness of perception itself were common. Without any external distraction, it became easier for participants to experience themselves as observers, and they may have even gotten a glimpse of the constructive nature of perception.

Looking at "impossible objects" is unlike looking at any other objects; they challenge our usual way of seeing. In particular, the installation prevents proper categorical perception by creating visual input that is characterized by a reduced availability of potentially corresponding external world categories. The slowly appearing and disappearing lines seem ambiguous, unfamiliar, unknown, unreal, ghostly, and spectral precisely because they are unlike any other kind of object category we usually encounter. While it is possible for us to see (almost) only highlights in the natural environment—for example, when only the reflections from a water surface are seen, but the water is barely visible—we usually have enough contextual factors that inform us about the stimuli that have caused our perception. We can categorize the object correctly and are satisfied with the explanation based on the identified physical object. When trying to explain what happens in this installation, on the other hand, our usual tendency to explain our perceptual experiences by referring to what is outside us and not what is within is almost certainly bound to fail. Even when we slowly start to see the monofilament structures, the causes of our phenomenology remain elusive. Our visual system seems unequipped to interpret highlights as objects in and of themselves when the corresponding object is invisible.

Surrounded by a never-ending flow of visual information in our everyday lives, we rarely, if ever, experience sensory rest. Complete darkness is rare, and observing and moving around in the dark are rather uncommon. The installation puts observers in exactly this position by taking them to the opposite pole of everyday experiences. It pits dark against bright, slow against fast, quiet against loud, and the unknown against the known, challenging our usual ways of seeing—of transiently paying attention and extracting relevant information as quickly as possible.

und etwas zu beobachten. Die Installation versetzt die Beobachter in genau diese Situation und führt sie an den Gegenpol der alltäglichen Erfahrungen. Sie stellt das Dunkel dem Licht gegenüber, langsam gegenüber schnell, leise gegenüber laut, das Unbekannte gegenüber dem Bekannten, und fordert so unsere Sehgewohnheiten heraus, flüchtig aufmerksam zu sein und die relevanten Informationen so schnell wie möglich zu erfassen. Wenn wir uns als Beobachter die Zeit nehmen, etwas länger hinzuschauen und genau zu beobachten, was wir erleben, werden wir höchstwahrscheinlich etwas anderes als für gewöhnlich sehen.

Eine Begegnung mit dem Unbekannten fordert uns auf, mentale Prozesse neu zu überdenken, die nicht-rational, spekulativ und intuitiv sind – Prozesse, welche vorherrschende Denkweisen ergänzen, die oft von Effektivitäts- und Produktivitätsanforderungen gelenkt sind –, ohne diese von vornherein als nutzlos, unnötig und ablenkend abzutun. Das Bekannte loszulassen, das scheinbar Unmögliche zu sehen, und dazu gezwungen zu sein, zu spekulieren und zu erahnen, und auf das Flüchtige, Fließende und Undeutliche zu achten, könnte uns dabei helfen, auch das Gewöhnliche als das zu sehen, was es letztendlich ist: unbekannt. Hier könnte eine Quelle für die Erweiterung herkömmlicher Denkweisen sowie für das Erwerben und Produzieren von Wissen liegen; eine Möglichkeit, einmal mehr zu überprüfen, aus was unsere Realität eigentlich besteht, und sich die Strukturen und Beziehungen zu vergegenwärtigen, in denen wir leben und die wir erzeugen.

When we as observers take our time, look a little longer, and observe closely what we experience, we will most likely see something different than usual.

An encounter with an unknown encourages us to reconsider mental processes that are non-rational, speculative, and intuitive—processes that complement general modes of thinking, which are often ruled by requirements of efficiency and productivity—without disqualifying them a priori as useless, unnecessary, and distracting. To lose the known, to see the apparently impossible, and to be pushed to guess and speculate, and attend to the transient, faint, and intangible may make us more open to seeing the ordinary as it ultimately is—unknown. This could be a source for expanding common modes of thinking and of acquiring and producing knowledge—the possibility to re-view what reality consists of and to imagine and explore the structures and relations that we exist in and create.

Reflektierende Strukturen

Reflecting Structures

Pierre Gallais

Zuerst – auch wenn dies lächerlich erscheinen mag – sollte daran erinnert werden, dass wir nur das sehen, was unser Auge erreicht. Anders gesagt: Wir nehmen nur die von einem Objekt ausgehenden Lichtstrahlen wahr, die auch unsere Netzhaut treffen. Wenn ein Lichtstrahl unsere Netzhaut trifft, stellt dies einen Punkt auf einer Ebene (der Netzhaut) dar, den wir erkennen. Daraus folgern wir dann, wo sich das Objekt befindet. Die Quelle (das Ausgangsobjekt) kann jedoch Lichtstrahlen in jede mögliche Richtung aussenden, und mit Hilfe eines im Raum platzierten Spiegels können mehrere Lichtstrahlen aus dieser Quelle unsere Netzhaut an unterschiedlichen Punkten treffen. Unser Gehirn wird bestätigen, dass wir mehrere verschiedene Objekte sehen. Das ist kein Fehler, aber es lässt uns annehmen, dass es mehrere Quellen (Objekte) gibt.

Um diese Illusion zu erzeugen, sollten die Spiegel präzise im Raum verteilt werden. Da jeder Spiegel fixiert ist, ist auch der reflektierte Lichtstrahl festgelegt. Wenn wir uns also bewegen, ergeben sich Situationen, in denen wir das Gefühl haben, dass wir mehrere Objekte sehen, während sie einen Schritt weiter zu verschwinden scheinen.

Stellen Sie sich einen reflektierenden Nylonfaden vor, der einen langen, zylindrischen Spiegel bildet. Ein Lichtstrahl könnte jederzeit meine Netzhaut treffen. Der Spiegelfaden besitzt eine kontinuierliche Oberfläche. Wenn ich mich bewege, gibt es deshalb auf diesem Faden immer einen Nachbarpunkt, der erneut wie ein winziger Spiegel wirkt und einen neuen Lichtstrahl reflektiert, der dann meine Netzhaut trifft. Da sich dieser Punkt von dem vorherigen unterscheidet, wird die Illusion erzeugt, dass sich das Ausgangsobjekt bewegt hat. Wenn ich viele Spiegelfäden platziere, wird der Eindruck mehrerer Objekte hervorgerufen. Basierend auf der Anordnung dieser Spiegelfäden werden diese Objekte – Spiegelungen einer einzigen Quelle – so im Raum verteilt beziehungsweise organisiert, dass sie eine Form bilden; und wenn ich mich dann bewege, nehme ich eine Verformung und Entwicklung dieser Figur im Raum wahr.

Wenn die Fäden so angeordnet sind, dass sich eine Figur bildet, die ich geometrisch definieren kann, dann wird es auch möglich sein, die Figur zu berechnen, die auf meiner Netzhaut gebildet wird. Eine veränderliche Figur, deren Form ich ebenfalls durch eine Berechnung bestimmen könnte. Dies ist aus physikalischer und mathematischer Sicht nur ein kleines Problem, aber da der Rechenvorgang sehr komplex ist, benötigt man einen Computer und ein Rechenprogramm für eine schnelle und fehlerfreie Berechnung.

Wenden wir uns nun dem physikalischen Vorgang der Reflexion und den mathematischen Berechnungen zu. Von Seiten der Physik genügt es, zu wissen: Wenn eine punktförmige Lichtquelle

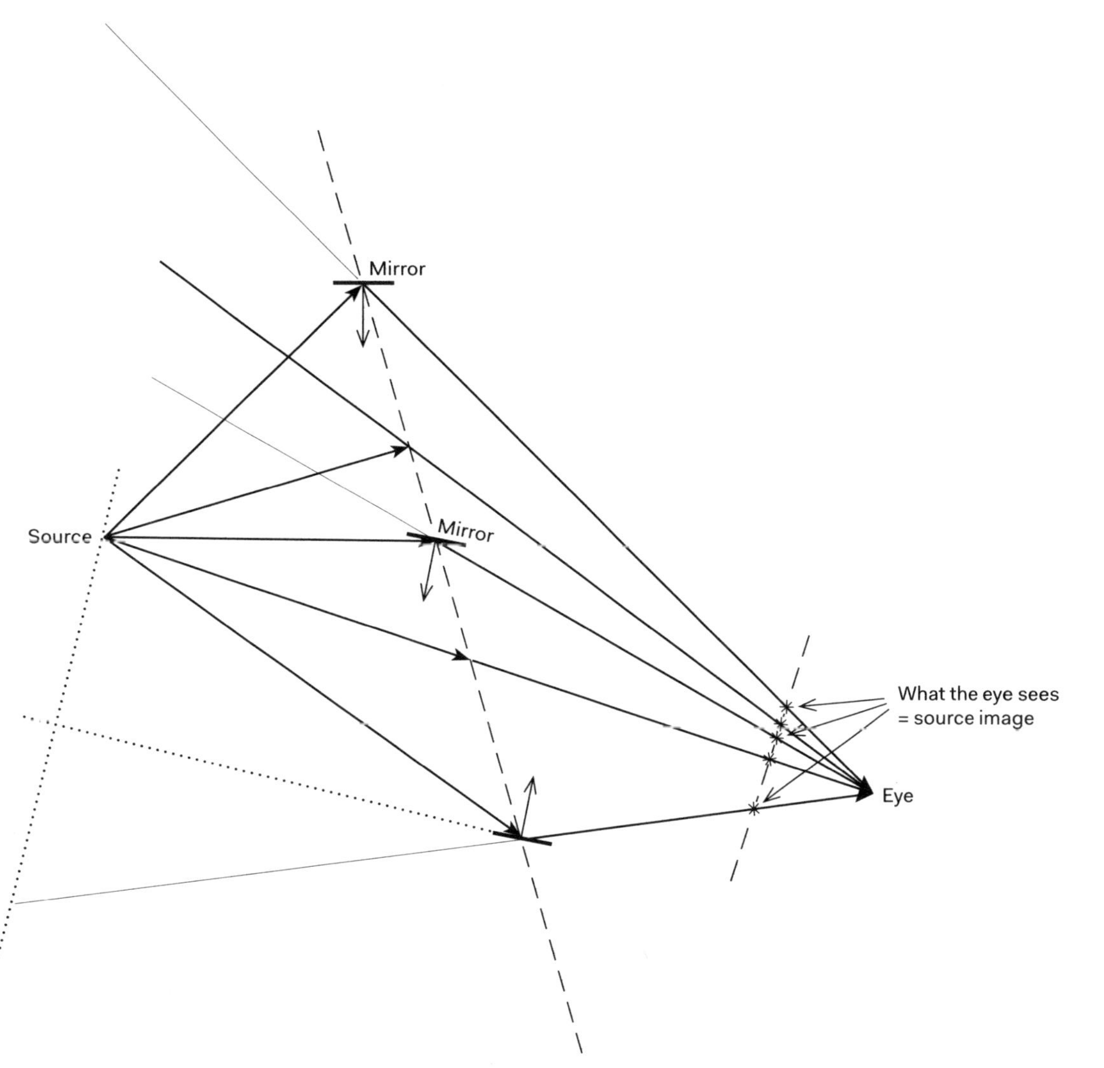

Fig · 1 Aufgereihte und ausgerichtete Spiegel. Achtung: Diese Spiegel sind nicht unser Faden. Sie wurden zur Vereinfachung der Abbildung aufgereiht.

Fig · 1 Mirrors aligned and oriented. Warning: These mirrors are not our string. They have been aligned to simplify the figure.

von einem Spiegel reflektiert wird und unsere Netzhaut trifft, dann sehen wir diesen Lichtpunkt als symmetrisch zum Ausgangspunkt der Lichtquelle relativ zum Spiegel (siehe Fig · 1).

Stellen sie sich einen Planspiegel vor.
Der einfallende Lichtstrahl **Ri** ist der Strahl, der von der Quelle **S** am Spiegel ankommt; der reflektierte Strahl **Rr** ist der Strahl, der unser Auge **E** erreicht. $\vec{\mathbf{W}}$ ist der Normalenvektor des Planspiegels (senkrecht zu jedem Vektor $\vec{\mathbf{F}}$ der Spiegelebene) im von **Ri** erreichten Punkt **m**. Wenn man die physikalische Eigenschaft in eine mathematische überträgt, bedeutet das, dass **Ri** und $\vec{\mathbf{W}}$ den gleichen Winkel bilden wie **Rr** und $\vec{\mathbf{W}}$; in anderen Worten, dass $\vec{\mathbf{W}}$ die Winkelhalbierende des Winkels **Ri m Rr** ist, oder $\measuredangle$**SmE**.

Es muss festgehalten werden, dass im Falle eines Fadens, der ja ein zylindrischer Spiegel ist, die jeweilige Spiegelfläche eine Tangentialebene an den Faden im Berührungspunkt **m** ist (Fig · 2).

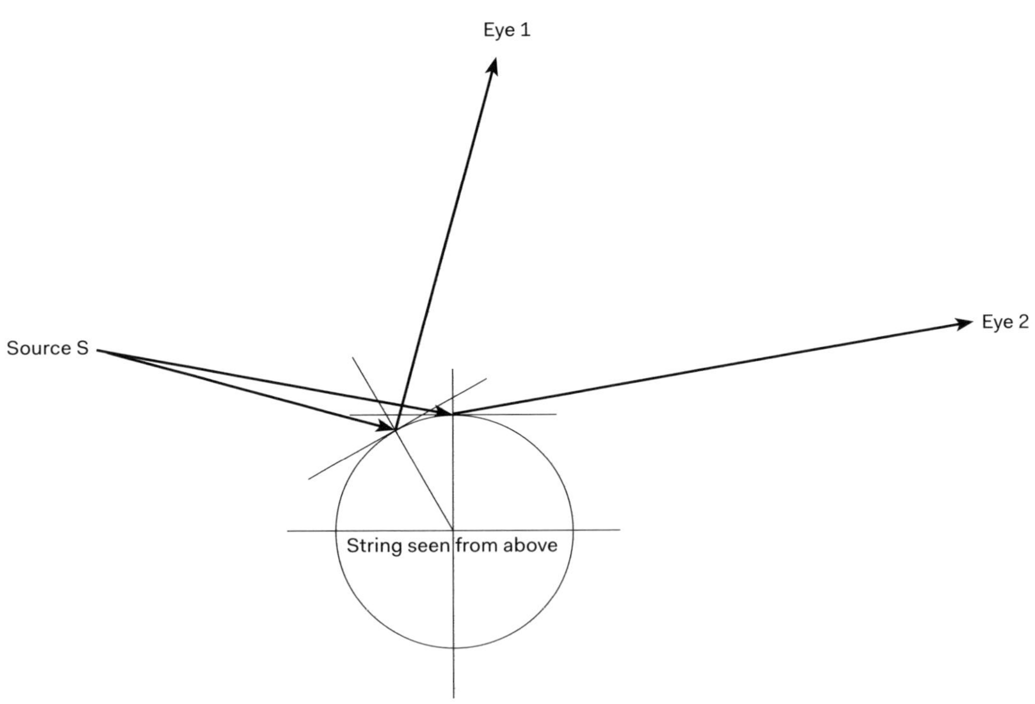

Fig · 2 Der Spiegeleffekt bei einem zylindrischen Spiegel, wie zum Beispiel einem Faden.

Fig · 2 A mirror effect on a string that is a cylindrical mirror.

First (and this may seem ludicrous), we should be reminded that we can only see what hits our eye. In other words, we perceive objects only as the rays of light that fall on our retina. When a ray of light hits our retina, it becomes a point on a plane (the retina). We detect this point and say that this is where the object is located. However, the source (source object) could send rays in every possible direction. Through mirrors placed within the space, several rays issued from that source can also hit our retina on different points, and our brain will confirm seeing several different objects. This is not a mistake, but it does lead us to consider that there are several sources (objects).

To create this illusion, mirrors should be carefully placed within the space. Because each mirror is fixed, the reflected ray is determined. Consequently, when we are moving, there are instances when we have the feeling that we are seeing several objects, while others, only steps away, seem to vanish.

Consider a reflecting nylon string. It is a long cylindrical mirror. At any given moment, a ray of light may hit my retina. When I move, because the mirror string is continuous, there will be a neighboring point on it that will function like a new little mirror and reflect another ray that will hit my retina. Since that point is different from the former, I will have the illusion that the source object has moved.

Because many mirror strings have been placed in the space, I will perceive the illusion of several objects. According to the disposition of these mirror strings, the objects—reflections of my unique source—will be distributed or organized according to a shape. Thus, through movement, I will see this shape deforming and evolving in space.

If the strings are organized according to a figure that I can geometrically define through calculation, it will then be possible to calculate the figure that it produces on my retina. This will be an evolving figure, the shape of which I could also determine through calculation. Although this is a small matter of physics and mathematical calculation, clearly such calculations are still sufficiently complex to require the use of a computer and program for fast and faultless performance.

We will now address the physical process of reflection and mathematical calculations. What we need to know beforehand regarding physics is that, when a punctual light source is reflected on a mirror and hits my retina, I see that spot of light symmetrical to the source relative to the mirror (see Fig · 1).

O, **i**, **j**, **k** the orthonormal coordinate system
S is on axis **S'** (a, 0, 0)
E (b, c, d)
m (0, 0, m)

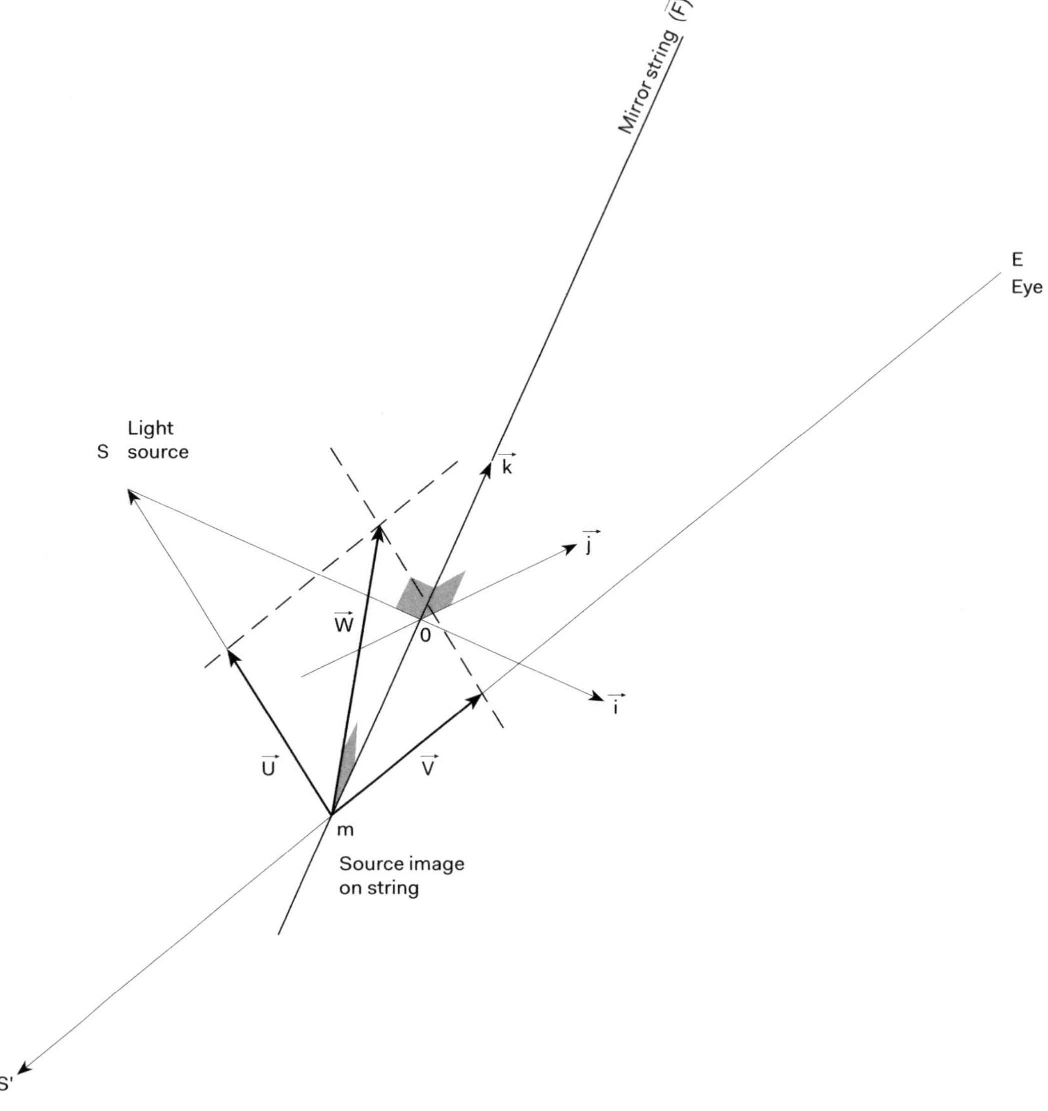

Fig · 3 Suchen Sie den Punkt **m** auf dem Faden, an dem der Vektor der Winkelhalbierenden $\widehat{S00e}$ rechtwinklig zum Faden ist.
Berechnen Sie $\vec{U}$, den Einheitsvektor von **mS**
Berechnen Sie $\vec{V}$, den Einheitsvektor von **mE**
Berechnen Sie $\vec{U} + \vec{V} = \vec{W}$
Bestimmen Sie **m** so, dass der Vektor $\vec{W}$ rechtwinklig zu $\vec{k}$ ist.

Fig · 3 Look for point **m** on the string such that the bisector vector of angle $\widehat{S00e}$ is perpendicular to the string.
Calculate $\vec{U}$ unit vector of **mS**
Calculate $\vec{V}$ unit vector of **mE**
Calculate $\vec{U} + \vec{V} = \vec{W}$
Determine **m** so that vector $\vec{W}$ is perpendicular to $\vec{k}$.

Consider a plane mirror.
The incident ray **Ri** is the ray that travels from source **S** to the mirror; the reflected ray **Rr** is the ray reaching my eye **E**. Next, $\vec{W}$ is the normal vector to the plane mirror (perpendicular to any vector $\vec{F}$ of the mirror plane) at point **m** reached by **Ri**. The physical property translated into a mathematical property is that the angle formed by **Ri** and $\vec{W}$ is equal to the angle formed by **Rr** and $\vec{W}$; in other words, $\vec{W}$ is a bisector of angle **Ri m Rr** or ∡**S m E**.

It must be noted that, in the case of a string that is a cylindrical mirror, what serves as mirror plane is the plane tangent to the string at point **m** (see Fig · 2).

Let us translate this mathematically and algebraically with an orthonormal coordinate system (**O**; **i**, **j**, **k**) in which the coordinates of source **S**, the eye **E**, and the equation of the reflecting string as a straight line whose direction is given by vector $\vec{F}$ are defined (see Fig · 3). $\vec{U}$ is the unit vector carried by ray **Ri**, and $\vec{V}$ is the unit vector carried by **Rr**. Vector $\vec{W}$, which defines the bisector of ∡**Ri m Rr**, is defined as the vectorial sum of $\vec{U}+\vec{V}$. To translate that $\vec{W}$ is perpendicular to $\vec{F}$, we use the scalar product of the two vectors $\vec{W}$ and $\vec{F}$, which must be zero in the case of perpendicularity. To translate our research visually, we could say that we are walking on the string (moving point **m** along string $\vec{F}$); each position of **m** determines a vector $\vec{W}$ that corresponds to the bisector. We perform the scalar product $\vec{W} \bullet \vec{F}$, stopping when it reaches zero. This way we obtain the position of point **m**, which is the position that our eye interprets as the image of the source. This is algebraically translated by investigating the solution(s) of an equation where the unknown is the parameter **x** of **m** on the string $\vec{F}$.

The equations presented on the manuscript page (see Fig · 4) correspond to a special case in which the string passes through the origin of the coordinate system. This special case is used to illustrate the process, because in reality, since there are many strings, an equation has to be determined for each, and these do not pass through the origin. This leads to numerical and computational complications and explains the need for a calculation program (though it can be also done manually with patience, time, and a risk of error). We then obtain the positions in space of the multiple points of our source image. This set of points defines the shape or the curve that our eye perceives. This figure is not an illusion, because all these rays do hit our retina and print the figure on it. This reality could, to a certain extent, be called an illusion, since we have a single source and multiple images of it. However, it is not an illusion in the psychological sense of the term, because if we were to take a photograph, these points would actually be present on the photographic image.

Nun übersetzen wir dies mathematisch und algebraisch in ein orthonormales Koordinatensystem (**O**; **i**, **j**, **k**), durch das die Koordinaten der Quelle **S**, des Auges **E** und die Gleichung des reflektierenden Fadens als eine gerade Linie, deren Richtung durch den Vektor $\vec{F}$ vorgegeben ist, definiert werden (siehe Fig · 3). $\vec{U}$ ist der Einheitsvektor, der vom Strahl **Ri** beschrieben wird, und $\vec{V}$ der Einheitsvektor, der von **Rr** beschrieben wird. Vektor $\vec{W}$, der die Winkelhalbierende ∡**Ri m Rr** definiert, wird durch die Vektorsumme $\vec{U}+\vec{V}$ definiert. Um zu übertragen, dass $\vec{W}$ senkrecht zu $\vec{F}$ ist, benutzen wir das Skalarprodukt der beiden Vektoren $\vec{W}$ und $\vec{F}$, das Null ergeben muss, wenn die beiden senkrecht aufeinander stehen. Als Veranschaulichung unserer Suche könnte man sagen, dass man auf dem Faden entlang läuft (den Punkt **m** entlang des Fadens $\vec{F}$ bewegt); Zu jeder Position von **m** gehört ein bestimmter Vektor $\vec{W}$, der der Winkelhalbierenden entspricht. Wir bilden das Skalarprodukt $\vec{W} \bullet \vec{F}$ und hören auf, wenn sich Null ergibt. So können wir die Position des Punktes **m** ermitteln, die der Position entspricht, die unser Auge als Bild der Quelle interpretiert. Die algebraische Übersetzung dafür ist die Berechnung der Lösung(en) einer Gleichung deren Unbekannte der Parameter **x** von **m** auf dem Faden $\vec{F}$ ist.

Die Gleichungen, die auf der Manuskriptseite (Fig · 4) präsentiert werden, beziehen sich auf einen Spezialfall, in dem der Faden den Ursprung des Koordinatensystems passiert. Dies ist aber ein Sonderfall, um die Vorgehensweise zu demonstrieren. Tatsächlich gibt es viele Fäden, weshalb für jeden von ihnen eine Gleichung bestimmt werden muss – und diese Fäden passieren nicht diesen Ursprung. Dies führt zu numerischen und rechentechnischen Komplikationen. Und das erklärt auch, warum man ein Rechenprogramm benötigt (obwohl es auch von Hand gemacht werden kann, mit Geduld, Zeit und einem gewissen Fehlerrisiko). So bekommen wir die Positionen der verschiedenen Punkte unseres Ausgangsbildes im Raum. Diese Anordnung von Positionen definiert die Form oder Kurve, die unser Auge wahrnimmt. Die Figur ist keine Illusion, weil alle Lichtstrahlen tatsächlich unsere Netzhaut treffen und die Figur auf ihr einprägen. Diese Realität kann bis zu einem gewissen Grad eine Illusion genannt werden, da wir nur eine Quelle haben und daraus verschiedene Bilder werden. Es handelt sich jedoch nicht um eine Illusion im psychologischen Sinn, weil die Punkte auch auf einer Fotografie erscheinen würden.

Bemerkung: Wenn die Fäden auf einer Ebene liegen, ist es klar, dass die Punkte unserer Ausgangsbilder auch auf dieser Ebene verortet sind und dass die Kurve flach ist. Wenn die Fäden eine Fläche in drei Dimensionen bilden, dann sind die Punkte unserer Ausgangsbilder auf diesen Fäden auch im Raum verteilt und bilden eine Kurve im Raum, die dann nicht länger flach ist.

Note: When the strings are in one plane, it is known that the points of our source image will be in that plane, and the curve will be flat. When the strings define a surface in three dimensions, the points of our source image that are on these strings will also be distributed in the space, where they will form a curve that will no longer be flat.

<u>Données</u> : Source $S \begin{vmatrix} -1 \\ 0 \\ 0 \end{vmatrix}$, oeil $O_e \begin{vmatrix} a \\ b \\ c \end{vmatrix}$

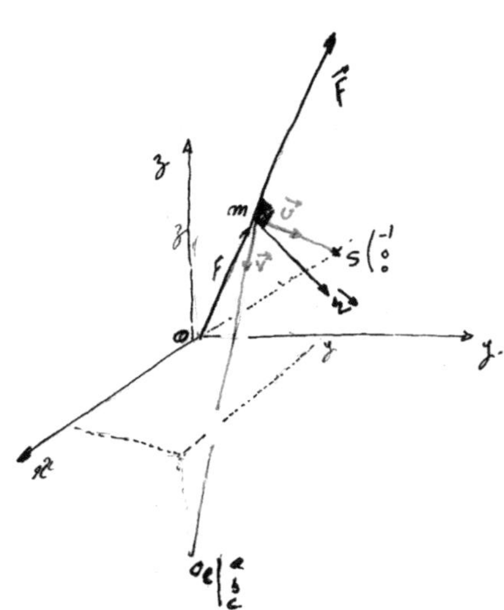

le fil $\vec{F} \begin{vmatrix} 0 \\ \cos\varphi \\ \sin\varphi \end{vmatrix}$; le point m sur le fil $m \begin{vmatrix} 0 \\ x\cos\varphi \\ x\sin\varphi \end{vmatrix}$

<u>Rayon incident Ri</u>

le vecteur unitaire $\vec{U} = \dfrac{1}{\sqrt{1+x^2}} \begin{vmatrix} -1 \\ -x\cos\varphi \\ -x\sin\varphi \end{vmatrix}$

<u>Rayon réfléchi Rr</u>

son vecteur unitaire $\vec{V} = \dfrac{1}{\sqrt{A}} \begin{vmatrix} a \\ b-x\cos\varphi \\ c-x\sin\varphi \end{vmatrix}$

où $A = a^2 + (b-x\cos\varphi)^2 + (c-x\sin\varphi)^2$.

le vecteur $\vec{W} = \vec{U} + \vec{V}$ bissectrice de l'angle $\widehat{SmO_e}$

$$\vec{W} = \frac{-1}{\sqrt{1+x^2}} \begin{vmatrix} -1 \\ -x\cos\varphi \\ -x\sin\varphi \end{vmatrix} + \frac{1}{\sqrt{A}} \begin{vmatrix} a \\ b-x\cos\varphi \\ c-x\sin\varphi \end{vmatrix}$$

le produit scalaire $\vec{F} \times \vec{W} = \dfrac{-x(\cos^2\varphi + \sin^2\varphi)}{\sqrt{1+x^2}} + \dfrac{(b-x\cos\varphi)\cos\varphi + (c-x\sin\varphi)\sin\varphi}{\sqrt{A}}$

exprimons de $\vec{F} \perp \vec{W}$ so $\vec{F} \times \vec{W} = 0$, on obtient l'équation assez compliquée

où $\boxed{x}$ est l'inconnue.

$$\boxed{\frac{x}{\sqrt{1+x^2}} = \frac{b\cos\varphi + c\sin\varphi - x}{\sqrt{a^2 + (b-x\cos\varphi)^2 + (c-x\sin\varphi)^2}}}$$

cette équation, bien que déjà compliquée à résoudre, correspond à la situation particulière où le fil passe par l'origine de notre repère.

Dans le cas de l'installation il y a plusieurs fils et aucun ne passe par l'origine. ce qui complique encore. Il est donc nécessaire d'avoir un programme de calcul. afin de résoudre rapidement et sans erreur ... Ceci lorsqu'on cherche à faire une simulation.

PIERRE GALLAIS

Fig · 4 Diese Gleichung, deren Lösung sehr komplex ist, entspricht dem Spezialfall, wenn der Faden den Ursprung des Koordinatensystems passiert.

In Ivana Frankes Installation gibt es viele Fäden, aber keiner passiert diesen Ursprung, wodurch es noch komplizierter wird. Man benötigt ein Rechenprogramm, um dies schnell und fehlerfrei zu berechnen, wenn man eine Simulation macht.

Fig · 4 This equation, though already difficult to solve, corresponds to the special case when the string passes through the origin of our coordinate system.

In Ivana Franke's installation, there are several strings, but none passes through the origin, which makes things even more complicated. It would be necessary to have a calculation program to be able to solve this quickly and without error when doing a simulation.

Lichtphänomene aus Sicht der Optik und der menschlichen Wahrnehmung – die »Brilliance« der Glühwürmchen

Optical and Perceptual Phenomena of Light—and the Brilliance of Fireflies

Sylvia C. Pont

Das Licht beeinflusst die Erscheinung

Ohne Licht können wir nicht sehen. Licht erlaubt uns, Objekte, Räume, Menschen und das Licht selbst zu sehen. Die Eigenschaften des Lichts, zum Beispiel seine Intensität, wie diffus es ist und aus welcher Richtung es kommt, haben einen großen Einfluss darauf, wie wir die Formen und Materialien dieser Objekte, Räume und Menschen wahrnehmen. Dieser Einfluss kann so groß sein, dass wir bei einem Objekt, das wir in verschiedenen Lichtverhältnissen sehen, nicht einmal erkennen können, ob es dieselbe Form hat und von gleichem Material ist. In Abbildung 1 (Fig · 1) ist dreimal dasselbe Objekt zu sehen (ein weißes Relief aus Papiermaché, A. J. Moerman, 2016), lediglich die Beleuchtung ist in allen drei Bildern anders. Im linken Foto scheint ein eher diffuses Tageslicht von links auf das Relief, in der Mitte wurde es von einem Strahler von links oben beleuchtet und das Foto rechts wurde mit dem Blitzlicht der Kamera aufgenommen. Die Form (und Materialien, Räume, Menschen usw.) kann also, je nach den Lichtverhältnissen, sehr verschieden erscheinen.

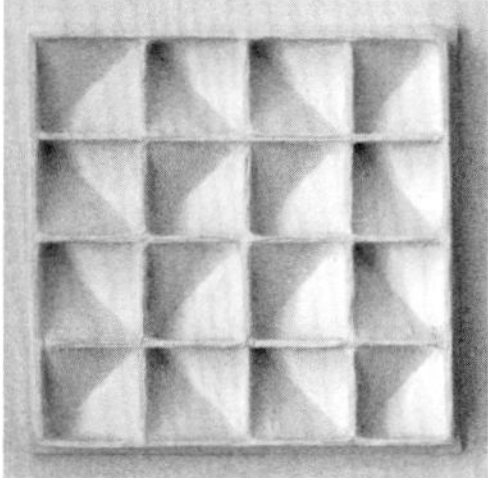

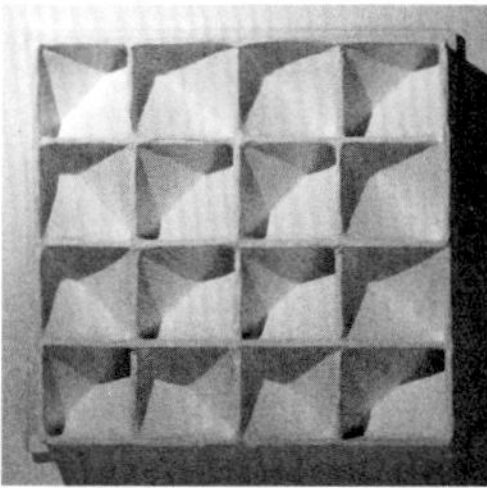

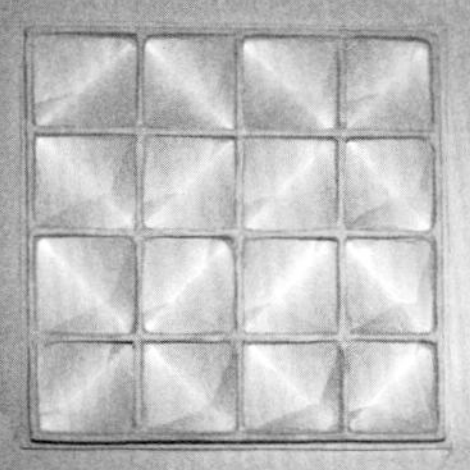

Fig · 1 Ein weißes Relief aus Papiermaché (A. J. Moerman, 2016) in drei verschiedenen Beleuchtungen, von links nach rechts: eher diffuses Tageslicht von links; ein Strahler von links oben; der Blitz einer Kamera.

Diese Erkenntnis haben wir in der Ausstellung *Kijk, Jan Schoonhoven,* Oktober 2015–Februar 2016 im Museum Prinsenhof in Delft, Niederlande,[1] genutzt. Für die geometrischen, weißen Papiermachéreliefs des Delfter Künstlers Jan Schoonhoven (1914–1994) entwarfen wir eine dynamische Lichtinstallation, die die Form der Kunstwerke vor den Augen der Besucher zu verändern schien. Aber es war lediglich die Beleuchtung, die sich änderte. Die Besucher waren überrascht und fasziniert und viele schrieben, dass »sie ihren Augen nicht glauben konnten«. Man könnte solche Effekte

1 Sylvia C. Pont / Marga Schoemaker / Hendrik van Leeuwen, *Jan Schoonhoven, Delft,* Delft: Stichting Licht op Schoonhoven, 2015.

2 Jan J. Koenderink, »The All Seeing Eye?«, in: *Perception,* 43 (2014) Nr. 1, S. 1–6.

Light Influences Appearance

There is no vision without light. Light makes us see objects, spaces, people, and light itself. The qualities of light—for instance, its intensity, diffuseness and direction—strongly influence how we perceive the shapes and materials of those objects, spaces, and people. This influence can be so strong that, if we put the same object in different light, we sometimes cannot even see that the shapes and materials are the same (see Fig · 1 for an example). The object in figure 1 is always the same (a white paper-mache relief, Moerman, 2016); only the illumination is different for the three images. In the left example, the relief is shown in rather diffuse daylight from the left, in the middle it is lit by a spotlight from above left, and the photograph on the right was made using the flash of the camera. Shapes (and materials, spaces, people, etc.) can thus look very different, depending on the conditions of illumination.

← Fig · 1 A white paper-mache relief (Moerman, 2016) under three types of illumination, from left to right: rather diffuse daylight from the left; a spotlight from above left; the flash of the camera.

We applied this knowledge in the art exhibition "Kijk, Jan Schoonhoven" shown October 2015–February 2016 at the Museum Prinsenhof in Delft, Netherlands.[1] We designed a dynamic lighting installation for the geometric, white, paper-mache reliefs of the Delft artist Jan Schoonhoven (1914–1994) that made the shape of the artworks seem to change in front of people's eyes. However, it was simply the lighting that changed. Visitors were surprised and intrigued, and many noted that they "could not believe their eyes." We might call such effects perceptual errors, implicitly assuming that it is possible to perceive the world veridically, or as accurately representing

1 Sylvia C. Pont / Marga Schoemaker / Hendrik van Leeuwen, *Jan Schoonhoven, Delft.* (Delft: Stichting Licht op Schoonhoven, 2015).

2 Jan J. Koenderink, "The All Seeing Eye?" *Perception* 43 (2014): 1–6.

Wahrnehmungsfehler nennen – und damit implizit annehmen, dass es möglich sei, die Welt realitätsgetreu wahrzunehmen, also als eine exakte Repräsentation der physischen Realität. Anders gesagt glauben die meisten Menschen an das »alles sehende Auge«, wie Jan Koenderink bemerkt hat[2]. Meiner Ansicht nach handelt es sich hier aber bloß um die Demonstration normaler Wahrnehmungsprozesse, da das Zusammenspiel unserer Wahrnehmung von Licht, Material, Form und Raum ein grundlegender und normaler Teil unserer Seherfahrungen ist. Sehen ist nicht umgekehrte Optik und die Wahrnehmung von Licht, Material, Form und Raum vermischt sich miteinander. Mit anderen Worten, wir können nie »unseren Augen glauben«.

Die Erscheinung und das Vermischen in der Wahrnehmung

Theoretisch ist es unmöglich, die äußere Welt auf der Basis des visuellen Inputs zu rekonstruieren, weil die Projektionen dieser Welt auf unserer Netzhaut uns einfach nicht genügend Informationen vermitteln.[3] Theoretisch können eine Bandbreite verschiedener Kombinationen aus Form, Material und Licht die gleiche Erscheinung ergeben, oder anders gesagt, das gleiche Bild auf der Netzhaut erzeugen. Folglich können wir aus dem Bild auf der Netzhaut nicht auf eine physisch einmalige Lösung (eine einzige Kombination aus Form, Material und Licht) schließen, daraus folgt, dass der Input des menschlichen, visuellen Systems mehrdeutig ist. Abbildung 2 zeigt ein Beispiel für diese Mehrdeutigkeit. Das Bild links zeigt einen Golfball in einem völlig diffusen Licht, auch »Ganzfeld-Beleuchtung« genannt (die Art von Licht, die man sieht, wenn man im Nebel Skifahren geht). In der Mitte und rechts sehen wir einen glänzenden, beziehungsweise einen matten Golfball im Licht eines Strahlers von links. Welcher dieser beiden Golfbälle wurde im linken Foto aufgenommen? Auf der Basis dieser Bilder können wir das nicht entscheiden, denn die Ganzfeld-Beleuchtung lässt glänzende Objekte matt erscheinen, weil die Glanzlichter nicht mehr zu sehen sind (das diffuse Licht lässt sie verschwinden). Das Ganzfeld-Bild ist also mehrdeutig in Bezug auf den Glanz des Materials. Dies ist nur ein Beispiel für die Interaktion zwischen Material, Form und Licht. Andere bekannte Beispiele sind die Mehrdeutigkeit bei der räumlichen Bewertung eines Flachreliefs (bas-relief ambiguity)[4] und die Mehrdeutigkeit bei der Wahrnehmung von konvexen und konkaven Formen (convex-concave ambiguity).[5]

3 Projizierte Bilder sind zweidimensional. Die Welt besteht aber aus dreidimensionalen Gebilden mit Materialien, die durch physikalische Funktionen beschrieben werden können, die für glatte, homogene und opake Oberflächen mindestens vier Dimensionen beinhalten (für die Beschreibung von rauen / geschichteten / durchscheinenden / fluoreszierenden Materialien brauchen wir sogar noch weitere Dimensionen). Sind diese Gebilde und Materialien in einem Lichtfeld, benötigen wir mindestens eine fünfdimensionale Beschreibung – wenn man die Farbe außer Acht lässt. Daher ist die »umweltbezogene Optik« der äußeren Welt hochkomplex. Die Form, das Material und das Licht erzeugen gemeinsam eine bestimmte Erscheinung. Das visuelle System der Menschen muss diese Erscheinung interpretieren. Die Rekonstruktion einer vier- oder höherdimensionalen Beschreibung eines zweidimensionalen Inputs auf der Netzhaut ist jedoch ein theoretisch unterdeterminiertes Problem und kann nicht zu einer einmaligen Lösung führen.

4 Peter N. Belhumeur / David J. Kriegman / Alan L. Yuille, »The Bas-Relief Ambiguity«, in: *International Journal of Computer Vision,* 35 (1999) Nr. 1, S. 33–44.

5 Vilayanur S. Ramachandran, »Perceiving Shape from Shading«, in: *The Perceptual World: Readings from Scientific American Magazine,* hg. von I. Rock, New York: W. H. Freeman & Co, Publishers, 1990, S. 127–138.

physical reality. In other words, as Jan Koenderink has stated, most people believe in the "all seeing eye."[2] However, I argue that these are just demonstrations of normal perceptual processes and that interactions between light, material, shape, and space perception form a basic, normal part of our visual experience. Vision is not inverse optics, and light-material-shape-space perception is confounded. In other words, we can never "believe our eyes."

Appearance and Perceptual Confounding

It is theoretically impossible to reconstruct the external world on the basis of our visual input, because we simply do not receive sufficient information via the projections of that world on our retinas.[3] Theoretically, ranges of combinations of shapes, materials, and light can result in the same appearance. In other words, multiple combinations of shapes, materials and light can result in the same retinal image. Thus, we cannot infer a physically unique solution (a single combination of a shape, a material, and light) from the retinal image, and for this reason input for the human visual system is ambiguous. Figure 2 shows an example of such an ambiguity. The image on the left shows a golf ball in completely diffuse or Ganzfeld illumination (the type of light you experience if you go skiing in the mist). In the middle and on the right we see a shiny golf ball and a matte golf ball in a spotlight from the left. But which of these two golf balls was also photographed on the left? On the basis of these images, we cannot decide, because in Ganzfeld illumination glossy objects also look matte, because the highlights disappear (are "diffused out"). The Ganzfeld image is thus ambiguous with regard to the glossiness of the material. This is just one example of the many different types of material-shape-light interactions. Other well-known examples concern the bas-relief ambiguity[4] and the convex-concave ambiguity.[5]

However, we do not experience the world as ambiguous under common conditions. Using visual intelligence,[6] we are usually well able to deal with ambiguous input. In order to do so, we (unconsciously) use knowledge about our natural environment—for instance, that light usually comes from above, and that most objects are convex. So, although the image of the golf ball on the left in figure 2 does not contain shading or shadowing cues from which we can infer that it is a sphere, we still perceive it as a sphere instead of a flat disk. Our visual system usually comes

3 Projected images are two-dimensional. The world contains three-dimensional shapes, with materials that can be described through physical functions that are at least four-dimensional for smooth homogeneous opaque surfaces (for rough / layered / translucent / fluorescent materials we need even higher-dimensional descriptions). Those shapes and materials are in a light field that requires a description that is at least five-dimensional if color is left out. Thus, the "ecological optics" of the external world is highly complex. Together, shape, materials and light result in a certain appearance. The human visual system must interpret that appearance. However, reconstructing four-dimensional or higher descriptions from a two-dimensional retinal input is a theoretically underdetermined problem and cannot lead to a unique solution.

4 Peter N. Belhumeur / David J. Kriegman / Alan L. Yuille, "The Bas-Relief Ambiguity," in *International Journal of Computer Vision*, 35 (1999): pp. 33–44.

5 Vilayanur S. Ramachandran, "Perceiving Shape from Shading," *The Perceptual World: Readings from Scientific American Magazine*, ed. Irvin Rock (New York: W. H. Freeman, 1990), pp. 127–138.

6 Donald D. Hoffman, *Visual Intelligence: How We Create What We See* (New York: W. W. Norton, 1998).

Unter normalen Umständen nehmen wir die Welt jedoch nicht als mehrdeutig wahr. Mit Hilfe unserer visuellen Intelligenz[6] sind wir gewöhnlich in der Lage, mit mehrdeutigem Input umzugehen. Dabei benutzen wir (unbewusst) unser Wissen über unsere natürliche Umgebung: zum Beispiel kommt Licht normalerweise von oben und die meisten Objekte sind konvex. Folglich sehen wir den linken Golfball in Abbildung 2 als eine Kugel und nicht als eine flache Scheibe, obwohl es keine Schattierungen oder keinen Schattenwurf gibt, aus dem wir die Kugelform ableiten könnten. Unser visuelles System erzeugt normalerweise angemessene Repräsentationen unserer Umgebung, die es uns erlauben wahrzunehmen, zu handeln und auf die Welt zu reagieren. Das heißt, wir können »unseren Augen trauen«, obwohl wir ihnen nicht »glauben« können.

6 Donald D. Hoffman, *Visual Intelligence – How We Create What We See,* New York: W. W. Norton & Company, Inc., 1998.

→ Fig · 2 Die Beleuchtung des linken Golfballs ist komplett diffus, auch »Ganzfeld-Beleuchtung« genannt. Der mittlere, glänzende Golfball und der rechte, matte Golfball werden von links angestrahlt.

Das Licht messen

Die Wahrnehmung der Form und des Materials ist also stark von den Eigenschaften des Lichts abhängig. Aber wie nehmen wir das Licht selbst wahr? Damit wir das untersuchen können, brauchen wir Methoden zur Beschreibung, Messung und Visualisierung des Lichts in komplexen, natürlichen und dreidimensionalen Räumen. Wir müssen die Optik und Wissenschaft des Sehens miteinander verbinden. Wir haben gezeigt, dass Licht in Räumen in Form von »Lichtfeldern« physisch (objektiv) und wahrnehmungsbezogen (subjektiv) gemessen werden kann.[7] Die physikalischen Messungen wurden mit einem »Plenopter« oder einem kubischen Beleuchtungsmesser[8] vorgenommen (siehe Fig · 3). Die Wahrnehmung wurde über eine Schnittstelle auf einem Computerbildschirm gemessen, dort wurde über dem Foto einer Szene eine künstliche, weiße Kugel eingeblendet. Die Beobachter sollten interaktiv die Intensität und die Richtung des Lichts steuern und festlegen, wie diffus das Licht auf die Kugel trifft, so dass alles zu der Atmosphäre des Lichts auf dem Foto passt (und damit zu der Szene). Die Kugel war auf einem Stab angebracht, der in der Szene verankert war, damit das Testobjekt in einer Leerstelle der Szene positioniert werden konnte. Die Parameter der Einstellungen der Probanden ergaben dann die Messdaten für deren Wahrnehmung. Die Beobachter hatten zumeist keine Probleme, diese Aufgabe zu erledigen. Dies zeigt, dass menschliche Betrachter ein gutes Gespür

7 Jan J. Koenderink / Alex A. Mury / Sylvia C. Pont, »Structure of Light Fields in Natural Scenes«, in: *Applied Optics,* 48 (2009) Nr. 28, S. 5386–5395; Jan J. Koenderink / Alex A. Mury / Sylvia C. Pont, »Representing the Light Field in Finite Three-Dimensional Spaces from Sparse Discrete Samples«, in: *Applied Optics,* 48 (2009) Nr. 3, S. 450–457; Tatiana Kartashova / Sylvia C. Pont / Huib de Ridder / Dragan Sekulovski / Susan te Pas, »Global Structure of the Visual Light Field and its Relation to the Physical Light Field«, *Journal of Vision,* 16 (2016) Nr. 10, S. 9.

8 Ingrid Heynderickx / Sylvia C. Pont / Ling Xia, »Light Diffuseness Metrics I: Theory«, in: *Lighting Research and Technology, doi:* 1477153516631391, 2016A; Ingrid Heynderickx / Sylvia C. Pont / Ling Xia, »Light Diffuseness Metrics II: Describing, Measuring and Visualizing the Light Flow and Diffuseness in 3D Spaces«, in: *Lighting Research and Technology, doi:* 1477153516631392, 2016B.

up with reasonable presentations of our environment, which allow us to perceive, act, and react to the world. Thus, we can "trust our eyes," although we cannot "believe our eyes."

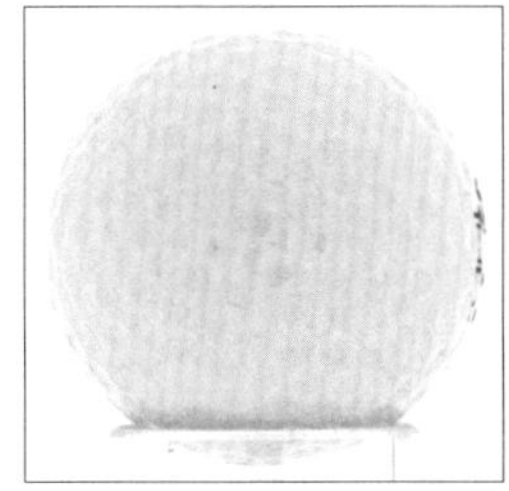
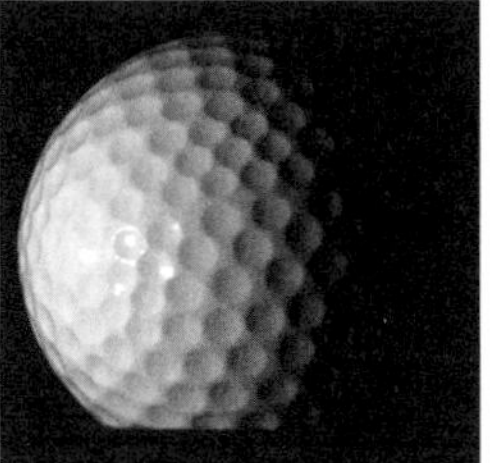
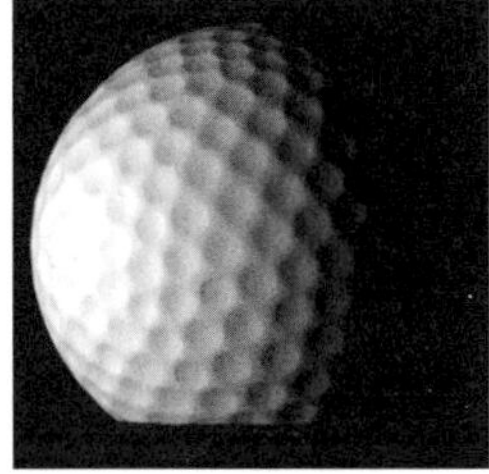

Fig · 2 Left, a golf ball in completely diffuse or Ganzfeld illumination; middle, a glossy golf ball; and right, a matte golf ball, both in spotlight from the left.

Measuring Light

Shape and material perception are thus strongly influenced by light qualities. But how do we perceive light itself? In order to study that, we need methods to describe, measure, and visualize light in complex, natural three-dimensional spaces. We need to integrate optics and vision science. We have shown that light can be measured in spaces as "light fields" both physically (objectively) and perceptually (subjectively).[7] The physical measurements were done using a "plenopter," or a cubic illuminance meter[8] (see Fig · 3). The perceptual measurements were conducted using an interface on a computer screen on which we superposed an artificial white sphere on a photograph of the scene. The observers had to interactively adjust the intensity, direction, and diffuseness of the lighting on the sphere so that it fit the luminous atmosphere of the photograph (and hence also the scene). The sphere was on a "monopod" stick that was grounded within the scene, positioning the probe in the empty space of the scene. The parameters of the observers' settings provided the measurements of their perceptions. Observers were, in general, well able to do this task. Thus, human observers have a good sense of the light in an empty space and can predict the appearance of a matte sphere in that space. This is what we call the "visual light field."[9] We have found that the visual light field is a simplified version of the "optical light field"[10] and can be described by four canonical modes or basic components of the light.[11]

7 Jan J. Koenderink / Alex A. Mury / Sylvia C. Pont, "Structure of Light Fields in Natural Scenes." *Applied Optics* 48 (28) (2009): pp. 5386–5395; Jan J. Koenderink / Alex A. Mury / Sylvia C. Pont, "Representing the Light Field in Finite Three-dimensional Spaces from Sparse Discrete Samples." *Applied Optics* 48 (3) (2009): pp. 450–457; Tatiana Kartashova / Sylvia C. Pont / Huib de Ridder / Dragan Sekulovski / Susan te Pas, "Global Structure of the Visual Light Field and Its Relation to the Physical Light Field." *Journal of Vision* 16 (10) (2016): p. 9.

8 Ingrid Heynderickx / Sylvia C. Pont / Ling Xia, "Light Diffuseness Metrics I: Theory." *Lighting Research and Technology* 49 (4) (2016A): 411–427; Ingrid Heynderickx / Sylvia C. Pont / Ling Xia, "Light Diffuseness Metrics II: Describing, Measuring and Visualizing the Light Flow and Diffuseness in 3D Spaces." *Lighting Research and Technology* 49 (4) (2016B): pp. 428–445.

9 Astrid M. L. Kappers / Jan J. Koenderink / Sylvia C. Pont / James Todd / Andrea J. van Doorn, "The Visual Light Field," *Perception* 36 (2007): pp. 1595–1610.

10 Kartoshova et al., "Global Structure of the Visual Light Field," p. 9.

11 Sylvia C. Pont, "Spatial and Form-giving Qualities of Light," in *The Wiley-Blackwell Handbook of Experimental Phenomenology. Visual Perception of Shape, Space and Appearance*, ed. Liliana Albertazzi (Chichester, West Sussex: Wiley-Blackwell, 2013), pp. 205–222.

für das Licht in einem leeren Raum haben und die Erscheinung einer matten Kugel im Raum vorhersagen können. Diese Eigenschaft bezeichnen wir als »visuelles Lichtfeld«.[9] Wir haben festgestellt, dass das visuelle Lichtfeld eine vereinfachte Version des »optischen Lichtfelds«[10] ist und dass es durch vier anerkannte Modi oder Grundkomponenten des Lichts beschrieben werden kann.[11]

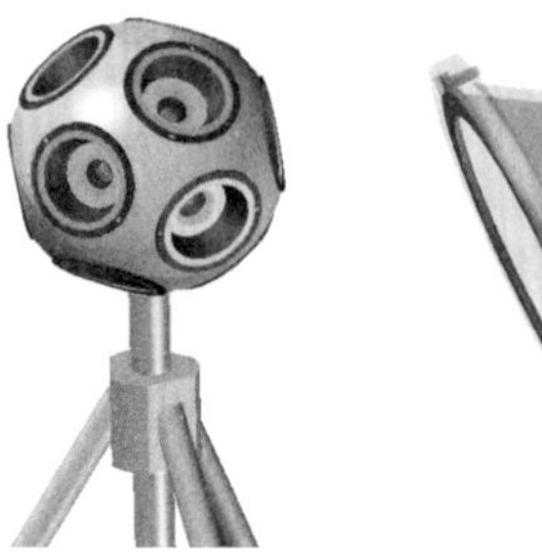

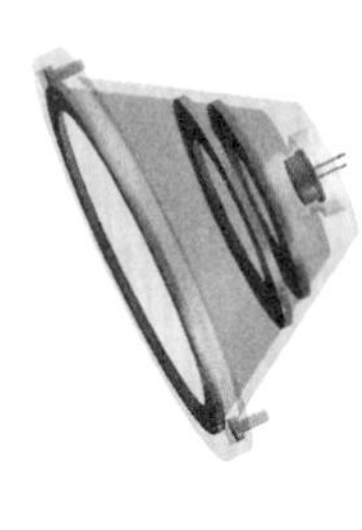

Fig · 3 Links der Plenopter, eine Spezialanfertigung, die mit 12 Sensoren das Licht messen kann, rechts ist einer dieser Sensoren in seinem Gehäuse zu sehen. Man kann die 12 Messungen zu einer Beschreibung des Lichts in Bezug auf die Lichtkomponenten Ambient, Focus und Squash-tensor kombinieren. Der Vorteil dieses Apparats ist, dass er dynamisch (einen Zeitverlauf) messen kann sowie mit einem extrem hohen Dynamikbereich (von sehr niedrigen zu extrem hohen Leuchtdichtewerten) – was bei Außenszenen nötig ist, besonders bei direkter Sonneneinstrahlung.

Licht entwerfen

Auf einer phänomenologischen Ebene konnte gezeigt werden, dass drei der anerkannten Lichtmodi mit den grundlegenden »Lichtschichten« übereinstimmen, die beim architektonischen Lichtdesign verwendet werden.[12] Diese Lichtschichten sind das sogenannte »Ambient (diffuse) Light«, »Focus Light« und das »Brilliance Light«, die in einer akzentuierten Weise übereinander gelegt werden können, um ein Beleuchtungskonzept zu erstellen. Ambient Light bestimmt die Gesamthelligkeit einer Szene oder eines Raumes. Focus Light erzeugt Schattenwürfe oder Schattierungen und Kontraste. Das Verhältnis zwischen dem Ambient und Focus Light bestimmt, wie diffus das resultierende Licht sein wird; je mehr Ambient Light, desto diffuser wird das Ergebnis, und je mehr Focus Light, desto gebündelter wird das Licht erscheinen. Durch das Brilliance Light kommen Variationen der Leuchtdichte beziehungsweise eine Lichttextur hinzu und im Fall von glänzenden Objekten erzeugt es viele Glanzlichter, siehe zum Beispiel den rechten Golfball in Abbildung 4. Fotografen verwenden auch den vierten Modus: das »Squash Light« oder »Clamp Light«, bei dem das Licht klammerartig von zwei Seiten gleichzeitig kommt.

9 Astrid M. L. Kappers / Jan J. Koenderink / Sylvia C. Pont / James Todd / Andrea J. van Doorn, »The Visual Light Field«, in: *Perception,* 36 (2007) Nr. 11, S. 1595–1610.

10 Tatiana Kartashova / Sylvia C. Pont / Huib de Ridder / Dragan Sekulovski / Susan te Pas, »Global Structure of the Visual Light Field and its Relation to the Physical Light Field«, in: *Journal of Vision,* 16 (2016) Nr. 10.

11 Sylvia C. Pont, »Spatial and Form-Giving Qualities of Light«, in: *The Wiley-Blackwell Handbook of Experimental Phenomenology. Visual Perception of Shape, Space and Appearance,* Hg. von L. Albertazzi, Hoboken, NJ: Wiley-Blackwell, 2013, S. 205–222.

12 Sylvia C. Pont, »Het licht zien – Lighting Design and Perceptual Intelligence«, Inaugural lecture, 2017: https://collegerama.tudelft.nl/Mediasite/Play/309167d7d02f45e6b0d60fb8afde4e1d1d (letzter Zugriff 27.10.2017).

← Fig · 3: Left, the plenopter, which is a custom-built apparatus for measuring light with 12 sensors, one of which is shown in its housing on the right. The 12 measurements can be combined to form a description of the light in terms of the ambient, focus, and squash tensor components of the light. The added value of this apparatus is that it can measure dynamically (over time) and with an extremely high dynamic range (from very low to extremely high luminance values), which is necessary for exterior scenes, especially if direct sunlight is present.

Designing Light

At a phenomenological level, three of the canonical light modes were shown to agree with the basic "light layers" that architectural lighting designers use.[12] These light layers are so-called ambient, focus, and brilliance lighting, which can be superposed in a weighted manner to compose a lighting plan. Ambient light refers to the overall brightness of a scene or space. Focus lighting provides shad(ow)ing and contrast. The ratio between ambient and focus light determines how diffuse the resulting light will be; the more ambient light, the more diffuse the result will be, and the more focus light, the more collimated the light will be. Brilliance light adds luminance variations or light texture, and in the case of glossy or shiny objects, it results in multiple highlights—see for instance the golf ball on the right in figure 4. Photographers also use a fourth mode, called a "light squash" or "clamp," In which the light is shown on the object from two sides, as if holding it in a clamp.

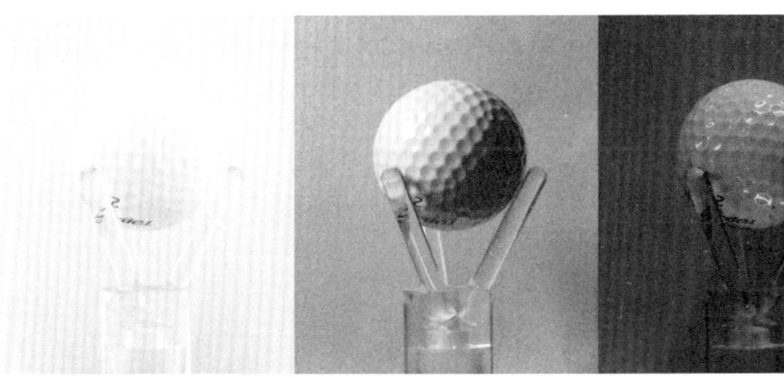

Fig · 4 A golf ball in examples of the three canonical light modes: left, ambient light; middle, focus light from above left; right, brilliance light or light texture.

Brilliance light concerns the angular high frequencies part of light. To describe brilliance light, our studies suggested that a statistical approach will suffice, while practical design experience suggests that its spatiotemporal dynamics are

12 Sylvia C. Pont, "Het licht zien – Lighting Design and Perceptual Intelligence," inaugural lecture held at the University of Delft in 2017, https://collegerama.tudelft.nl/Mediasite/Play/309167d7d02f45e6b0d60fb8afde4e1d1d (accessed October 27, 2017).

↗ Fig · 4 Ein Golfball, aufgenommen in den drei anerkannten Lichtmodi: links Ambient Light, in der Mitte Focus Light von links oben und rechts Brilliance Light oder Lichttextur.

Brilliance Light bezieht sich auf die hohen Kreisfrequenzen im Licht. Unsere Untersuchungen legen nahe, dass ein statistischer Ansatz ausreicht, um Brilliance Light zu beschreiben, und Erfahrungen aus der Lichtdesign-Praxis lassen vermuten, dass seine raumzeitliche Dynamik ein wichtiger Faktor ist. Inspiriert von Ivana Frankes Installation möchte ich das Beispiel eines Waldes voller Glühwürmchen heranziehen. Bei Tag wird ein Teil des Lichts durch das Laub der Bäume gestreut und erzeugt ein diffuses, grünliches Licht unter dem Dach der Baumkronen – Ambient Light. Wenn die Sonne durch ein Loch in dem Blätterdach scheint, entsteht ein gebündelter Strahl – Focus Light. Die kleinen Lichtblitze der Glühwürmchen erzeugen Lichtmuster – Brilliance Light. Bei Tag wird das Ambient und Focus Light sehr viel heller sein und wahrscheinlich das Brilliance Light überstrahlen. Bei Nacht wird jedoch das Ambient und Focus Light schwach sein (weil anstelle des Sonnenlichts nur das Mondlicht scheint) oder ganz verschwinden (bei einem bewölkten, dunklen Himmel) und das Brilliance Light der Glühwürmchen wird hervorstechen. In Ivana Frankes Installation gibt es nur Brilliance Lichtmuster, die sichtbar werden, wenn man sich an die Dunkelheit angepasst hat (was bis zu 20 Minuten dauert).

Im Lichtdesign wird Brilliance Light meistens durch die Verwendung von Lampen erzeugt. Wir neigen dazu, nicht direkt auf eine Lampe zu schauen, sondern auf die beleuchtete Szene. Deshalb konzentriere ich mich in meiner Forschung auf die Erscheinung, darauf, wie Menschen das Endresultat des Lichts und seine optischen Interaktionen mit der Szene wahrnehmen. Solche Interaktionen sind zum Beispiel Schattenwurf oder Körperschatten, gegenseitige Reflexionen zwischen Objekten, diffuse Streuung matter Objekte und Reflexionen glänzender Objekte. In einer vollständig matten Welt könnte man Brilliance Light nicht wahrnehmen, weil das diffuse Licht dieses durch die Streuung »verschwinden« lässt. Brilliance Light kann man in einer (teilweise) glänzenden Welt beobachten, weil diese durch Reflexionen Lichtmuster auf glänzenden Objekten erzeugt. Die Menschen achten auf Form, Intensität, Kontrast, Schärfe und relative Größe von Reflexionen.[13] Also müssen im Design der »Lichttestobjekte« – den Gegenständen, die Lichtdesigner in Leerstellen einer Szene einfügen, um die Qualitäten des Lichts sichtbar zu machen – die Materialien der Testobjekte optimiert werden, um bestimmte Eigenschaften des Lichts hervorzuheben. In Abbildung 5 sehen wir ein mattes, weißes Testobjekt und ein glänzendes, schwarzes Testobjekt, die in demselben Licht fotografiert wurden. Das matte Testobjekt betont das Ambient

13 Sylvia C. Pont / Jan Jaap R. van Assen / Maarten W. A. Wijntjes, »Highlight Shapes and Perception of Gloss for Real and Photographed Objects«, in: *Journal of Vision,* 16 (6), 2016, S. 1–14; Barton L. Anderson / Philip J. Marlow, »Generative Constraints on Image Cues for Perceived Gloss«, in: *Journal of Vision,* 13 (14), 2013, S. 2.

important determinants. I will consider the example of a forest full of fireflies, inspired by Ivana Franke's installation. In daytime, some light will scatter through the tree leaves and create a diffuse, greenish light under the canopy: ambient light. If the sun shines through a hole in the canopy, it will create a collimated beam: focus light. The small sparks of light created by the fireflies form patterns of lights: brilliance light. In the daytime, the ambient and focus light will be much brighter and probably over-radiate the brilliance light. However, at night, the ambient and focus light will be weak (due to moonlight instead of sunlight) or they will disappear (under a cloudy, dark sky), and the brilliance light of the fireflies will become salient. In Ivana Franke's installation there are only brilliance light patterns that become visible after our eyes adapt to the dark (which takes up to 20 minutes).

In lighting design, brilliance light is usually created using lamps. We tend not to look at lamps directly, but at scenes. Therefore, in my research, I focus on appearance, on how humans perceive the final result of light and its optical interactions with scenes. Such interactions are, for instance, cast and body shadows, mutual reflections between objects, the diffuse scattering of light from matte objects, and reflections from glossy and shiny objects. In a completely matte world, brilliance light cannot be seen, since it is "diffused out" by the light scattering. Brilliance light can be observed in a (partly) glossy/shiny world, because reflections will cause highlight patterns on glossy and shiny objects. Humans are sensitive to the shape, intensity, contrast, sharpness, and relative size of reflections.[13] Thus, in the design of "light probes"—objects that lighting designers can put in the empty space of a scene to make light qualities visible—we need to optimize the probes' materials to bring out specific light qualities. In figure 5 we see a white matte probe and a black shiny probe, which were photographed in the same light. The matte probe brings out the ambient and focused light, while the shiny probe clearly shows the brilliance light. In Ivana Franke's installation, the light patterns are caused by reflections of the light from three tiny, weak, directed beams on a composition of transparent shiny threads. Thus, the fundamental optical and perceptual mechanisms behind Ivana Franke's installation can be well understood. However, humans are not sensitive to the geometry of reflection pathways.[14] Therefore, in Ivana Franke's installation, we cannot perceive the causal relations of the reflection patterns.

13 Sylvia C. Pont / Jan Jaap R. van Assen / Maarten W. A. Wijntjes, "Highlight Shapes and Perception of Gloss for Real and Photographed Objects," *Journal of Vision* 16 (6) (2016): p. 6, pp. 1–14; Barton L. Anderson / Philip J. Marlow, "Generative Constraints on Image Cues for Perceived Gloss." *Journal of Vision* 13 (14) (2013): p. 2.

14 A. Blake / H. Bülthoff, "Does the Brain Know the Physics of Specular Reflection?" *Nature* 343 (6254) (1990): pp. 165–168.

und das Focus Light, während das glänzende Testobjekt klar das Brilliance Light hervorhebt. Die Lichtmuster in Ivana Frankes Installation werden durch Reflexionen dreier schwacher Lichtstrahlen ausgelöst, die auf eine Konstellation transparenter, glänzender Fäden gerichtet sind. Das bedeutet, dass die grundlegenden optischen und wahrnehmungsbezogenen Mechanismen hinter ihrer Installation gut nachvollziehbar sind. Allerdings sind Menschen nicht in der Lage, die geometrischen Bahnen der reflektierten Strahlen zu erkennen.[14] Deshalb schaffen wir es nicht, in Ivana Frankes Installation die kausalen Verbindungen der Reflexionsmuster wahrzunehmen.

→ Fig · 5 Ein glänzendes, schwarzes Testobjekt und ein mattes, weißes Testobjekt, in demselben Licht fotografiert. Beachten Sie, wie verschiedene Facetten des Lichts betont werden.

Die »Brilliance« der Glühwürmchen

Wie kann man also die Eigenschaften beschreiben, welche die Brilliance Lichtschicht bei Glühwürmchen ausmachen? Glühwürmchen leuchten auf und verlöschen. Sie fliegen herum. Einige ziehen einander an. Andere nicht. Das Resultat sind unregelmäßige Strukturen winziger Lichtblitze, die aufscheinen und faszinierende Muster erzeugen. Wir können sie von nah oder von fern betrachten, wodurch das Licht mehr oder weniger hell erscheint. Wir können sie anschauen, wenn unsere Augen an das Licht oder an die Dunkelheit angepasst sind, was bedeutet, dass wir entweder Dunkelheit oder eine Welt voll von Brilliance Light wahrnehmen – so wie in Ivana Frankes Installation. Man kann sie mit dem bloßen Auge oder einer Kamera anschauen. Die Belichtungszeit der Kamera kann verändert werden. Wenn wir eine kurze Belichtungszeit wählen, erhalten wir Momentaufnahmen der Glühwürmchen als helle Punkte, während eine lange Belichtungszeit uns die Flugbahnen der Insekten zeigt (siehe Abbildung 6 für einige Simulationen). Die letztere Methode wird in der »Lichtmalerei« verwendet, einer fotografischen Technik, mit der eine dynamische Beleuchtungssituation in einer Standfotografie festgehalten wird. Die meisten Menschen kennen Beispiele einer langen Belichtungszeit von Fotografien des Sternenhimmels, die die Bahnen der Sterne zeigen, oder von Straßen, die die Bewegung der Autolichter nachzeichnen.[15] Echte Glühwürmchen-Fotos lassen sich leicht googeln – im Internet gibt es viele faszinierende Bilder dazu, mit kurzer und langer Belichtungszeit, die die Brilliance der Glühwürmchen in verschiedenen räumlichen und zeitlichen Maßstäben zeigen.

14 A. Blake / H. Bülthoff, »Does the Brain Know the Physics of Specular Reflection?«, in: *Nature*, 343 (1990) Nr. 6254, S. 165–168.

15 Für Beispiele zur Lichtmalerei, siehe http://lightpaintingphotography.com/light-painting-artist/ (letzter Zugriff 30.08.2017).

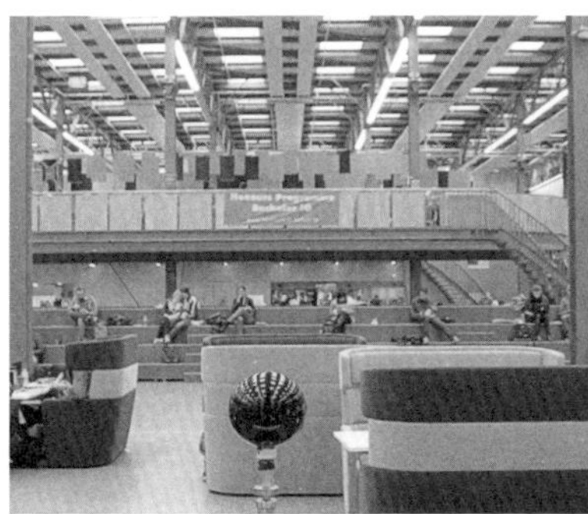

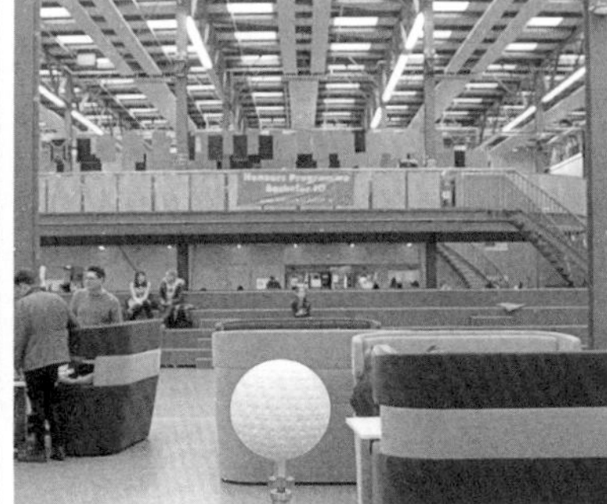

Fig · 5 A black shiny probe and a matte white probe. Both were photographed in the same light. Note that they bring out different light qualities.

The Brilliance of Fireflies

So how can we describe the characteristics of a firefly's brilliance light layer? Fireflies flash on and off. They fly around. Some attract others. Some don't. Altogether, this creates irregular patterns of tiny sparks of light, flashing on and off and creating intriguing motifs. We can view them from close-up or from far away, which results in more, or less, bright light. We can watch them after our eyes have adapted to the light or dark, which will enable us to see darkness or a world full of brilliance—as in Ivana Franke's installation. We can take in a view with our bare eyes or with a camera. The camera's exposure settings can be varied. If we choose a short exposure time, we will get instantaneous images showing the flies as bright spots, while a long exposure will capture the flies' flight paths—see figure 6 for simulations. The latter method is used in "light painting," which is a photographic method used to capture dynamic lighting in a still image. Most people have seen examples of long exposure photographs of night skies showing stars' pathways, or of highways resembling arteries of car lights.[15] To look at real photographs of fireflies, you only have to google them—the Internet has many intriguing images with short as well as long exposure times that show the brilliance of fireflies at different scales of space and time. Some clearly show the temporal dynamics, some the spatial dynamics. So what makes these light paintings so intriguing? Is it the magic of showing a world that is invisible to the naked eye—the unknown on the scale of human vision?

15 For examples of light painting art, see for instance http://lightpaintingphotography.com/light-painting-artist/ (accessed August 30, 2017).

Einige von ihnen betonen die zeitliche und andere die räumliche Dynamik. Was macht diese Lichtmalereien so faszinierend? Ist es der magische Moment einer Welt, die für das bloße Auge unsichtbar ist – das Unbekannte im Bereich des menschlichen Sehens?

→ Fig · 6 Lichtmalereien – ein Versuch, (echte) Glühwürmchen-Fotos zu simulieren. Alle Bilder wurden in einem dunklen Raum gemacht, mit einer kleinen, punktuellen LED Taschenlampe, einer Pflanze und mit einer Belichtungszeit von mehreren Sekunden. Links oben: Ein Bild, in dem das LED-Licht an verschiedenen Punkten an- und ausgeschaltet wurde. Rechts oben wurde das LED-Licht in Kreisen bewegt, links unten in geraden Bahnen und rechts unten in Kurven.

An die Grenzen des menschlichen Sehens und darüber hinaus: die Neugier und das Unbekannte

Mit dem berühmten Maler Johannes Vermeer und dem Wissenschaftler Antoni van Leeuwenhoek blickt Delft auf eine lange Geschichte im Bereich der Optik und der Visualisierung zurück. Vermeer benutzte eine Camera obscura (wie genau ist nicht bekannt), die es ihm erlaubte, eine Szene durch Projektionen auf einer zweidimensionalen Fläche zu betrachten. Heute sind wir an zweidimensionale, bewegte Bilder gewöhnt, aber es muss aufregend gewesen sein, dies zum ersten Mal zu sehen. Van Leeuwenhoek hat das Mikroskop erfunden und herausgefunden, dass jenseits der räumlichen Bereiche des menschlichen Sehens eine andere Welt existiert. Stellen Sie sich einmal vor, wie es war, das erste Mal Wasser durch ein Mikroskop zu betrachten und darin sich bewegende Organismen zu entdecken! Diese neuen Möglichkeiten, sich ein Bild von der Realität zu machen, dehnten die visuellen menschlichen Erfahrungen auf andere Welten aus, die bis dahin unbekannt gewesen waren.[16] In jüngerer Zeit wurde in Delft der sogenannte Synopter, oder Kunstbetrachter, entwickelt. Der Synopter ist ein Gerät zum Sehen, das die räumliche Tiefenwirkung von Gemälden verstärkt.[17] Es projiziert das gleiche Bild auf das linke und das rechte Auge, wodurch die stereoskopischen Anhaltspunkte wegfallen, aus denen wir ableiten können, dass das Bild in Wirklichkeit flächig ist. Für die meisten Betrachter treten dann die bildlichen (gemalten) Hinweise (wie Farbverläufe und Verschattungen) in den Vordergrund, wodurch eine künstliche, stereoskopische Tiefe entsteht – und tatsächlich sollte man es einfach einmal selbst probieren, um eine richtige Vorstellung davon zu bekommen.

16 Laura J. Snyder, *Eye of the Beholder – Johannes Vermeer, Antoni van Leeuwenhoek, and the Reinvention of Seeing*, New York: W. W. Norton & Company, 2016.

17 Tyas Deetman / András Füzy / Sylvia C. Pont / Maud E. S. Verheij / Maarten W. A. Wijntjes, »The Synoptic Art Experience«, in: *Journal of Art and Perception*, 4 (2016) Nr. 1–2, S. 73–105.

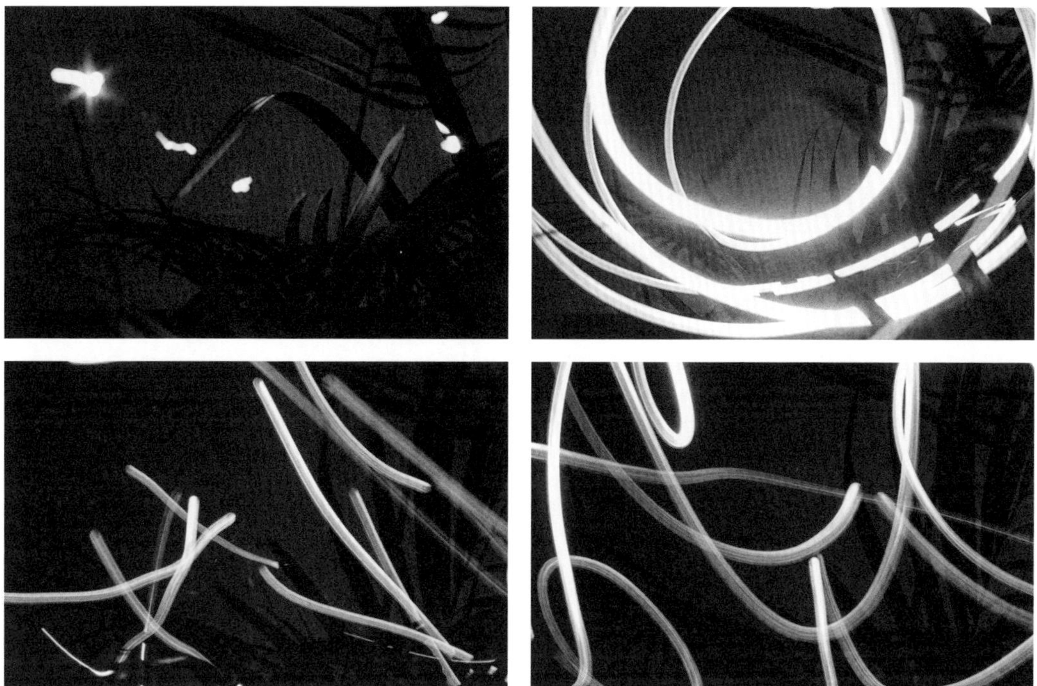

Fig · 6 Light paintings, or an attempt to simulate (real) photographs of fireflies. All images were made in a dark space with a small, punctate LED flashlight and a plant, using a shutter speed of several seconds. Above left, an image in which the LED light was flashed on and off in different locations; above right, the LED light was moved in circles; below left, the LED light was moved in lines; and below right, the light was moved in circles.

The Limits of Human Vision and Beyond: Curiosity and the Unknown

The city of Delft in the Netherlands has a history in the field of optics and visualizations and was home to the famous painter Johannes Vermeer and the scientist Antoni van Leeuwenhoek. Vermeer used a camera obscura (how precisely we do not know), which enabled him to look at scenes via projections on a two-dimensional plane. Nowadays, we are used to two-dimensional, moving images, but seeing them for the first time must have been thrilling. Van Leeuwenhoek also invented a microscope and discovered that another world exists beyond the spatial scale of human vision. Just imagine looking at water through a microscope for the first time and detecting moving organisms! These novel ways of imaging the world extended the human visual experience to worlds previously unknown.[16] More recent work from the city of Delft concerns, for instance, the synopter or

16 Laura J. Snyder, *Eye of the Beholder: Johannes Vermeer, Antoni van Leeuwenhoek, and the Reinvention of Seeing* (New York: W. W. Norton, 2016).

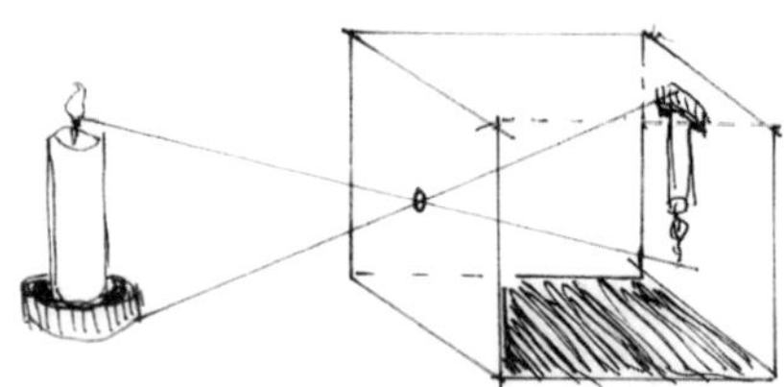

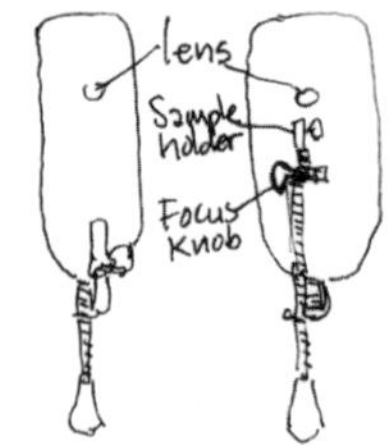

Fig · 7 Links eine schematische Zeichnung einer einfachen Camera obscura; eine Schachtel mit einem kleinen Loch, durch das ein auf dem Kopf stehendes Bild auf die Rückseite des Inneren projiziert wird. Camerae obscurae gab (gibt) es in verschiedenen Größen und mit verschiedenen Projektionsmechanismen, einige nutzen Spiegel und Linsen. Rechts eine Zeichnung eines Mikroskops von Antoni van Leeuwenhoek aus zwei Blickwinkeln. Seine Mikroskope waren höchstens fünf Zentimeter lang.

Ivana Frankes *Retreat into Darkness. Towards a Phenomenology of the Unknown* machte mich neugierig, weil das Projekt ähnliche Fragen aufwarf wie die oben beschriebenen Phänomene. Diese aufregenden, faszinierenden und überraschenden visuellen Erfahrungen erinnern uns an das Rätsel des Lebens, wie sie sagt. Sie mögen auf den ersten Blick eher unerklärlich und unbekannt erscheinen. Die Phänomene, die in diesem Beitrag angesprochen werden, haben alle gemein, dass sie Erkenntnisse über die Optik und Wahrnehmung sowie Kunst und Design verbinden. Hinzu kommt, dass sie alle das Ergebnis von einzigartigen Einsichten, Aha-Momenten und – was am wichtigsten und wertvollsten ist – neuen Fragen sind, die unsere Neugier beflügeln.

art viewer. The synopter is a viewing device that enhances the depth perceived in a painting.[17] It projects the same image to the left and right eyes, which removes the stereoscopic cues from which it can be inferred that the painting is actually on a flat plane. For most observers, the image cues (such as color gradients and occlusions) "take over," creating artificial stereoscopic depth. Indeed, you should experience this for yourself in order to fully appreciate the idea.

← Fig · 7 Left, a schematic drawing of a basic camera obscura: a box with a small hole in which the reversed and upside-down image is projected on the back of the interior. Camera obscuras exist(ed) in various sizes and with various projection mechanisms, some using mirrors and lenses. Right, a drawing of a microscope designed by Antoni van Leeuwenhoek from two perspectives. His microscopes were at most five centimeters long.

Ivana Franke's "Retreat into Darkness" piqued my curiosity because it triggered similar questions about the phenomena described above. These thrilling, intriguing, and surprising visual experiences, as she calls them, remind us of the mystery of life. They may seem rather inexplicable and unknown at first sight, but the phenomena addressed in this essay all have in common that they combine knowledge about optics and perception, as well as art or design. They also all result in novel insights, aha moments, and most importantly (and most valuable of all), novel questions that feed our curiosity.

17 Tyas Deetman / András Füzy / Sylvia C. Pont / Maud E. S. Verheij / Maarten W. A. Wijntjes, "The Synoptic Art Experience." *Journal of Art and Perception* 4 (1–2) (2016): pp. 73–105.

Biografien

Biographies

ELENA AGUDIO ist Kunsthistorikerin und Kuratorin, sie lebt und arbeitet in Berlin. Ihr Forschungsschwerpunkt ist das Teilen und Austauschen von Wissen und Fähigkeiten über die Grenzen von Disziplinen und Kulturen hinweg, jenseits der westlichen Episteme. Sie ist die künstlerische Leiterin der gemeinnützigen Association of Neuroesthetics: A Platform for Art and Neuroscience, einem gemeinsamen Projekt der Charité – Universitätsmedizin Berlin und der Berlin School of Mind and Brain, das sowohl einen kritischen Dialog als auch eine dauerhafte Kooperation zwischen zeitgenössischen Künstlern und Kognitionswissenschaftlern fördert. Seit 2013 ist sie stellvertretende künstlerische Leiterin des SAVVY Contemporary, einem Kunstraum in Berlin, gegründet und unter der Leitung von Bonaventure Soh Bejeng Ndikung. Zu ihren jüngsten kuratorischen Projekten gehören: *SAVVY FUNK*, ein Teil von *Every Time A Ear di Soun* – ein Radioprogramm im Rahmen der *documenta 14*, kuratiert zusammen mit Bonaventure Ndikung und Marcus Gammel; *Speaking Feminisms*, eine Veranstaltungsreihe, gemeinsam kuratiert mit Nathalie Mba Bikoro und Federica Bueti; und *That, Around Which The Universe Revolves*, kuratiert zusammen mit Anna Jäger und Saskia Köbschall. Im Moment ist sie Gastprofessorin an der Hochschule für bildende Künste (HFBK) Hamburg und »Curator-in-Residence« am Helsinki International Curatorial Programme (HICP), das vom HIAP (Helsinki International Artist Programme) organisiert wird.

JIMENA CANALES ist Inhaberin des Thomas M. Siebel Lehrstuhls für Wissenschaftsgeschichte an der University of Illinois, Urbana-Champaign. Sie ist die Verfasserin der Bücher *A Tenth of a Second: A History* und *The Physicist and The Philosopher: Einstein, Bergson, and the Debate That Changed Our Understanding of Time* (laut National Public Radio, USA, unter anderem eines der besten Wissenschaftsbücher im Jahr 2015). Sie hat zahlreiche Veröffentlichungen in Fachzeitschriften publiziert und schreibt auch für ein breiteres Publikum *(The New Yorker, The Atlantic, WIRED*, BBC, *Aperture* und *Artforum)*. Sie präsentierte ihre Arbeiten im Centre Georges Pompidou, dem SFMOMA und bei der 11. Shanghai Biennale. Zuvor war sie Privatdozentin für Wissenschaftsgeschichte an der Harvard University und Senior Fellow am IKKM (Internationales Kolleg für Kulturtechnikforschung und Medienphilosophie) in Weimar. 2013 wurde ihr der Charles-A.-Ryskamp-Preis des American Council of Learned Societies verliehen. Canales hat an der Harvard University ihren MA und ihre Promotion in Wissenschaftsgeschichte abgeschlossen und wurde mit dem Preis für Nachwuchswissenschaftler der International Union of the History and Philosophy of Science ausgezeichnet.

IVANA FRANKE ist eine bildende Künstlerin, die in Berlin lebt und arbeitet. Sie hat an der Akademie der Künste in Zagreb, Kroatien, studiert und nahm an einem Forschungsprogramm für Postgraduierte am Zentrum für zeitgenössische Kunst in Kitakyushu, Japan, teil. Ihre Arbeiten, zumeist Lichtinstallationen, untersuchen die Schnittstelle zwischen Wahrnehmung, Kognition und Umwelt, wobei sie sich auf Grenzbereiche der Wahrnehmung konzentrieren. Mit ihrer Einzelausstellung *Latency* repräsentierte sie Kroatien bei der 52. Biennale Venedig. Weitere Projekte waren u.a. *Disorientation Station* (11. Shanghai Biennale) und *Seeing with Eyes Closed* (Peggy Guggenheim, Venedig; Deutsche Guggenheim, Berlin); weitere Ausstellungen: u.a. *Manifesta 7*, Museum für zeitgenössische Kunst in Zagreb und MoMA P.S.1 in New York. Bei ihrem Projekt *Seeing with Eyes Closed* hat sie mit der Neurowissenschaftlerin Ida Momennejad zusammengearbeitet.

ELENA AGUDIO is a Berlin-based art historian and curator. Her research is focused on the sharing and exchange of knowledge and skills across disciplines and cultures beyond the Western episteme. She is the artistic director of the non-profit Association of Neuroesthetics (AoN): A Platform for Art and Neuroscience, a project in collaboration with the Medical University of Charité and the Berlin School of Mind and Brain that encourages both a critical dialogue and a long-term cooperation between contemporary artists and cognitive scientists. In 2013, she became artistic co-director of SAVVY Contemporary, a Berlin-based art space founded and directed by Bonaventure Soh Bejeng Ndikung. Among her last and still running curatorial projects are *SAVVY FUNK*, an iteration of *Every Time A Ear di Soun—a documenta 14* Radio Program, curated together with Bonaventure Ndikung and Marcus Gammel; *Speaking Feminisms*, a series curated with Nathalie Mba Bikoro and Federica Bueti; and *That, Around Which The Universe Revolves*, curated with Anna Jäger and Saskia Köbschall. She is currently a visiting professor at HFBK (University of Fine Arts) Hamburg and a curator-in-residence at Helsinki International Curatorial Programme (HICP) organized by Helsinki International Artist Programme (HIAP).

JIMENA CANALES is the Thomas M. Siebel Chair in the History of Science at the University of Illinois, Urbana-Champaign. She is the author of *A Tenth of a Second: A History* and *The Physicist and The Philosopher: Einstein, Bergson, and the Debate That Changed Our Understanding of Time* (listed as one of the Best Science Books of 2015). She has published widely in specialized journals, writes for general audiences (in *The New Yorker*, *The Atlantic*, *WIRED*, BBC, *Aperture*, and *Artforum*), and has presented her work at the Centre Georges Pompidou, the SFMOMA, and at the 11th Shanghai Biennale. She was previously an associate professor of the history of science at Harvard University and a senior fellow at the IKKM (Internationales Kolleg für Kulturtechnikforschung und Medienphilosophie) in Germany. She was a recipient of the Charles A. Ryskamp Award given out by the American Council of Learned Societies (2013). Canales received her M.A. and Ph.D. from Harvard University in the History of Science and was awarded the Prize for Young Scholars by the International Union of the History and Philosophy of Science.

IVANA FRANKE is a visual artist based in Berlin. She studied at the Academy of Fine Arts in Zagreb, Croatia, and participated in a postgraduate research program at the Center for Contemporary Art Kitakyushu, Japan. Her works, often in forms of light installations, investigate the interface between perception, cognition, and environment, focusing on perceptual thresholds. She represented Croatia at the 52nd Venice Biennale with the solo exhibition *Latency.* Her other projects include *Disorientation Station* (11th Shanghai Biennale), *Seeing with Eyes Closed* (Peggy Guggenheim in Venice, Deutsche Guggenheim in Berlin), and projects at *Manifesta 7*, the Museum of Contemporary Art Zagreb, and MoMA P.S.1. With neuroscientist Ida Momennejad, she collaborated on her project *Seeing with Eyes Closed* and co-organized interdisciplinary symposiums and panel discussions. In collaboration with the vision scientist Bilge Sayim, she exhibited and lectured at the European Conference of Visual Perception in Liverpool (2015) and at the Science of Consciousness Conference in Tucson, Arizona, (2016).

Sie war bereits an der Organisation von mehreren interdisziplinären Symposien und Podiumsdiskussionen beteiligt. In Zusammenarbeit mit Bilge Sayim, Professor für visuelle Psychophysik und Experte für visuelle Wahrnehmung, war sie bei der »European Conference of Visual Perception« in Liverpool (2015) mit einer Ausstellung und einem Vortrag vertreten, genauso wie bei der »Science of Consciousness Conference« in Tucson, Arizona (2016).

PIERRE GALLAIS (*1950 in Frankreich) ist Künstler und Mathematiker. Nach seinem Diplom in Mathematik (1977) wandte er sich der Kunst zu und arbeitet seitdem in den Medien Zeichnung, Skulptur und Installation, häufig in Kooperation mit Mathematikern und Komponisten, stets eng an der Schnittstelle zur Mathematik. Gallais realisiert Kunst im öffentlichen Raum und hat seit 1987 regelmäßig auf Festivals und Konzerten in Frankreich, Belgien, Luxemburg und in den Niederlanden die Lichtszenografie verantwortet, darunter am IRCAM, Centre Pompidou, Paris, im Rahmen der Akusmatikkonzerte des ina-GRM am Maison de Radio France, Paris, und wiederholt beim Festival »L'Espace du Son« (Neue Musik Festival) des Théâtre Marni, Brüssel.

HEIKE CATHERINA MERTENS ist Kuratorin und geschäftsführender Vorstand der Schering Stiftung. Sie studierte Kunstgeschichte, Philosophie und Soziologie und nach einer wissenschaftlichen und publizistischen Tätigkeit im Bereich der zeitgenössischen Kunst arbeitete sie von 2000 bis 2007 als Kuratorin für Kunst im öffentlichen Raum. 2001 gründete sie in Berlin den Verein »stadtkunstprojekte« zur Förderung von Kunst im Stadtraum. Seit 2007 ist sie künstlerische Leiterin der Schering Stiftung. Neben ihrer Stiftungstätigkeit lehrt sie regelmäßig im Rahmen des Weiterbildungsprogrammes »Kuratieren« an der Universität der Künste Berlin und publiziert Bücher zur zeitgenössischen Kunst. Sie ist Mitglied im Hochschulrat der Hochschule für bildende Künste Hamburg, Mitglied im Vorstand des Bundesverbandes Deutscher Stiftungen, Mitglied im Kuratorium zur Vergabe des KAIROS-Preises der Alfred Toepfer Stiftung F.V.S. und Kuratoriumsmitglied von Common Purpose Berlin.

KATJA NAIE ist wissenschaftliche Programmleiterin der Schering Stiftung. Geboren in Dinslaken begann sie nach ihrem Biologiestudium ihre berufliche Laufbahn an der Charité in Berlin, wo sie in den Neurowissenschaften promovierte. Nach ihrer wissenschaftlichen Tätigkeit an der Eidgenössischen Technischen Hochschule in Zürich wechselte sie 2007 zur Gemeinnützigen Hertie-Stiftung. Dort initiierte und leitete sie das Informationsportal www.dasGehirn.info und teilte ihre Begeisterung für das Gehirn und seine Bedeutung für unser Fühlen, Denken und Handeln mit einer breiten Leserschaft. Sie ist Mitautorin eines Fotosachbuches über das Gehirn für Kinder und Gutachterin für den KlarText!-Preis der Klaus Tschira Stiftung. Der Brückenschlag zwischen Wissenschaft und Gesellschaft ist ihr ein persönliches Anliegen, das sie in ihrer täglichen Stiftungsarbeit umsetzt.

SYLVIA C. PONT ist seit 2016 Inhaberin der Antoni-van-Leeuwenhoek-Professur an der Delft University of Technology, Niederlande, wo sie seit 2008 im Bereich des Industrial Design Engineerings arbeitet. Sie leitet eine Forschungsgruppe, die am Perceptual Intelligence-Labor, zu dem ein Lichtlabor und ein Sehlabor gehören, an Studien zum Design, der Wahrnehmung und der Optik des Lichts, Materialien und Formen, sowie deren Interaktionen arbeitet. Sie ist für den Masterstudiengang Lichtdesign verantwortlich und unterrichtet unter anderem

PIERRE GALLAIS (born 1950 in France) is an artist and mathematician. After earning a Diploma in Mathematics (1977), he began making art, concentrating on the media of drawing, sculpture, and installation. He also often collaborates with mathematicians and composers, always working at the crossroads of mathematics. Gallais also creates art in public spaces, and since 1987, he has been designing the stage lighting for festivals and concerts in France, Belgium, Luxemburg, and the Netherlands—for example, at the IRCAM of the Centre Pompidou in Paris, for the acousmatic concerts of ina-GRM at the Maison de Radio France in Paris, and numerous times at the Festival (New Music Festival) of the Théâtre Marni in Brussels.

HEIKE CATHERINA MERTENS is the curator and managing director of Schering Stiftung. She studied art history, philosophy and sociology. After completing academic work in the field of contemporary art, she worked as a curator for public art from 2000 until 2007. In 2001, she founded stadtkunstprojekte, a Berlin-based association for the promotion of urban public art. In 2007, she became the head of the Cultural Department of Schering Stiftung. Alongside her work at the Foundation, she regularly teaches Curating in the further education program at the Berlin University of the Arts and also publishes books on contemporary art. She is a member of the University Council (Hochschulrat) of the University of Fine Arts of Hamburg, the board of directors of the Association of German Foundations, the board of trustees of the KAIROS Prize awarded by the Alfred Toepfer Stiftung F.V.S., and the board of trustees of Common Purpose Berlin.

KATJA NAIE is the director of the science program at Schering Stiftung. She was born in Dinslaken, Germany. After studying biology, she began her career at the Charité in Berlin, where she earned a Ph.D. in Neuroscience. After working as a researcher at ETH Zurich, she moved to the Hertie Foundation in 2007. There she initiated and directed the Internet information portal www.dasGehirn.info, on which she shared her enthusiasm for the brain and the role it plays in our emotions, thoughts, and actions with a broad audience. She is the co-author of an illustrated non-fiction children's book about the brain and serves as an expert advisor for the KlarText! Award given out by the Klaus Tschira Foundation. Her personal passion is to build a bridge between science and society, and she strives to achieve this goal in her everyday work at Schering Stiftung.

SYLVIA C. PONT is the Antoni van Leeuwenhoek Professor at Delft University of Technology, Netherlands (2016), where she has worked in the Faculty of Industrial Design Engineering since 2008. In the light and vision labs, which are part of the Perceptual Intelligence Lab, her research group studies the design, perception, and optics of light, materials, and shapes, and their interactions. She coordinates the master's degree program in Lighting Design and teaches courses in such subjects as visual perception and research methods. From 1999 to 2008, Sylvia worked in the Physics of Man group in the Helmholtz Institute at Utrecht University. Her postdoctoral research in ecological optics was partly conducted at Columbia University and Stanford University and included studies in reflectance, texture, and light fields. January 2004 she was appointed an assistant professor and built a research group studying the

visuelle Wahrnehmung und Forschungsmethoden. Zwischen 1999 und 2008 hat Sylvia Pont am Helmholtz Institut der Universität Utrecht zur Physik des Menschen gearbeitet. Nach ihrer Promotion hat sie zu »ökologischer Optik« geforscht, zum Teil an der Columbia University und der Stanford University, dazu gehörten Studien zum Reflexionsgrad, Texturen und Lichtfeldern. Ab Januar 2004 baute sie als Assistenzprofessorin eine Arbeitsgruppe auf, die sich mit der Erscheinung von natürlichen Materialien und Lichtfeldern beschäftigte. Ihre Dissertation befasst sich mit der haptischen Wahrnehmung. Von 1997–99 arbeitete sie an einem Institut für sehbehinderte Menschen.

BILGE SAYIM hat Psychologie und Informatik an der Universität in Kiel und der University of California, San Diego, studiert. Er wurde in den Neurowissenschaften an der École Polytechnique Fédérale de Lausanne (EPFL) in der Schweiz mit einer Dissertation zum Thema *Grouping and Gestalt in Visual Contextual Modulation* promoviert. Nach der Promotion arbeitete er als Forscher an der Université Paris Descartes und der Universität Leuven, bevor er als Gastprofessor an der Königlichen Akademie der Künste in Antwerpen tätig wurde. Zurzeit hat er eine Förderungsprofessur des Schweizerischen Nationalfonds (SNF) an der Universität Bern inne, wo er das Psychophysics of Appearance Laboratory leitet (appearancelab.org). Außerdem ist er CNRS-Forscher im SCALab der Université de Lille, Frankreich. Seine Forschungsschwerpunkte sind das periphere Sehen und »Crowding«, kontextuelle Modulation, erscheinungsbasierte Methoden und Kunst.

ANIL K. SETH ist Professor für Kognitive und Computerbasierte Neurowissenschaften an der University of Sussex und Stellvertretender Leiter und Mitgründer des Sackler Centre for Consciousness Science. Er ist zudem Engagement Fellow des Wellcome Trust und Senior Fellow des Canadian Institute for Advanced Research. In seiner Arbeit untersucht Anil Seth die biologischen Grundlagen des Bewusstseins, indem er Forschungsergebnisse aus den Neurowissenschaften, der Mathematik, künstlichen Intelligenz, Informatik, Psychologie, Philosophie und Psychiatrie zusammenbringt. Er hat mehr als 110 wissenschaftliche Publikationen veröffentlicht und ist der Chefredakteur der akademischen Zeitschrift *Neuroscience of Consciousness* (Oxford University Press). Er ist Redakteur und Mitautor von *30 Second Brain* (Ivy Press, 2014), war Berater für *Eye Benders* (Ivy Press, 2013; Gewinner des Jugendbuchpreises der Royal Society 2014) und *Brain Twisters* (Ivy Press, 2014). Er verfasst regelmäßig Beiträge für verschiedene Medien, darunter der *New Scientist, The Guardian* und die BBC, die in ihrer renommierten Sendung »The Life Scientist« ein Porträt über ihn präsentierte.

appearance of natural materials and light fields. Her Ph.D. project concerned haptic perception, and she also worked at an institute for visually disabled people from 1997 to 1999.

BILGE SAYIM studied psychology and computer science at Kiel University and the University of California, San Diego. He obtained a Ph.D. in Neuroscience at the École Polytechnique Fédérale de Lausanne (EPFL) in Switzerland with a dissertation on *Grouping and Gestalt in Visual Contextual Modulation*. After postdoctoral research at the Université Paris Descartes and the University of Leuven, he served as a visiting professor at the Royal Academy of Fine Arts in Antwerp. Currently, he is Swiss National Science Foundation (SNSF) Professor at the University of Bern, Switzerland, where he heads the Psychophysics of Appearance Laboratory (appearancelab.org). He is also a National Center for Scientific Research (CNRS) research scientist in the SCALab (Cognitive & Affective Sciences Laboratory) at the Université de Lille, France. His research interests include peripheral vision and crowding, contextual modulation, appearance-based methods, and art.

ANIL K. SETH is Professor of Cognitive and Computational Neuroscience at the University of Sussex and founding co-director of the Sackler Centre for Consciousness Science. He is also a Wellcome Trust Engagement Fellow and a Senior Fellow of the Canadian Institute for Advanced Research. In his work, Anil seeks to understand the biological basis of consciousness by bringing together research across neuroscience, mathematics, artificial intelligence, computer science, psychology, philosophy, and psychiatry. He has published more than 110 research papers and is editor-in-chief of the academic journal *Neuroscience of Consciousness* (Oxford University Press). He is editor and co-author of *30 Second Brain* (Ivy Press, 2014), was consultant for *Eye Benders* (Ivy Press, 2013; winner of the Royal Society Young People's Book Prize 2014), and co-author of *Brain Twisters* (Ivy Press 2014). He contributes regularly to many media, including the *New Scientist*, *The Guardian*, and the BBC, for which he was profiled on their flagship show *The Life Scientific*.

DANK

Ein herzliches Dankeschön an alle, die zu dem Projekt *Retreat into Darkness. Towards a Phenomenology of the Unknown* beigetragen und dabei geholfen haben, dass die Ausstellung in der Schering Stiftung, das Symposium in Zusammenarbeit mit Savvy Contemporary, das Panel in der Schering Stiftung im Rahmen der Langen Nacht der Wissenschaften sowie diese Publikation realisiert werden konnten.

Mein aufrichtiger Dank geht an Heike Catherina Mertens, die an dieses Projekt geglaubt und geduldig alle Schwierigkeiten bei seiner Umsetzung auf sich genommen hat. Danke für ihre unermessliche intellektuelle Neugier und ihr Einfühlungsvermögen. Ein besonderer Dank an Elena Agudio, Kuratorin der Ausstellung, für ihre engagierten Gespräche nicht nur im Rahmen dieses Projekts, sondern während unserer langjährigen Zusammenarbeit. Diese Gespräche sind für mich enorm wichtig und inspirierend. Die anhaltenden, anregenden Dialoge mit Bilge Sayim und unsere Kollaborationen waren grundlegend für die Konzeption des Symposiums.

Dafür, dass sie sich mit dem Thema beschäftigt und unseren intellektuellen Horizont erweitert haben, bedanke ich mich von tiefstem Herzen bei allen Autoren dieses Buchs, bei den Referenten des Symposiums – Jimena Canales, Patricia Reed, Sylvia C. Pont und Pierre Gallais – und bei den Teilnehmern des Panels – Michael Pauen, Anil K. Seth, Philipp Sterzer und Melanie Wilke.

Martina Schrammek gebührt mein Dank für ihre großzügige Geduld, ihre stete Unterstützung und ihre akribische Organisation, die für die Umsetzung des Projekts unerlässlich war. Danke auch an Katja Naie für die Konzeption und Organisation des Panels im Rahmen der Langen Nacht der Wissenschaften, und an Andrea Bölling für ihre freundliche Unterstützung bei der Kommunikation und Koordination der Veranstaltungen. Für ihre Hilfe bei dem Besucherexperiment und dafür, dass sie stundenlang im Dunkeln ausharrten, danke ich Katja Sommerfeld und Wencke Schubert. Vielen Dank auch an die Teilnehmer des Experiments.

Ich bedanke mich bei Elena Chronopoulou für ihren Einsatz im Rahmen der Ausstellung sowie dieser Publikation. Ein besonderer Dank an Sara Ferrer, Alexander Bouchner, Sophia Tang, Felix von Haselberg, Serra Öner und Mark Pennock, die ebenfalls einen großen Beitrag zur Realisierung der Ausstellung geleistet haben.

Für ihre Unterstützung danke ich der Schering Stiftung, Savvy Contemporary und dem Ministerium für Kultur der Republik Kroatien. Des Weiteren geht mein Dank an Jeebesh Bagchi und das Raqs Media Collective, Mario Furčić, Vanja Žanko, Vedran Franke, Dora Šribar, Ljiljana Franke, Tomás Saraceno, Željka Himbele, 3LHD.

Ivana Franke

ACKNOWLEDGMENTS

A warm thank you to everyone who has contributed to the project *Retreat into Darkness. Towards a Phenomenology of the Unknown* and helped realize the exhibition at the Schering Stiftung, the symposium in collaboration with Savvy Contemporary, the panel event at the Schering Stiftung as part of the Long Night of the Sciences, and this publication.

My sincere thanks go to Heike Catherina Mertens for her belief in the project, for bearing with all the difficulties in realizing it, and for her immense intellectual curiosity and sensitivity. Special thanks to Elena Agudio, curator of the exhibition, for her engagement in conversations, not only during this project but throughout our long years of collaboration. Those conversations have been immensely important and inspiring for me. Long-term thought-provoking dialogues with Bilge Sayim and our collaborations have been foundational for the conceptualization of the symposium.

For their engagement with the theme and for enlarging our intellectual horizons, I would like to deeply thank all the contributors to this book, the speakers at the symposium—Jimena Canales, Patricia Reed, Sylvia C. Pont, and Pierre Gallais—and the participants in the panel—Michael Pauen, Anil K. Seth, Philipp Sterzer, and Melanie Wilke.

I am indebted to Martina Schrammek for her generous patience, her enduring support, and her meticulous organization which was indispensable for the realization of this project. Thanks to Katja Naie for conceptualizing and organizing the panel event at the Long Night of the Sciences, and to Andrea Bölling for her kind support in communicating and coordinating the events. For helping with the experiment and enduring long hours in the darkness, Katja Sommerfeld and Wencke Schubert. Many thanks to all the participants in the experiment.

I am grateful to Elena Chronopoulou for her efforts in realizing the exhibition as well as this publication. Special thanks to Sara Ferrer, Alexander Bouchner, Sophia Tang, Felix von Haselberg, Serra Öner, and Mark Pennock, who have greatly contributed to the making of the exhibition.

I would like to thank the Schering Stiftung, Savvy Contemporary, and the Ministry of Culture of the Republic of Croatia for their support. Additional thanks to Jeebesh Bagchi and the Raqs Media Collective, Mario Furčić, Vanja Žanko, Vedran Franke, Dora Šribar, Ljiljana Franke, Tomás Saraceno, Željka Himbele, 3LHD.

Ivana Franke

Dieses Buch erscheint anlässlich der Ausstellung *Ivana Franke: Retreat into Darkness. Towards a Phenomenology of the Unknown* in der Schering Stiftung (27. April – 16. Juli 2017) sowie des gleichnamigen Symposiums am 27. Juni 2017 bei Savvy Contemporary.
This book was published on the occasion of the exhibition *Ivana Franke: Retreat into Darkness. Towards a Phenomenology of the Unknown* at Schering Stiftung (April 27–July 16, 2017) and the symposium of the same title on June 27, 2017, at Savvy Contemporary.

Herausgeber **Editors**
Ivana Franke, Heike Catherina Mertens, Dr. Katja Naie

Redaktion **Managing Editor**
Martina Schrammek

Lektorat **Copyediting**
Michelle Miles
Martina Schrammek

Übersetzungen **Translations**
Dr. Ingo Maerker
Michelle Miles
Frédérique Destribats (P. Gallais)

Grafische Gestaltung und Satz
Graphic Design and Typesetting
Studio Pandan – Ann Richter & Pia Christmann, Berlin

Papier **Paper**
Gmund Colors 87, 300 g/m², Maxioffset 110 g/m², Heaven 42 absolutweiß 150 g/m²

Bildbearbeitung **Image Processing**
Joscha Bruckert, RGBerlin

Druck **Printed by**
druckhaus köthen

Bildnachweis **Image Credits**
pp. 1–9, 14–24, 72–79, 111 (Fig · 3), Cover: Roman März, © Schering Stiftung; pp. 10–13, 50–55, 111 (Fig · 1–2), 112, 115: © Ivana Franke; p. 95: © Edward H. Adelson; p. 101: Courtesy of Keisuke Suzuki (Sackler Centre for Consciousness Science); pp. 80–85: Julia Zimmermann, © Schering Stiftung; pp. 138–147: © Pierre Gallais / Studio Pandan; pp. 150–165: © Sylvia C. Pont
Sollten trotz intensiver Recherche Rechte an den Bildern nicht ausreichend berücksichtigt worden sein, können sich Anspruchsberechtigte an den Verlag wenden.
In compiling this book, an attempt was made to credit all sources of the scanned photo material. If, however, an acknowledgement is incomplete, the copyright owner may contact the publisher.

Aufgrund der besseren Lesbarkeit wird in den deutschen Texten in diesem Buch die männliche Form verwendet. Die weibliche Form ist selbstverständlich immer mit eingeschlossen.

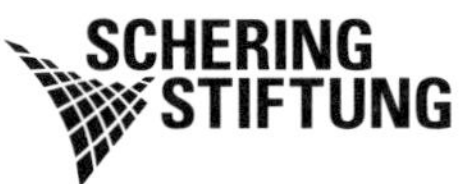

Schering Stiftung
Unter den Linden 32–34
10117 Berlin
www.scheringstiftung.de

Erschienen bei **Published by**
Spector Books
Harkortstr. 10
04107 Leipzig
www.spectorbooks.com

Vertrieb **Distribution**
Germany, Austria: GVA, Gemeinsame Verlagsauslieferung Göttingen GmbH & Co. KG, www.gva-verlage.de
Switzerland: AVA Verlagsauslieferung AG, www.ava.ch
France, Belgium: Interart Paris, www.interart.fr
UK: Central Books Ltd, www.centralbooks.com
USA, Canada, Central and South America, Africa, Asia: Artbook / D. A. P., www.artbook.com
Australia, New Zealand: Perimeter Distribution, www.perimeterdistribution.com

Printed in Germany
ISBN: 978-3-95905-212-2